Ideals, Beliefs, Attitudes, and the Law

Ideals, Beliefs, Attitudes, and the Law

Private Law Perspectives on a Public Law Problem

GUIDO CALABRESI

Sterling Professor of Law, Yale University

SYRACUSE UNIVERSITY PRESS   1985

Library of Congress Cataloging in Publication Data

Calabresi, Guido, 1932–
    Ideals, beliefs, attitudes, and the law.

    (The Frank W. Abrams lectures)
    Bibliography: p.
    Includes index.
    1. Public law—United States.   2. Civil law—United
States.   3. Law and ethics.   4. Accident law—United
States.   I. Title.   II. Series.
KF385.C35   1985   344.73   85-2590
ISBN 0-8156-2309-7   347.304
ISBN 0-8156-2310-0 (pbk.)

To Morris and Eugenie Crosby Tyler

GUIDO CALABRESI is an authority on torts, legal process, and on the relationship of law and economics. A 1958 graduate of the Yale Law School, he served as a law clerk for Supreme Court Justice Hugo L. Black before returning to Yale in 1959 as a member of the law faculty. In 1978, Professor Calabresi was appointed Sterling Professor of Law at Yale and in 1985 Dean of the Yale University Law School.

Professor Calabresi was born in Milan, Italy and came to the United States with his family in 1939. He earned a B.S. degree in analytical economics at Yale in 1953, attended Oxford University as a Rhodes Scholar, and received both bachelor's and master's degrees from Magdalen College.

Professor Calabresi is a fellow of the American Academy of Arts and Sciences and a Corresponding Fellow of the British Academy.

Among his books are *A Common Law for the Age of Statutes*, *Tragic Choices* (with P. Bobbitt), and *The Costs of Accidents: A Legal and Economic Analysis*.

Contents

Foreword

THE ABRAMS LECTURE SERIES has added a new and substantial component to the richness of academic life at Syracuse University. The 1982 series by Guido Calabresi sparked great interest among members of the faculty and the student body.

The Abrams Lecture Series is financed by a grant from the Exxon Education Foundation in memory of the late Frank W. Abrams, former chairman of the board of the Standard Oil Company (New Jersey), the predecessor of Exxon, and former chairman of the board of trustees of Syracuse University.

A member of Syracuse University's Class of 1912, Mr. Abrams was a life-long leader in support of higher education. He was a founder of the Council for Financial Aid to Education, chairman of the Ford Foundation's Fund for the Advancement of Education, and a trustee for the Alfred E. Sloan Foundation.

Mr. Abrams was one of the key pioneers who awakened American business, both through education and landmark legal precedents, to the need for financial support by business for private higher education. It was a contribution by Mr. Abrams, the importance of which cannot be overemphasized, which makes it particularly appropriate that this lecture series be presented in his name.

A special thank you is due the members of the Abrams Lecture Series Planning Committee, headed by Guthrie S. Birkhead, Dean of the Maxwell Graduate School of Citizenship and Public Affairs. Working with Dean Birkhead are Michael O. Sawyer, Vice Chancel-

lor of the University and Professor of Constitutional Law; L. Richard
Oliker, Dean of the School of Management; Richard D. Schwartz,
Ernest I. White Professor of Law; Chris J. Witting, Chairman of the
Syracuse University Board of Trustees; and Robert L. Payton, Presi-
dent of the Exxon Education Foundation.

MELVIN A. EGGERS
Chancellor
Syracuse University

Acknowledgments

THIS BOOK is derived from five Frank W. Abrams lectures I gave at Syracuse University in March of 1982. I am grateful to the Chancellor of the University, Melvin A. Eggers, and to Dean Guthrie Birkhead of the Maxwell School for the opportunity those lectures gave me to pull together thoughts and ideas I had long wished to write. An earlier version of some of these ideas was the basis of the Jessie and John Danz lectures I delivered at the University of Washington in 1980. In the summer of 1982, the Center for the Study of Public Choice permitted me to submit the first draft of the Abrams Lectures to close criticism at a Liberty Fund Conference. I am grateful to Professor James M. Buchanan, the General Director of the Center, for his invitation, as well as for his own very helpful comments at the conference.

A large number of my friends and colleagues have read and commented on parts of this book. They are too many to list. I thank them all and know they will recognize the changes they led me to make and will accept my gratitude.

The staff of the Yale Law Library, and especially Morris Cohen, Librarian and Professor of Law at Yale University, have been extremely helpful. Susan Lucibelli, my secretary at the Yale Law School, has, in her work on this book, as in all I write, been superb. Her kindness, patience, speed, and cheerfulness never seem to fail and cannot be sufficiently acknowledged. The Dean of the Yale Law School, Harry H.

Wellington, has been generous in his support, both institutional and personal. It is a pleasure to thank him also.

In most of my books I have had many student research assistants. In this book Kenneth Christman did the bulk of auxiliary research. I am enormously grateful to him, as I am also to Jamie Star, who did the source and cite check with speed, care, and wonderfully good humor.

Finally, I thank Anne, my wife and dearest friend.

Woodbridge, Connecticut   GC
Fall 1984

Introduction

I AM a torts teacher. I deal in accidents and the like, and from there to ideals, beliefs, and law may seem like quite some distance. Yet some years ago, starting from torts and how our legal system deals with accidents, I ended up talking and writing about how law, how societies and legal systems, make those choices, those decisions, which cannot be made decently, let alone well. I called those choices "tragic."[1] Who gets the artificial kidney when there are not enough to go around, and how do we decide not to have enough to go around? Who gets picked to serve in a limited war, a war in which it is much safer to stay home than to go to the front?[2] Who gets to have children when a society implicitly or explicitly decides that unlimited procreation is no longer acceptable? All those questions, however, were dealt with not in the abstract but as a result of musing about torts, about how our laws seem to decide how many people — and who, most likely — will be killed in accidents.[3]

More recently, also starting from torts and from observing how statutes have come to pervade this traditionally common law area, and from considering how such statutes have been treated by tort law generally, I started wondering about the role of courts and common law in an age when statutes and written law have become dominant. All this led to a book about the change in our political system brought about by the prevalence of legislative law making, and about how the relationships among law-making institutions in our country have to be reconsidered in the light of the increasing role played by statutes in our law.[4] Once again, the discussion was not derived from abstract political theory, but arose, rather, from real cases and situations in which courts tried to deal with the effect of statutes in areas which had once been statute free.[5] Because my field is torts, many of these situations involved accident cases.

In this book, I would like to start on another journey and again begin from torts, from accidents. What I would like to do is to try to consider the place of beliefs, attitudes, and ideals in our legal system. But as before, instead of beginning with a theory about the general place of beliefs in our law, I shall try to use examples of how torts has dealt with different kinds of beliefs and attitudes in order to derive some insights into the significance of such things in our system of law.

In the next chapter, I shall describe a way of looking at the problem of accidents which will give us a framework, a context to help us understand the cases I shall discuss later. It is a way of thinking about what is going on when we decide to stop some accidents, but not others, that also will be helpful in the last chapter, when we shall be very far indeed from accident law. In the second chapter, I'll examine how our law treats idiosyncracies and idiosyncratic attitudes which arise out of social or physical disadvantages or handicaps. This will lead us to consider, in the third chapter, how accident law treats idiosyncracies which stem directly from beliefs. I shall there be dealing with some quite peculiar cases — which many find amusing, even though they all involve people getting hurt. They are all situations which concern beliefs outright, that is, where people do things which we would not think would be sensible, indeed which often would strike us as quite mad, were it not for the fact that they are justified or explained by their beliefs.

In the fourth chapter, I'll be dealing with still other kinds of attitudes and beliefs, those that are not idiosyncratic, which, in fact, we all share to some extent, and yet which appear to be disfavored in the law. I shall be treating the feelings of pain that we all have when we see someone run down on a highway or even just hear of a terrible accident, and that special sense of loss I would have if my watch was destroyed, because it was given to me by my Great-aunt Amnesia Calabresi, for whose memory I have a special affection.

I hope from all these to draw forth a sufficient number of ideas or impressions so that I can then discuss more generally the role of

ideals, attitudes, and beliefs in our legal system. In the last chapter
I will try to put these together with some notions derived from my
earlier book on tragic choices in order to look at the most complicated, the most searing, issue of beliefs and the law that is now before
us — that is, the abortion question. I shall not hope to come up with
any solutions to the abortion issue, but I will try to see how the things
we will have discussed in the earlier chapters relate to that particular
problem. If they have something to say about that most intractable
question, they may be of more use in other areas which are less complicated and less difficult.[6]

It is a long journey, and many other areas of law have much to
say about the issues involved. For that reason this book will be only
one view of the problems discussed. Others, starting from different
areas of law, will take very different approaches. This will be especially true in the last chapter dealing with abortion. Still, I feel more
comfortable approaching a topic like this in common law fashion, trying
to build up from cases, hypothetical and real, than by working down
from great principles. I would rather approach the issues from a specific field of law — itself affected by other fields of law as well as by
its own peculiar problems and questions — and see where that leads
us, than to try to deal with the topic as if I — or anyone — knew *all
law* and was ready to describe it in terms of an abstract theory. There
are dangers in such an approach — call it common law or casuistry[7]
— for the results are apt more to be, or to justify, a series of essays
on how a problem is dealt with in a particular field than a book which
supports broad generalizations. One can be too impressed by the way
specific cases were decided when instead those decisions reflected no
more than the need to deal with the special doctrinal requirements
of an area. Then one is likely to assume, mistakenly, that some more
general themes are at play.[8] Yet, the dangers of starting from general
notions in dealing with issues like these are equally great and too often
ignored,[9] and the insights of the common law method, if they are treated
with caution, can be a helpful antidote against those very dangers.[10]
For this reason, then, even if for no other, this kind of approach jus-
tifies itself.

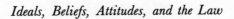

Ideals, Beliefs, Attitudes, and the Law

The Gift of the Evil Deity

AFTER ABOUT A MONTH of studying cases, I put to my first term torts students a couple of hypothetical questions. The first concerns an "evil deity."[11] "Suppose," I ask my students, "such a deity were to appear to you, as president of this country or as controller of our legal system, and offer a gift, a boon, which would make life more pleasant, more enjoyable than it is today. The gift can be anything you want — be as idealistic, or as obscene, or as greedy as you wish — except that it cannot save lives." Later I will drop even that requirement. "The evil deity suggests that he can deliver this gift in exchange for one thing . . . the lives of one thousand young men and women picked by him at random who will each year die horrible deaths."

When I ask; "Would you accept?" my students almost uniformly answer, "No." Indeed, they are shocked that one could even ask the question. I then ask, quietly, what the difference is between this gift and the automobile, which takes some fifty-five thousand lives each year. My students immediately come up with various differences, a few of which are worth examining.

The first difference they mention is that no one chooses the automobile for all society. It is not the president, or even our legal system, which imposes the automobile on us. An evil deity may offer it, but the president does not choose to accept it in exchange for all those lives. Rather, individuals decide for themselves whether they wish to drive or not, and if they decide to drive and happen to get killed, well, it's their own choice, and not that of our society, as such. The evil

1

deity, however, would say that that was not much of an answer. The president or our legal system can, after all, prohibit cars, and by barring individual choices, save all those lives.[12] "Indeed," the deity would say, "all I am asking is that you, as president, allow individuals to choose for themselves whether to accept the gift that I offer. You need not impose the gift, simply give people freedom to accept it. That's all I need from you, president or legal system."

"In all honesty, however," the evil deity goes on (because even if evil, he is honest), "I should point out to you that those who do not accept the boon may, nevertheless, be picked as victims." Not just people who drive are killed in automobile accidents; pedestrians are, too. And though even these have accepted some of the gift (their food, et cetera, may be delivered to them by cars), they have not made the same acceptance choice as drivers.[13] Of course, their chances of being picked as victims are considerably less, but then no one has that high a chance of being picked. After all, in the proposed boon only one thousand people would be killed each year. "A mere trifle, a mere trifle," he whispers.

"Still, if pressed, I even would be willing to concede safety to all those who reject the gift *altogether,*" the deity continues, "even though that isn't the way it works with cars. But remember, though the gift is wonderful, and makes life better for almost everyone (except in retrospect for those who get picked as victims), if someone rejects the gift and most people in the society accept it, *that* person's life is much worse off than it was before the gift was offered!" That is to say, one can live quite decently in a world without automobiles, but it is extraordinarily difficult to live tolerably in a society organized around automobiles and totally reject all the benefits that come from them. Consider the effect of the general acceptance of cars on public transportation systems and on the location of stores. It is quite easy to see that an individual choice to reject the automobile and all its pomp is harder than one may think.[14]

In other words, while there is some choice in the case of cars, which the evil deity is now more than willing to match, it is a tricky choice. The question of how *real* the choice is remains far from answered in both the automobile and the evil deity situation, as does the question of whether we can avoid responsibility for permitting "unreal" choices. Morally speaking, one might argue, in these situations the president and our legal system accept the gift for us the moment they decide to allow it to be offered.

Two examples of this problem of choices, though they appear to be slightly to one side, suggest the key may be less the existence of nominal choice than what is at stake behind the choice. The first involves a medical experiment.[15] A distinguished oncologist was treating some inoperable cancer patients whose only hope lay in the chemotherapeutic drug being administered to them. Since this drug was not yet approved for general use, the doctor was the only person available to these patients who could treat them with the drug; in a sense, the doctor held their lives in his hands. The appropriate treatment, as best could be discerned at the time, was to be on the drug for a week and then to be off it for four weeks. So far no special problems of choice were presented.

Later, however, the researcher decided there was a good chance this drug could prove to be the first systemic treatment for viral diseases. Viruses had been treated locally before, but not successfully throughout the body. Thorough and careful preliminary experiments had, of course, been done which permitted the oncologist to reach his conclusions that this might be a successful treatment for some viral diseases. Let me add that showing that this drug could cure some viruses would be of great importance. Among the diseases he thought it might treat were smallpox (though this would have been a very expensive way to deal with smallpox given the existence of a vaccine) and, more importantly, herpes meningitis, which was at the time almost 100-percent fatal to babies who contracted it, as well as a variety of other diseases for which there was no treatment then available. It is even more crucial, perhaps, that should the drug treat this "family" of viruses successfully, evidence would be adduced linking those types of cancers (which were treatable by this drug) with this class of virus. (Some suggestions to that effect had previously been made, in fact, but they had not been demonstrated.)

The researcher then thought up an experiment.[16] Most of the patients were elderly and either had never been vaccinated against smallpox or had been vaccinated ages ago. If he could give them cowpox (that is, vaccinate them against smallpox) while they were on the drug and the vaccination did not take, that would be good evidence that the drug was effective against the cowpox virus. If he vaccinated them again when they were off the drug and the vaccination took, the evidence would be very strong indeed.[17] The only trouble with all this was, of course, that vaccinating these people was in no sense in their interest. The likelihood that the elderly in the United States, with inoperable cancer, would contract smallpox was nil. So the vaccination was useless, and dangerous besides! Let us assume that one elderly person in a thousand would die as a result of vaccination. Under the circumstances, the researcher could not proceed without their consent, and so he sought to offer them a choice.

He explained to them the importance of the experiment as well as its dangers to them, and asked them if they would be willing to take part without hope of benefit. He assured them they could refuse to participate and he would, of course, continue to treat them. (Had he not said that, they would have had no choice, for one chance of death in a thousand against certain death is not much of a choice.) I asked him whether they believed his assurance. His answer was chilling. "Yes, they believed me," he said. "They believed me more than most people believe someone when they say, 'I believe you,' for I am a very convincing person." (And he is.) But he added, "Still, if you were to ask me what, while believing me, they thought the chances that I might be lying would be, I'd have to say, one in a hundred at least. For even when one believes someone wholeheartedly, one always assumes *a chance* that the person is lying, and I have to assume the same for them." "In other words," I said, "in their own view, if they went along with the experiment, they had one chance in a thousand of dying; if they turned it down, they had at least one chance in a hundred. That isn't much of a choice, is it?" "Yes," he said, "perhaps so, *but the experiment was worth doing, and I did the best I could to give them a true choice.*"

The experiment was a great success. All agreed to participate. No one was injured. The drug treated the viruses, and some herpes meningitis babies now survive. All ends best in this best of all possible worlds. Nevertheless, the question remains — was that which was treated by all concerned (including the hospital experiment committee which approved the experiment[18]) as a free choice in fact a free choice, or was it a decision — worth making perhaps, but made by the researcher and the committee — in which individual choices played little role, except to ratify the fact that the researcher had done "the best he could" and the experiment was worthy?[19]

Let me compare this non-choice with a choice that was examined in the so-called doctors' trial at Nuremberg after World War II.[20] The "doctors" were charged with having subjected some women to perfectly dreadful sexual experiments.[21] A woman who survived and who allegedly had agreed to participate in these experiments, had been asked by one of the defendants why she had "volunteered." Her reply was: "Rather half a year in a brothel than half a year in a concentration camp." The prosecution argued that in these circumstances "[n]one of the victims of the atrocities perpetrated by the defendants were volunteers."[22] The "doctors" were, of course, convicted.[23] The choice may have been "free," but they could not avoid responsibility for the situation which created that "free" choice. The same responsibility may instead justify our treating as free the very limited choice the researcher could offer. Similarly our president or our legal system cannot avoid responsibility for permitting people to accept the boon of the evil deity. The moment the president knows that for someone to reject the boon when most others accept it would create an intolerable situation for those who refuse, he or she must decide whether the offer itself is morally permissible, and cannot hide behind the illusion of individual free choice.

The second answer my students give is that we already have automobiles, and we did not know of the slaughter they would bring when we accepted them. The gift of the evil deity, instead, now offers us a clear choice between life and convenience. But in fact that *choice* is always present even if the gift had previously been accepted. We can prohibit cars—even if they now exist. The cost in convenience may be greater, but that's only haggling over the price. We in fact prohibited fireworks—which kill far fewer people than automobiles—even though they had been around a long time.[24] In England a couple of years ago the government forbade medicine bottles which were not childproof. They did this for the wonderful reason that non-childproof bottles were costing the National Health Service too much, because of the accidents they brought about. As a result, the government, which did not wish to pay the costs, forbade what had previously seemed convenient, and mandated childproof bottles.[25]

Nor is it true that we never choose something new when it involves the loss of life. When we chose to permit nuclear energy (in peace time), the issue was put quite explicitly—even if it then was somewhat lost in the hearing transcripts of a Congressional committee.[26]

A congressman asked how many accidents had occurred during early research on nuclear energy. The answer was that the accident rate had been quite modest. The congressional reaction, in effect, was "Oh, is that all? Then it's all right."[27] Unfortunately, then, we cannot distinguish cars from the deity's boon on the ground that one is already here while the other is a choice for the future.

The third answer my students give is deeper. It is that automobiles take "statistical" lives, while the deity wants "real" lives. I have never run into a "statistical" life anywhere, in my car or anyplace else. But it is certainly the case that there is an important difference in attitude toward lives that are described only in statistical terms and those that seem to represent real, flesh and blood people. Perhaps because we hope ordinary accidents will somehow not occur, or perhaps because we do not know who the victims will be, we treat the case of a hostage who will die unless we act, or even of a fool who chooses to row—solo—across the Atlantic Ocean, differently than a run of the mill accident.[28] We do spend millions of dollars to save the lives of clearly identified individuals who are in immediate danger—dollars, which, if applied to generalized safety, would protect and preserve many more.[29] Indeed, in *Tragic Choices* I had something to say on why it even may be correct to save the fool in the rowboat, why there is something which society gains by saving those who are in known peril, even at the cost of more numerous, unknown, lives.[30]

Still, in the temple of truth all lives are real, whether originally described in statistical terms or not. There is in fact no difference between the fifty-five thousand people killed in automobile accidents and the thousand lives sought by the evil deity. In retrospect, we could show their pictures in newspapers just as we would the deity's victims. We could as easily describe their grieving families. We also can be sure that such accidents will occur, and that such lives will be lost.[31] We are awfully sure when we build a tunnel that we will kill a certain number of workers per kilometer of tunnel or, it used to be said, in skyscrapers, a certain number of people per story—and these too, I fear, are *real* lives.[32]

The evil deity, however, does not wish to argue. If certainty and statistics matter to us, his gift can be made to comply: "If you don't like so certain a number of lives, I'll make it a statistic. I will take between eight hundred and twelve hundred lives each year. The variance can be even greater if you wish. The number will deviate according to something I'll propose to you in a bit to make the decision even more palatable. But on *average* it will still come out at a thousand or so."

At this point my students came up with a distinction that will prove to be the most crucial for this book. It is not cars that kill people; it is individual bad behavior in driving that does. The evil deity takes victims regardless of how people behave; automobiles only kill when people misbehave. If everyone drove carefully, built cars well, acted *reasonably* (a crucial phrase), we would have no accidents. If only people acted as they should — *reasonably* (that word again) — no one would need to be killed.

The deity, acting as though he believed that was true with respect to automobiles, but with a look on his evil face that suggests that he knows better,[33] says, "I can match that too. I will give you a game. We'll call it Guido's Roulette, and depending on how well you play this game and the type of wheel you use — whether it is cheap and shoddy or expensive and well made — the chance of being picked as a victim will vary. In fact, that is what will determine whether in any one year fifty or nineteen hundred fifty victims will be taken. But remember that the more expensive the wheel is and the more carefully you play the game, the less pleasure you get from the boon I offer you and the less of the gift you receive. Still, that leaves you some 'choice,' some chance perhaps of avoiding the evil altogether."

There is no doubt that this kind of uncertainty makes such "boons" more acceptable. We all prefer "perfectible" standards, things which seem as if they could result in no harm at all, because they fool us into thinking we are not accepting the gift of the evil deity.[34] If, of course, by accepting a "perfectible" standard we get results which are manifestly worse than under a mathematical or certain standard, we are in trouble. If it turned out that to say someone must be guilty "beyond a reasonable doubt" meant that one in one hundred people convicted was clearly innocent, we might prefer (I do not say we would, for there is more at stake in this than the point I am making) a standard which openly announced that one innocent person would be convicted for every thousand guilty ones.[35]

I was at a conference in Boston when Dr. Henry Beecher was first promoting the brain death, flat EEG, definition of death.[36] Someone asked him how often a flat EEG would give a wrong prognosis, resulting in someone being buried alive who could have returned to what all of us would consider life. He immediately gave an answer. I do not recall the figure and have no idea if it was correct. It was, in any event, quite low. Yet everybody there was shocked that this "new" approach would allow people to be buried alive in so definite, if limited, a number of cases. We were so shocked that somebody had to step in to relieve the tension. Someone did just that by telling us that we no longer bury people alive. It was a great worry in the nineteenth century, and all sorts of devices were developed to avoid it. But embalming cured all that. Now if people are wrongly diagnosed as dead we kill them when we embalm them, and so never bury them alive.[37]

Then someone asked, But what is the current definition of death, and how often is *it* mistaken?" Naturally, everyone turned to the lawyers who grandly said that a death occurs when doctors certify that it has. The doctors then were questioned and they, less grandly, spoke of "vital signs" and of "when someone is visibly dead." They added that, as a practical matter, it is when the nurses say the patient is dead, and that if everyone is *careful* the system works quite well. So we turned to the nurses and asked again: "How often do you think this impressionistic test will turn out to be a wrong prognosis?" The figure they gave (again I have forgotten it), though uncertain since based on human error, was far larger than that which Beecher gave for the flat EEG test. We were lost. We had eaten the fruit of the tree of knowledge and could no longer, it seemed, remain complacently hiding behind a false "perfectible" standard.

In fact, this is not a good example because it is an area in which one can achieve improvements and still maintain the illusion of perfectibility. A flat EEG can be made a necessary, but not sufficient, condition of death and an impressionistic, nominally perfectible, "vital signs" test can be added as a second requirement before a death is certified.[38] At the moment, however, we suffered both the shock of facing a test which told us that in a precise number of cases we would be "killing" someone — something we could not tolerably accept — and the shock of realizing that if we didn't accept this, we would have to stay with a "perfectible" standard which would in practice be worse!

The problem as posed by the evil deity is even more difficult; though we may wish to have "perfectibility" (to foster the illusion that we have not accepted the deity's gift),[39] we do not, in fact, desire perfection. The deity would in all honesty tell us, "I will give you a game of roulette, which, if you spend enough money on the wheel, and play it carefully enough, would mean that the lives I would claim could, conceivably, drop to zero. Though, given my knowledge of human nature, I can assure you that the average will still hover around a thousand. I can say this because such a well-made wheel would cost a great deal, and such a carefully played game would deprive the players of all the pleasure of the gift I offered." We could make cars which are built like tanks, or even just built like racing cars (in their capacity to protect driver and passengers) but which cannot go faster than ten miles per hour. Such cars would cost a great deal, but with them we would have virtually no serious automobile accidents. We could build such cars, but we do not wish to do so.[40]

In fact, most accident-causing behavior is *not* valueless to its originator. Safety costs! And when we don't choose the safest car at any cost, we are doing exactly what the evil deity knew all along we would do. We are accepting some of the boon he offers. Moreover, if we deny we are accepting the gift but put the blame for the "victims" on those who "misbehave," as if good behavior could avoid all accidents without unacceptable costs, we are not only hiding from ourselves that we have accepted the gift, but are indulging in ugly scapegoatism as well![41] And so we speak of carelessness in driving, of well and poorly designed cars, and of speeding. Yet the very definition of each of these in effect represents a decision of how much of the evil deity's gift we have chosen to accept, and how much we have rejected. For the more we increase standards of safety, the more we decrease pleasure or increase costs, and the more we decrease the number of victims taken.

In this book I am concerned with beliefs and attitudes, and so far I have said little or nothing about them. I would like to approach this subject by suggesting that such beliefs and attitudes must themselves be viewed as gifts of the evil deity. They are things which have value in our society, either in themselves or because protecting the right of people to hold such beliefs, free from pressures to which others are not subjected, is considered important. Yet, as a result of these beliefs some people will be injured or killed and there will be some suffering. And so we will have to make a decision with respect to ideals, beliefs and attitudes, on the extent to which we wish to encourage them or discourage them as "unreasonable" choices, as undesirable acceptances of the gift of the evil deity.

Ultimately we must conclude, not cynically but sadly, that the issue is not *whether* we accept the gift of the evil deity—call it progress if you wish to sound cynical—but *which* and *how much* of many such gifts offered we will accept and which and how much we will reject. This, then, immediately raises the questions of who will win and who will lose as a result of our acceptance or rejection of these gifts, of who will bear their burden, and how we can refine the choices between acceptance and rejection so as to make the results more tolerable.

But one devil remains to be exorcised. If one calls the gift "technological progress" and says we have accepted that gift, it seems easy to conclude that despite all the lives that the deity has claimed, we have, *on lives saved,* come out ahead. Despite all the early deaths brought on by automobiles, environmentally caused cancers, industrial accidents and what have you, life expectancies have continued to rise.[42] And so, one could say, the gift has saved more lives than it has taken! Even environmental cancers and fifty-five thousand automobile deaths a year become insignificant as the price paid for a technologically progressive society which, *because* it is committed to such progress, cures diphtheria and pneumonia and a host of past plagues and accidents.[43] Can one then be complacent in the belief that we have won the game, that we have fooled the evil deity?

Unfortunately, however, that is too simplistic a view. It does not consider at least three things that cannot be ignored. The first is that quality of life (a trite, but still valid expression) is crucial, perhaps as crucial as life itself. The second is that we may be able to pick and choose *within* progress; we need not, necessarily, put up with environmentally caused cancers in order to develop life-saving penicillin. The third is that the winners and the losers are *not* the same people, and we may not be indifferent as to who wins and who loses, whether in extra years of life or in quality of life, when we accept or reject some part of some boon offered by the evil deity.

Let me say just a bit more about each of these. First, there are things other than life-years which we *do* value more than life. The very fact that we accept some boons of the evil deity (whether material ones, like dangerous automobiles; or spiritual ones, like costly freedom) shows this. But beyond that, since we all *must* die, the issue has to be: are some *ways* of living sufficiently important to us that we would sacrifice some years of life to have them? In accepting and rejecting the deity's offers, and in deciding whether or not we have "come out ahead of the game," mere life expectancies cannot be enough. Have we treated the mentally ill decently—at the cost of some lives? Have the lives we have prolonged been, in some sense, fruitful and rewarding (even if terribly handicapped)? Have we adhered to those beliefs, ideals and attitudes (including the ideal of letting people hold to their own kooky ideals) which may be dearer to us than an extra month on a life expectancy table? These are the questions which we must face — together with the number of lives and life years we *have* saved — in deciding whether we have "come out ahead" on the deity's offer.

Second, we need not accept the notion that progress, "technological" or otherwise, is indivisible. If we accept cars, we need not, for that, accept terribly unsafe cars, cars which run at any speed, or cars which do not have air bags or seat belts.[44] That we are committed to letting science run freely — in order to develop new life-favoring inventions — does not necessarily mean that we can do nothing about hazardous wastes.[45] Even if life-expectancy maximization *were* our only goal, choices among "progress" would still be available to us and some offers of the evil deity would be appropriately rejected. Life expectancy *has* increased, but had we been more careful in our dealings with the deity it could have increased still more, for "progress" is, to some extent at least, divisible.

Finally, we do care a great deal about who wins and who loses as a result of our acceptances and our rejections of the evil deity's offers. A great increase in life-years for the very rich, achieved at the cost of brutalizing and shortening the lives of the very poor, is not a gain — even if the total of additional life-years comes out "in the black."[46] It is on this point that I would like to dwell further in the rest of this chapter. I will do this mindful of the fact that I have not discussed many other differences between the gift of the evil diety and the automobile. There is not time to discuss each of them, even those which my students regularly raise, especially since the deity has "answers" for all of them and since these answers are not greatly different from those already given.

To focus our thinking on the issue of who gains and who loses — and on the relationship between this and when and how much of the deity's gifts we accept, I would like to turn to the second hypothetical that I put to my students. In this situation, the students become common law judges or legislators and a widower or widow appears before them. The relict (to use the old, non-sexist, term for both) is followed by thirteen children and says: "My late spouse and I accepted the boon of the evil deity.[47] Perhaps we had little choice, since all were going along with it, but still I'll admit we accepted it and got benefits from it. The benefits were about the same as those which all the others who accepted the boon got — no more, no less. But now it has happened that my spouse was picked as one of the victims. Why should I and my children bear the bulk of the loss when we only gained what everyone else gained? Why," the relict plaintively asks, "should society's gain be at my total expense?" In other words, the relict asks for social insurance for survivors of evil deity victims, and wants to know why common-law judges, or legislators (whichever are the appropriate lawmakers) should not give it to them. "Let *all* those who gain bear some of the burden, not just those selected by the deity, those who have already lost what cannot be compensated for!" the relict pleads.[48]

The traditional answer to this plea was the one given by Oliver Wendell Holmes. He suggested that such social insurance would *compel* all to buy insurance. It would be better, instead, to let people who wished to do so buy "evil deity" insurance and leave those who did not free to "enjoy" the risk they choose to take. Anyone who accepts the boon could go out in the "free market" and purchase, from a local insurance company, coverage against being selected as a victim. That person's relict and children would collect if the deity struck, and all would be well. Or so Holmes seems to have thought.[49]

If this were the only answer to the relict's plea, however, it would not seem very satisfactory today. If the only object of accident law, of torts, were to compensate victims for losses which, since they derive from evil deities, are unavoidable, then most people today would probably opt for compulsory social insurance (whether rightly or wrongly). This is not, necessarily, due to a prevalence of paternalism — in the sense of my knowing what is best for you and hence compelling you to insure yourself.

It may arise from what I call self-paternalism, which is something that even those who live in that state (of mind) called Chicago may find acceptable.[50] That is, "I wish to be required to buy evil deity insurance because I know that unless I am compelled, I will be too tempted to buy other things instead and regret having spent the money on short run pleasures rather than on long run security. I want to force myself to "maximize" in the long run, because I know that if I am not so forced, I will yield to desires for short run maximizations which will satisfy me less.[51] And I, dear Chicago friend, have as much right to opt for long run maximization and to compel it for myself, as you have to opt for short run maximization if you wish." When Ulysses tied himself to the mast in order to avoid falling prey to the sirens' song, the intellectual ancestors of Chicago did not, indeed could not, complain that "freedom of choice" was hampered.[52]

The problem, however, is that often I cannot do what is best for me without compelling you to do the same. I cannot tie myself to the mast without also tying you. If you have your way, I lose my freedom to tie myself; if I have mine, you lose your freedom to be untied. For me to affirm my long run choices deprives you of the freedom to effectuate your short run ones, and vice versa. Either way, compulsion is inevitable.

An example may help: Should we allow contracts made by drunks to be valid? There are those who wish to drink and who are terrible at making contracts when drunk. There are others who either do not drink or who are superb negotiators when seven sheets to the wind. Those who are bad at making drunken contracts might well desire a law which made such deals invalid.[53] Those who are good at them would wish the opposite. Unless a badge to differentiate good drunken contractors from bad ones were feasible, the law would have to make all such contracts good, or all of them void. One group, in other words, would inevitably impose its way on the other, however the law came out on the issue.[54] Which group would end up compelling which would, in our society, most likely depend on the numbers in each group as well as on the intensity of feeling in each.[55]

The same would be true concerning compulsory evil deity social insurance. My guess is that if all there were to it was the question of spreading of losses and private choice in the purchase of insurance in today's society (though not necessarily in Holmes' time) enough people would wish to compel *themselves* to be covered so that evil deity social insurance would be the rule, and the relict would be compensated automatically.[56] This would be true notwithstanding any other reasons (including paternalistic and wealth distributional ones) that would lead some to favor such insurance.[57]

Unfortunately, that is not all there is to it. The problem is that social insurance paid out of general taxes is of little or no use in inducing individual decisions which would control the boon. One of the things that accident law does is to put pressure on people to decide how much to drive, what kinds of cars to drive and, to some extent, perhaps even how carefully to drive. That is to say, it converts into financial incentives the price the evil deity exacts for his gift, and hence helps people to decide somewhat more wisely whether accepting any particular boon offered is worthwhile.[58] Earlier I joked about the government in England deciding to require childproof medicine bottles because it cost the government (that is, the National Health Service) too much not have them.[59] While that remains something of a joke, it is not joking to say that if the manufacturer of the evil deity's roulette wheel were liable in damages for the lives of the additional victims selected when "cheap" roulette wheels were made, he or she would be very concerned with what kind of roulette wheels were put on the market. He or she at least would make the "cheap" wheels more expensive in order to cover the extra "damage-liability" costs they entailed.[60]

Similarly, it is often said that if the injurer or the victim is held responsible for the costs of accidents (rather than having them paid out of general taxes through a social insurance fund),[61] this will affect, in the direction of greater safety, all sorts of decisions made by that person.[62] Placing the costs of accidents or of being selected as evil deity victims on one or more of the people involved leads those people not necessarily to reject the gift altogether, but at least to consider which of the gifts offered are worth accepting and which are not. It leads them to choose more intelligently—that is, based on more tangible information[63]—whether to use "cheap" or more expensive roulette wheels, whether to play as much at 16 or 80 as at 45, and perhaps whether to play "reasonably" (that word again) or to take a chance.[64] It may even (to return to accidents) induce the potential injurer to act like a great 19th century English lord chancellor, Lord Westbury, who, when his horses bolted, leaned out of the carriage and instructed his groom to "hit something cheap."[65]

If, instead, we accept social insurance, then *individual* decisions on whether and how much of the evil deity's gifts are to be accepted become much less significant. Then the decision of which gifts to accept falls right back to the government.[66] That is, we would be back to the first hypothetical in which the evil deity appears to the president or to legislators and asks them to accept or reject the gift—at the cost of a thousand lives. If we have no more diffuse, individual methods for deciding when and to what extent safety is worth its costs —methods like those which tort law gives us—then that same decision must be made by the state. The state will decide which safety standards are "worth" having and which are not. But the latter decision would, inevitably, represent a clear choice by the whole polity that some lives are not worth saving. That is, it would be precisely the kind of decision my students rejected when the situation was first proposed.

Of course, as I argued earlier, the state is always in that position, even when it just allows the market—or tort law if you will—to influence the level of safety which prevails. The state always could have required *more* safety. Nevertheless, the failure of the state to impose more safety—to save more lives—than individuals informed through the market would choose, is not as blatant an anti-life choice by the state as would be an out and out acceptance of the evil deity's offer. (Cars seemed different from the deity's gift, my students argued, because the state's choice to permit individual decisions about cars was not so blatantly an anti-life choice.) Blatancy in dealing with the evil deity, in accepting his offers, is very, very dangerous.

One of my favorite examples of this came up when the Pentagon Papers case was being argued before the Supreme Court.[67] My late colleague, Alexander Bickel, was presenting the case in favor of permitting publication. Justice Potter Stewart asked whether he could still argue against a prior restraint blocking publication if it were the case that one hundred young men and women would surely die if the papers were printed. For a court to allow publication under such circumstances, Justice Stewart suggested, would amount to a judicial death sentence for those young men and women. Alex started to say that in such a case he would not argue for publication, but he backed away. He remembered that he was being a lawyer, not a law professor, and said, in effect, "That isn't this case, Mr. Justice, so don't worry about it now."[68] Justice Stewart took his advice and wrote an opinion which permitted publication without worrying about such possible "tragic" situations not then before the Court.[69]

Justice Hugo Black, for whom I had clerked, would have said something quite different. Indeed, I am told he did say it in private, though not in the elegant, short opinion which he wrote and which turned out to be his last.[70] His position was that the problem was precisely "the *judicial death sentence*," rather than the hundred lives lost. A hundred lives are given up all the time in our society for values far less worthy, in his view, than freedom of the press. What made Justice

Stewart's hypothetical, had it come to pass, answerable only in favor of the lives, is that we rarely can tolerate having the state decide *clearly, coldly,* and *unequivocally* that a hundred lives are not "beyond price" and "can be sacrificed."[71]

Justice Black drew a rather grisly conclusion. He believed there ought to be an absolute rule forbidding any and all prior restraints on publications, and that such a rule should be promulgated in a case where *no* lives were at stake. If that were done and a situation involving lives ever came up, the lives would be lost before the case got to court. The court would never be in the situation of either openly and coldly decreeing that a hundred people must die or limiting what Black deemed the greater value — freedom of the press. Once one allows hostages to be taken, one is bound to reach a bad result. Better, then, that the potential hostages be killed before a demand for ransom can be made!

I do not mean to imply that I necessarily accept Justice Black's position. I only wish to emphasize — a bit dramatically perhaps — that when the choice of the evil deity is clearly put on *the state,* the question becomes not only whether the boon is worth the lives, but also what it does to the state and to all of us — in the rest of our existence — if we can so coldly, openly and collectively sacrifice lives.

All this is not to say that state regulation of safety — state prohibition of some evil deity gifts — ought to be insignificant. In fact, all societies make many of these decisions at a collective, governmental level.[72] We do not allow two-year-olds to drive merely because their parents think it worthwhile and are willing to pay the huge insurance premiums needed to cover their possible accidents. On the other hand, we *do* allow sixteen-year-olds to drive; but that decision *is* muddied, mitigated even, by the fact that tort law and insurance premiums will influence and limit how much they drive and what kinds of cars they drive. The decision to let them drive cannot be seen simply as a statement by the government that if one is sixteen, one has a right to claim a certain number of victims. Conversely, the decision to bar driving by those younger than sixteen, can readily be seen — even if that is illusory — as the state demanding more safety, being more pro-life, than individuals would be on their own.[73]

As a result, we return to the fact that the answer the common-law judge or legislator gives to the relict must take into account not only the desire to ease the survivors' loss and to burden all gainers equally,[74] but also the desire to induce possible recipients of the evil deity's bounty to act advertently when they choose whether and how much of the gift to accept. If this incentive is put on all possible recipients, the choice, *by the whole society,* of how much of the deity's gift will be accepted will itself be automatically effected and affected. (Unfortunately, of course, this desire to influence choices intelligently often runs counter to our desire to place the burdens on those most suited to bear them from a wealth distributional point of view, or from the point of view of other values of that society. It gets in the way of our wish to ease the relict's plight.)[75]

There currently are two broad approaches to placing such incentives to choose wisely on individuals and groups without violating our distributional concerns. They are the "strict liability" approach and the "fault" or "reasonableness" approach. Under the first, the cost of compensating victims is put on what can roughly be called an insurance category involved in the loss,[76] regardless of the reasonableness of the behavior of the parties concerned. This category may be a manufacturer of evil deity roulette wheels, the category to which the victim belongs, or the category in which we place those whom, in the context of accidents, we define as injurers.[77] Under such "strict" or "no fault" liability systems we place the cost of compensating victims in this way because we want those whom we are willing to burden, those who belong to the burdened category, to decide whether spending more on safer roulette wheels is worth the lives it saves, whether playing roulette at a particular age is worth the pleasure it gives in view of the cost in lives, and so forth. We do not ask whether someone behaved badly, was unreasonable, was at fault. We simply say: "You are in the best position to make the choice between lives and convenience. By making you bear the costs imposed by your decision, we induce you to choose to the best of your ability.[78] Like Lord Westbury, we urge you to urge yourself and those in your control to 'hit something cheap.'"

Under the second of these approaches, we put the cost of the harm — the burden of compensating the victim or of remaining uncompensated — on one of the parties involved in the loss because we think that party has done something "unreasonable." He or she has chosen to risk harming himself or herself or others, in circumstances in which we believe no such risk should have been taken. Too much of the evil deity's boon has been accepted, and we — judge, jury, or legislators — want to express our disapproval of the choice and discourage other people who play roulette, or other manufacturers of the deity's roulette wheel, from making analogous choices. We call that, fault liability.

I have written at great length on why, in a variety of areas, I do not like fault liability.[79] I think it emphasizes choices that are often illusory and makes use of scapegoats. I believe society often deals better with the evil deity if it uses non-fault systems for choosing how much of what gifts proffered are taken. Still, much of tort law hinges — even today — on fault and on reasonableness of behavior.[80] More important, many of the cases that best serve to suggest the role of beliefs, ideals, and attitudes arose in a fault context. And so, for this book, I will act as though the issue of who bears the burden of the evil deity's gifts is to be answered in terms of the "fault" and "reasonableness" of behavior of the parties.[81]

In fact, both the "fault" and "strict liability" approaches raise analogous questions with respect to the significance of beliefs, attitudes, and ideals in the allocation of injury burdens. Non-fault systems raise the issue of belief because, before we decide that someone is in the best position to choose whether to do something which can cause injury to others, one of the things we must ask ourselves is what weight to give to that person's beliefs and attitudes. Is this person *really* best suited to make the choice or will this person's belief system impede him or her from chosing well? And, if the person is impeded from making choices for or against safety because of beliefs, is there another party available who, if faced with the incentives can make an appropriate choice at little or no costs to beliefs? Does the existence of beliefs make someone other than the believer a better decision maker, a better vicar for society, in opting whether or not to take the deity's boon?[82] Or is modification of beliefs a relatively easy or cheap way to avoid the harm, and ought we then put the burden on the believer precisely because that is where the possibility of the cheapest avoidance of accident costs lies?

The way the issue of beliefs and attitudes enters into the "fault" approach is not very different. In deciding whether someone chose reasonably, do we take into account that the person was motivated by beliefs, attitudes arising from cultural differences, or economic or other handicaps? Ought we say that what is "reasonable" behavior is independent of belief systems, or is "reasonableness" itself affected by what a person's beliefs and ideals are? Should we, in deciding how much of the evil deity's gifts to accept, ignore the harm to beliefs that acceptance or rejection may entail, or do we wish those to be made part of the calculus, of our definition of a "reasonable" decision with respect to the deity's offer? If we do not include them in the calculus — if we treat "reasonableness" as being apart from beliefs — we in effect say that we wish to burden, and hence discourage, such beliefs whenever they entail risk of harm. We declare that those who hold beliefs should either give them up or pay for them, even if a non-believer could also, at relatively little cost, have avoided the harm.

In the next chapters, I shall treat the issue of beliefs, attitudes and ideals as if the question is one of "reasonableness," rather than one of who ought to bear non-fault, or strict liability burdens. As I said, I do this because that is what the cases I shall discuss focus on, not because the issue is limited to fault systems. I shall look at situations in which beliefs and attitudes seem to affect what is considered reasonable and situations in which they do not. I shall address this question not only with respect to religious ideals, beliefs and faith but also with respect to attitudes arising from handicap or disadvantage, and with respect to non-religious moralisms and emotions (including the particular value many of us would give to some objects because of the special sentimental attachments they have for us). I shall do it in the narrow context of torts, of how beliefs affect how much of the evil deity's gifts we accept with respect to accidents. I hope, nonetheless, to derive some notions from this of the role beliefs play in the broader legal context as well.

2

Reasonable Prudence and the Disadvantaged

I WOULD LIKE TO BEGIN the discussion of beliefs and attitudes by focusing on the weight given to personal idiosyncrasies *not* based on religious beliefs in determining what our society deems unreasonable or not worthwhile behavior. I will first consider physical handicaps as a way to lead us to the main theme of this chapter — the weight given to attitudes arising from social handicaps, status, or disadvantage. These last should be of interest in themselves, and also will prove to be a useful way to approaching the role played by other attributes and attitudes — those which we call faith or belief. These in turn will lead to a discussion of conflicts of beliefs and ideals, especially when notions of life and faith are involved.

In order to understand the cases I will be discussing, a miniscule background in tort law is needed. Fortunately, however, torts is a simple subject. As far as doctrine is concerned, one could teach most of the subject in two days, and so I will hit the main points in just a couple of pages. To the extent that losses are allocated on the basis of fault (and for the purposes of this book I am staying with that assumption), a person is required to act "reasonably" to avoid injury to self and others.[83] If he or she does not act reasonably, the loss stays entirely on him or her. And this remains true even if he or she was injured by someone who also acted unreasonably.[84] That means if I was an accident victim and I behaved unreasonably, the whole of the damages would lie on me, even though I was injured by someone whose behavior in injuring me was also unreasonable. This was known as

21

the *contributory negligence* rule. It was a profoundly silly rule, and has been dropped in many states.[85] But it was in effect at the time of the cases we will be discussing, and we must take it, foolish or not, as a given in our discussion.

Moreover, one not only was bound to act reasonably to avoid injury in the first place, one was also required to act reasonably to lessen, to *mitigate,* damages once one was injured. Thus, if my car was damaged as a result of your carelessness, it was my responsibility to act reasonably and rent another car if I could, rather than take taxis all the time and incur a greater cost. I could, of course, take taxis if I wished, but I could only charge you for the reasonable cost of my injury and, if it was reasonable for me to have rented another car rather than take taxis, the rental fee would be the limit of the damages I could charge you.[86]

Reasonableness, then, was the key at various stages. The test of reasonableness was not necessarily passed if one behaved to the best of one's ability, in "good faith." One could act in good faith but still be unreasonable, be at fault.[87] To act reasonably one had to do more than do the best one could, at a minimum one also had to behave as a reasonably prudent man would have behaved under the circumstances.[88] I know that requirement sounds sexist; that is because it probably was. From this point of view I would urge you to look at a devastating little essay by A. P. Herbert (who wrote such wonderful other things about law as *Holy Deadlock*[89] to urge reform of the English divorce law and who was not a bit sexist) on why the law did not believe there was any such thing as a reasonably prudent woman.[90] In any event, I use the term in its traditional way, "reasonably prudent man," rather than as many do today, "reasonably prudent person,"[91] precisely because that is part of the story I wish to tell. That is, I'll have more to say later in this chapter on whether the law was in fact talking about the generic when it said "man," and was applying nonsexist standards of behavior under that sexist language, or whether the law was not using the generic but was, in fact, imposing a male standard of what was reasonable on both men and women.

We are, after all, talking about attitudes in this book, about ways of looking at what is reasonable and what is not. These inevitably derive from the point of view of those who dominate law-making in a given society. Given that, it would be foolish just to assume that when the law *said* "reasonably prudent man" it meant "reasonably prudent person." One should at least examine the issue of whether reasonableness was being defined, *as the words said,* according to purely male standards of appropriate behavior.

The reasonably prudent man was invariably described rather vaguely, but always in male terms. In England, he was defined as the man on the Clapham Omnibus[92] — a definition which has always left me utterly cold since I have never met the Clapham Omnibus or any man on it, and have no idea why reasonableness should attach especially to those males who ride that line. In Roman law (and, by derivation, in most civil law countries) the analogous figure was "the good father of the family."[93] I have met many good fathers of families in my time, and I suppose some of them were even reasonable. In America, the definition — perhaps the most startling of all — was given by courts and commentators as "the man who takes the magazines at home and in the evening pushes the lawn mower in his shirt sleeves.[94] I must say I have never understood what this (like riding the Clapham Omnibus) has to do with reasonableness of behavior — stereotypical masculinity perhaps, but reasonableness? One has to wonder at the glory of the law! In any event, all these people whose attributes seem, in Europe and America, to define reasonableness are unmistakably male. It would not be surprising, then, if "reasonable man," at law, meant reasonable *male* and not reasonable *person.*

The victim, moreover, had to do more than act reasonably. He or she was also bound not to take risks of harm which he or she had no *right* to take.[95] Regardless of whether behaving that way was reasonable, there were risks which one had no special right to take and which one took only at one's peril. Of course, the key to all that was the word *right* — what risks did one have a right to take without thereby "assuming" the risk of injury, without taking on oneself the burden if harm occurred? It all depended on how one's "rights" were defined.[96] As in so many things in law, that definition and the whole exercise turned out to be circular, it is as if one put a rabbit into a hat, took it out, waved it around and said, in mock surprise, "Look, there's a rabbit!"[97]

This brings us back to the question of this chapter. Where do these rules leave the person who is *not* the *ordinary, reasonable man*? What happens to someone who, because he or *she* is not an ordinary reasonable man, behaves in ways different from those which one can expect of an ordinary reasonable man? Where does this leave a person who, because of physical or mental handicap, or because of age, sex, social status, or disadvantage, does not (*could* not, would be too strong)[98] do what the man on the Clapham Omnibus would have done in like circumstances?

It is important to distinguish this person as "victim" from this person as "injurer." The premise is that unreasonable behavior bars a victim from recovery and also is the basis of liability of injurers to innocent victims. But it does not follow that what is reasonable or unreasonable will be the same for both injurers and victims.[99] In fact, *some* (but not all) of the deviations from the standard of the reasonable man have different effects depending on whether the person deviates from the standard in such a way as to injure others or only in such a way as to injure himself or herself. Some idiosyncrasies that are unreasonable in an injurer are not so treated in a victim.

At law this concept is expressed by the phrase that "one takes one's victim as one finds him or her." Thus, if someone taps me on the shoulder offensively, or negligently drives into me with the result that, because I happen to have a thin skull or shoulder or a weak leg, or privates, I am grievously hurt, it is not only tough on me physically, it is also tough on the injurer financially.[100] The injurer must pay my losses. He or she takes me as he or she finds me. It is no answer to say that had the injurer hit someone else (who had an ordinary, thick or strong skull, shoulder, or privates) in the same way, much less harm would have occurred. Nor is it an adequate answer at law that I might have stayed home, or worn a steel yarmulke, or armor-plated underwear to avoid being injured more seriously than the average victim would have been. It is not viewed as reasonable, to require victims to protect themselves from the effects of these kinds of idiosyncrasies.[111] And so the injurer is stuck, and takes these victims as he or she finds them.

There are limits to this notion. Suppose, for example, I am a great violinist-composer. I want to write the great proletarian symphony, and in order to write that symphony, I go to work in a steel mill. It is necessary for me to do this so that I can be "one with the workers" and thereby be properly inspired. I cannot tell the workers or the mill owners that I am a violinist, for to do so would ruin the proletarian relationship essential to my inspiration and hence to the writing of the opus. My behavior in doing this may be perfectly reasonable.[102] Still, if my hand is mangled in the steel mill, it is unlikely that I will recover more than the value of an ordinary worker's hand, even though my hand is worth an enormously greater amount because I am a great violinist.[103]

In this case the injurer does not take me as he or she finds me, but rather as if I were an ordinary worker free of my expensive musical idiosyncrasy. This would not be the case if I, still a great violinist, were driving about town and suffered a mangled hand as a result of someone else's negligent driving. Then the injurer would take me as he or she found me and be liable for my very expensive hand.[104] In the steel mill something is different, the idiosyncrasy is treated in a different way. In the steel mill I am treated as assuming the risk of my handicap (my valuable hand). I can do more about it. I can best decide if, given the value of my hand, working there is really worth the risk to write the great proletarian opus. In the street, it is assumed that there is little I really can do (and remain an ordinary citizen) to protect my hand. As a result, it is best to make injurers aware (by making them liable) that sometimes the hand they mangle when they drive carelessly will be a cheap one and at other times it will be an immensely expensive one.

For this reason, when injuries occur in ordinary places like a street, the question is usually put as: "Did I behave reasonably *given* my handicap?" It is not put (as it was for the violinist injured in the steel mill) as "Were my attributes and my behavior those of the *ordinary*, reasonably prudent man?". As a result, eccentricities of this sort are typically not a burden on me but rather on those who negligently injure me.

The same is by and large true for age. Children below a certain age are frequently held, as a matter of law, to be incapable of contributory negligence.[105] Age and maturity also can be taken into account in deciding whether children between that minimum age and adulthood behaved reasonably when they were accident victims.[106] It is not quite as neat at the other end. It is not precisely clear at what point age can be considered a handicap which affects whether actions that would be unreasonable in a younger victim may nonetheless be acceptable in an older one.[107] The same lack of clarity exists concerning mental handicaps,[108] but, by and large, the approach remains the same. The question for purposes of contributory negligence is, "Did I behave reasonably given my handicap and limits?" rather than "Did I overcome my limitations and act up to the standard of the man on the Clapham Omnibus who, lucky man, is free from all my handicaps?"

All this would seem sensible, even obvious. After all, why should we put a greater burden on the limited? Why should we demand superior behavior from those who are physically or mentally handicapped, or simply too young to know or do better? Why should we place heavy expenses on them when they fail to live up to standards that are appropriate for those who are more mature or more gifted? Why should we put more of the harm and give less of the benefit of the evil deity's gift to these "little ones" of society? It would seem sensible except that, as a matter of law, this rule does not seem to hold when the handicap is of a slightly different sort, nor does it hold when the disadvantaged person is the injurer. In that situation the typical rule is to burden the injurers even though they have done the best they can, given their physical or mental limitations.[109]

Let us stay, however, with the so-called disadvantaged as victim and consider what happens if the behavior under scrutiny is not that of a child or of a physically limited person, but is rather that of a woman or of a black or of a member of another minority group. Is the test of reasonableness adjusted to the cultural attributes of the particular victim, or is it one that ignores these and asks only what the lawn-mowing man on the Clapham Omnibus would do? Is the test, in other words, that of a reasonably prudent *person,* with all the ethnic, sexual, and cultural diversity such a phrase implies, or is it, in practice, that of a reasonably prudent white Anglo-Saxon male? (For this chapter I will leave Protestant out of the usual phrase: White Anglo-Saxon Protestant. The question of whether reasonableness is defined in terms of the traditional beliefs, and unbeliefs, of "respectable" American protestantism, or whether, instead, it can or must encompass the views of many other, "odd," sects, is a large part of this story. I shall return in the next chapter to whether such non-establishment beliefs are somehow outside the pale in our society which, in its highest document, prohibits any establishment of belief! However, let us leave the issue of religions to the side for now.)

As far as physical attributes are concerned, the victim need not have, or behave as though he or she had, the physical characteristics of the white Anglo-Saxon male in order to be deemed reasonable. It is not contributory negligence for an Italian, for example, who is short to fail to do something which a person of average height (in an Anglosociety) could easily do, and would be unreasonable for not doing. Similarly, a small woman physically incapable of doing something which would lessen her injuries after an accident would not have failed to mitigate damages simply because the "average" man could have done so and would be properly charged with unreasonableness should he fail to do it and mitigate the loss. The standard, then, insofar as physical attributes of victims are concerned, is a fairly individualized one and hence rarely sexist or racist. [110]

The issue becomes clouded, however, when one moves beyond physical attributes. When the key question is whose *attitudes* are reasonable, the answer the law gives is much less certain. Is reasonableness defined by the attitudes and points of view of the dominant ethnic, racial, or sexual groups in the society, or are those who do not share these views to be tested by their own standards? Different still, are the standards, though unitary and applied to all, a mixture of those of all groups—of all reasonable persons and not merely of white reasonable fathers riding Clapham Omnibuses while mowing their lawns in their shirt sleeves? And if the attitudinal differences are so great that such a mixture is impossible (as it would be, *physically*, between the blind and the seeing), which attitudes should be considered reasonable, and for whom?

Let us assume that for cultural reasons women drive differently than men. It is not impossible—though I doubt it. My wife drives far better than I do, but she drives well in a somewhat different way than I drive. I do not believe that either her greater skill or her different style are because she is a woman and I am a man. It seems more likely to me that it is due to those who taught her to drive and to those who taught me, not to mention our personality differences. Still, if it were the case that women *qua women* drove differently than men, it would not be all that surprising. If a society *is* sexist—and ours surely is—it would not be odd that people within that society who were characterized as *different* and treated *differently* would react to different treatment by behaving differently in a wide variety of everyday contexts. Driving is such a context, so it should not be outside the range of possibility that in our sexist society women as a group would drive differently than men as a group. [111] If this were so, would it be appropriate to consider how reasonable *women* drive in deciding whether a woman had behaved reasonably when her driving led her to be a victim in an accident? Or should the test instead be that of driving behavior of reasonable men or of a combination of the two?

To move the context only slightly—is it reasonable to drive the way Italians stereotypically are said to drive? Again, one need not be a racist to admit the possibility that the stereotypes may have some truth to them. I don't believe in race, but if people are treated badly in a racist society on account of an irrelevant characteristic such as color or language, it should not be surprising if they react to that treatment in their everyday behavior. Is it then just, or even decent, to punish them or burden them for that behavior because it deviates from the behavior of those who have treated them as different in the first place? Is it fair to designate a group as different, and then require them to act as though they had never been so designated?

More important perhaps, behavior also is the product of cultural differences which have value and might persist (and incidentally might well be desirable) even if our society were not racist or ethnically biased. It is just possible that the stereotype that Italians drive fast, and squiggle between cars, and act as though they are perennially involved in a sporting event, is such a cultural attribute. Some who have travelled to Italy seem never to tire of saying so.[112] Is such driving reasonable, or is the standard we would impose that of some other culture, of some other group, whose values stereotypically give rise to stodgy, plodding driving? If we can lightheartedly impose standards of another culture, what happens to the culture of ethnic groups in America? Is it bound, in the name of equality of standards, to be melted into a single culture which is usually dominated by the attributes and attitudes of those who happened to arrive here earlier?

This, I would suggest, is a crucial issue in America today. The tradition of our society has been the tradition of the melting pot. It is a fine tradition in that it promises (even when it does not deliver) equality.[113] But even the *promise* of equality comes at a significant price. The term "melting pot" implies that equality will not be granted until the group which seeks equality is melted into the pot. Equality, therefore, is based on the capacity of the newly arrived group to learn to behave like the previously dominant group.[114] Simply to state this is to suggest its deep problems, for equality then becomes the gift that is given when diversity of cultural attributes is eliminated. That, in a society that wishes to be pluralistic, is a very troublesome notion. Consider for a moment what that means to religion — is the price paid for equality to be the willingness to give up significant religious difference? The constitution says no—but our ordinary laws and our mores are less clear on the matter.

This problem is even more significant and dramatic today because it is fundamental to the issue of women's liberation. It is the question of whether equality is being achieved at an appropriate price when one moves from the "reasonable prudent man," to the "reasonable prudent person." If all that has happened is a verbal change and women are now expected to act as reasonable *men* did before (in order to qualify as reasonable persons), rather than men being expected to act, at least in part, as reasonable women did, then equality may be there—but at the cost of cultural subjugation!

I do not think I am exaggerating this tendency of the previously dominant group to offer equality, but only when the group seeking it accepts the culture of the group granting it. Ask yourselves, for example, why, when an objection is made to the designation of toilets as "Men's Room" and "Ladies' Room," the difference is usually corrected by a change to "Men's Room" and "Women's Room" rather than to "Gentlemen's Room" and "Ladies' Room." It may be, of course, that the reason for this is that we don't like gentility in toilets, and that both the terms "ladies" and "gentlemen" connote something to which we object. That would be fine. But it may also be that equality will be granted only if we are willing to conform to the male stereotype and *therefore* the female stereotype of gentility becomes unacceptable, even if it is the better ideal to which both men and women ought to aspire.[115]

Similarly, in our society there traditionally has been a double standard in acceptable sexual behavior. At long last we are moving away from such a double standard, but the tendency has invariably been to undermine the double standard by all moving into the kind of promiscuity that too frequently characterized stereotypical male behavior.[116] Again that *may* be fine; it may be sexual freedom. Thus, it may be desirable for women to be as openly concerned with the size, shape, and visibility of the sexual parts of movie actors as men stereotypically were with those of movie actresses.[117] But it also may be possible that a previous, rather tawdry stereotype of male behavior is being imposed on women as the price of equal treatment. Men in effect say, "We *won't* change and we are socially powerful enough so that, even if you don't like the way we behave, you can't make us change.

If you want equality, the answer is simple. *Perhaps* you can have it, but you must act like us." The irony, of course, is that when it is put this way women may be the ones who have to *ask* to be allowed to abandon what stereotypically was female behavior to gain equality, even if they believe it should be men who modify *their* cultural attitudes.[118]

Just as Italians were, in effect, told they could be accepted in American society when they stopped drinking wine,[119] and Hispanics and Blacks are told that learning "good English" as a primary language is the price of equality,[120] so it may be that women can get equal treatment in the higher work force only if they are willing to act, dress, fight, and keep working hours (regardless of family), just as men supposedly do.[121] If so, those cultural values which women have traditionally nurtured and protected in our sexist society will come to be abandoned in order to have equality. This will happen even if some of these cultural values are highly desirable and should be nurtured and equally protected by *both* men and women.

All this is not terribly important if the only thing that happens is that we end up getting male strippers and burlesque shows for women, because men are unwilling to forego female strippers.[122] It becomes more dangerous when the issue becomes the care of children. If equality in parenting is gained by accepting the notion that both men and women should behave, with respect to children, as stereotypical American men did, we may have lost something of great value for the sake of equality.[123] Let me re-emphasize that I am not for a moment saying we should forego equality. The issue is, rather: Equality on *whose terms, under which standard?* If stereotypical American men ignored their children in order to work long hours, perhaps equality should be gained by inducing men (and their employers) to adopt another stereotype in which they become caring parents as women traditionally have been. Here, the melting pot should give rise to an amalgam in which women's values win out, and not the usual one in which the values of the previously dominant group are taken for granted as setting the standard for all!

The destruction of almost any cultural value is a loss in a pluralist society. We are poorer for having too readily, too callously, and too totally "Americanized" the poor migrants of the nineteenth and twentieth century. The Mediterranean attitude toward life, toward other human beings, is little seen in American culture today, despite the enormous numbers of immigrants who once held that view.[124] Once lost it is not something one can reestablish easily. When the third generation of those immigrants tried to find its cultural roots, it could not recreate these fundamental attitudes, and, too readily, settled for pasta, pizza, and good wine.[125] And while these trivial, though not irrelevant things did become a part of American culture and did enrich us, the deeper values were lost, and we are all poorer for it.

In like manner we may lose those values traditionally preserved in American society by women, but with one fundamental difference. If we lose these values, we take a far greater risk than when we lost the values associated with immigrant groups. Some societies have survived reasonably well without Jewish mothers, and without Italian anarchical notions of the individual human being as central.[126] Such attitudes did not prevail in the northern lands which by and large shaped —and still shape—American culture. Those lands do quite well despite it.[127] It is far more doubtful whether any society has so far survived without preserving those cultural values, without safeguarding that cultural luggage, which in this country has (perhaps improperly and certainly in a sexist way) been assigned to women.[128] That is especially true with respect to parenting, but it may even be true to lesser matters like gentility, gentleness, and perhaps even a bit of reticence in sexual matters.

Do not misunderstand me. There are plenty of stereotypically male values that I, rightly or wrongly, like and would like to see prevail in an equal society. But I may be wrong even as to these. There are others which even a fully socialized male like myself, in thoughtful moments, has to wonder and have doubts about. I would suggest that we be very careful before we move to a *universal* stereotype, to a universal cultural model, which is the previous male stereotype. I also would suggest that if the danger of such a move is far greater than it was in the analogous destruction of immigrant cultures, the need for such a move in order to establish equality for women may be less than it was in the traditional melting pot. Each immigrant group was inevitably a social and political minority. As a result, they all had to accept equality, or the illusion of it, on the terms offered by the majority.[129] Women are not a minority, and might, if so disposed, be able to demand equality on their own terms. They might, in other words, be able to require men to adopt at least some patterns of behavior, some cultural values, which previously were stereotypically theirs.

All of this argues that before we move to the standard of a reasonably prudent person, *linguistically,* we must make sure that what we have put into that standard is not simply a carryover of male attributes. We must be careful lest we simply apply sexist precedents and cases.[130] We must not just take the old lawn-mowing man on the Clapham Omnibus, call him a person, and think we have done the job. We must work to define a *person* who is reasonably prudent, and give that person attributes which, in terms of past stereotypes of proper, reasonable behavior, may be male in some regards, but will in other regards be female. We must do this not because tort law *directly* shapes much of the behavior or many of the attitudes that are important to society. We must do it, rather, because what is done in one area of law affects other areas of law, and what law does in general *is* crucial to shaping fundamental societal attitudes and behavior.

This is not to say, once the society, the legal system, works its way toward this new, non-sexist standard, that the standard should not apply *equally* across the board, to men and women both. It is not to say that reasonable prudence should be different for men and women. That is a different issue altogether and I am more than inclined to accept the notion that the standard should be the same for men and women. We should, I think, have either men's and women's rooms *or* ladies' and gentlemen's rooms. (Though when we come to deal with other cultural and religious attitudes we may well decide that at times a single, unitary standard is less desirable than several more diverse ones applying to different groups.) It is just that in choosing such a single standard we ought not simply and mindlessly choose the previous male one (or, for that matter, the previous female one), but should work toward a new standard that might include the better parts of both past stereotypes.

Up to this point, I have been discussing attitudes and physical attributes insofar as they define "reasonableness" of behavior in accident victims. I will return to that in a bit to consider how our legal system deals with an attitude, like love of fast driving, which, let us assume, is culturally linked to a particular group. Before I come to that, I must deal with how attitudes, and even idiosyncratic physical attributes, come into play in defining what behavior is deemed reasonable for an injurer in an accident.

When a person who has a handicap—be it physical, mental, or simply age-related—is an injurer, the traditional attitude as been "tough on him or her." The burden to compensate victims lies on him or her.[131] At first glance, the reason for the difference between the law's treatment of handicaps in victims and injurers seems clear enough. When victim behavior is being judged, there is, by hypothesis, an injurer involved who behaved unreasonably and who (in a sense) ought to pay. The injurer was at fault or the issue of compensation would not have come up at all.[132] The only question then is whether, despite the injurer's wrongdoing, he or she should be exempted from paying because there was victim wrongdoing as well. When it is put this way, it seems almost natural to deny a windfall to the wrongful injurer since the only ground for it would be that the victim behaved differently from most of us — but only because of handicap or age. Under the circumstances, it would seem very odd to say that the victim "deserves" to lose and not be compensated.[133]

The situation seems quite different when we are dealing with injurer behavior. In this context, again by definition, the issue is whether an *innocent* victim should bear the loss or whether it should fall on an injurer who behaved idiosyncratically and below society's average standards. (If the victim had not been innocent, the injurer would have been shielded from liability regardless of whether the injurer had acted reasonably.)[134] Put this way the question, why should the innocent victim suffer, rather than the injurer who, for whatever reason, failed to live up to society's expectations for normal behavior, becomes quite difficult to answer.[135] We are back, in fact, to the relict who asks why he or she should bear the burden of society's acceptance of the deity's boon when he or she behaved reasonably. Why should the loss not be borne by the injurer, the person whose driving or working was more dangerous than the norm. Why should this not be so regardless of the reason, age, sex, handicap, or simple wrongheadedness, which made the injurer's behavior unusually dangerous.

If the object is to find a way of reducing accidents, then those with the greatest incidence of accidents should be discouraged from taking part in the activities which give rise to them.[136] The story— which, let me hasten to add, I do not fully buy — goes on. If the handicapped are more prone to accidents in some activities they should be given incentives to enter others where their handicaps are less perilous. Do we not wish to induce less driving by the young and the aged since they are involved in more accidents? Should not those who come from groups which, for whatever reasons, are accident prone be steered away from those activities in which their propensities create the great-

est dangers?[137] And this, in fact, has by and large been the attitude
of the common law. Courts have said, if you don't behave reasonably
—where reasonableness is defined by a common societal standard—
and are an injurer, you (or your insurance company) must pay even
though you are disadvantaged, handicapped, or have, in other ways,
acted to the best of your limited capacity. In this way, one may assume, the law sought to make more expensive, and hence less common, participation in dangerous activities by those who belong to categories whose participation was most prone to accidents.[138]

Although understandable, this traditional approach is simplistic. We may not wish to exclude groups from activities which are central to citizenship (in a broad sense) even if their participation is dangerous to others. The unfettered participation of people from such
risky categories in driving, jobs, and other activities that are essential
to being a part of our society may be as important to the society (and
the groups involved) as the lives that such participation may take. Jobs
for the handicapped and driving by the young and aged may be sufficiently important to all of us so that their freedom to take part on
the same terms as anyone else may well be a gift of the evil deity we
want to accept, even though, as with all such gifts, there will be a price
in lives and accidents.[139]

It is important to realize that both the cost and the benefits of
such unfettered participation are real. It would be nice if it were the
case that the cost was false—if it were a fiction (as may be the case
with respect to the physically and mentally handicapped in many jobs)
that arises out of prejudice and ignorance.[140] But all too often, the
cost is even greater than people may believe. Thus when I say more
accidents by the young, I mean *many* more accidents. The figures given
by the U.S. Department of Transportation on automobile fatalities in
which one of the drivers was between the ages of 16 and 24 are *stagger-
ing.* Such a driver was involved in about 40 percent of all fatal accidents.[141] The person killed was not always between 16 and 24, but such
a youth was driving one of the cars involved.[142] If we were honest,
then, we would focus on this fact and admit that while drink and other
things that are apparently hard for society to control may be a part
of the problem, the one pressure point that is both visible and readily
controllable is the mass participation in a death dealing activity, like
driving, by those of that risky age.[143] Still, honesty does not require
us to conclude that members of this group should be excluded from

driving, or even limited in their driving by making them pay very high insurance rates in order to take part. The slaughter — to be blunt — may be worth it in order to include them without discrimination!

When common-law courts have faced this problem, they found themselves in a terrible jam. Since injurer behavior was at stake, the only way they could have ensured full participation of high risk groups would have been to apply a lower standard of reasonableness to members of such groups. But to do that would have meant that the burden, the cost of paying for society's desire to subsidize equal rights and equal participation, would fall on the innocent victim. It would be he or she who would pay for the evil deity's boon — financially as well as physically. It would be the relict who would go uncompensated in order to ensure "equal access" for the members of the accident prone category.[144] That always seemed unfair for, after all, while all of us gain from being part of a non-discriminatory society, the victim gains very little from it and stands to lose a lot. Why should the whole burden of the common gain fall on him or her?

It may be this seeming unfairness that has been responsible for the failure of those relatively few attempts by common-law courts to place lower standards on those who could not — as a group — be expected to comply with normal societal notions of reasonable prudence. Thus, New Hampshire's attempt to gauge driving by minors according to what could be expected of them — while promulgated into law[145] — was apparently ignored by juries. These keepers of popular morality evidently found youths "at fault" by ordinary standards and assessed liability accordingly.[146] Not surprisingly, New Hampshire gave up and adhered, in law as well as results, to the general approach.[147]

If courts have not done well with the problem, legislatures have not done much better. Some have tried to favor equal access by forbidding age, sex, or racial discrimination in auto insurance.[148] That sounds very simple. It says insurance companies may not charge people more because they are part of a racial, sexual, or age group which is characterized by being more accident prone than other groups. They must charge them the same price they charge all others. If that worked, the equal access subsidy would not be paid by the victim, but would be borne broadly by all insured drivers in the less accident prone categories.[149] Unfortunately, merely passing a statute, despite an overwhelming American tendency to think so, does not always solve a problem.[150] Without the statute it is true that the disadvantaged would pay more — as a group. But what happens with such statutes; who then pays more?

The answer is, or should be, troubling. When states prohibit discrimination in insurance by sex, age, or race the effect is that the discrimination persists, but the higher premiums are paid mainly by groups that are surrogates for the group previously charged. Insurance companies try to define and surcharge people who are accident prone in ways which do not require categorization based on the prohibited characteristic. They seek to identify groups who have more dangerous attitudes toward driving and charge them more, without basing the insurance category on race, sex, or age.[151] Thus, to pick a particularly fanciful example, if age classifications were prohibited they might charge more to those who like rock and roll music. This is a high risk group, let us assume, not because that characteristic has much to do with accident proneness in driving, but because it happens that there are relatively few safe 50-year-old law professors in that group and many 16- to 18-year-olds. To pick a more realistic example, insurance companies charge more to those who live in large metropolitan areas. Again it is not because this identifies a greater risk; if anything, such people drive less and ought to have fewer accidents. Rather, it is because this is a good surrogate for prohibited categories, and charges more to supposedly high risk ethnic and racial groups who predominantly live in inner cities.[152] If the law ultimately forbids *this* surrogate, they will just move on to the next best one and categorize, for example, by occupation.[153]

And what, one may ask, would we expect insurance companies to do?[154] Their job is to define and charge according to actuarially predictable risk. They look for the best predictor of future accidents, definable at the cheapest price, and charge accordingly. If that is forbidden, they look for the next best. But if what was forbidden was in fact intimately linked to accidents, the next best will probably simply be a less offensive — and more inaccurate and perhaps more expensive — way of identifying the same group whose identification was meant to be forbidden. I do not mean to say that some, or even much, racial, sexual, and age classification in insurance was not biased or based on false data and prejudice. That may well be the case. If so, laws barring such classifications properly speed us in learning what the profit motive ultimately might have led even biased companies to learn anyway.[155] I do mean that if we are — and we are — a racist, sexist, wealth-

and age-biased society, then it is not improbable that driving and accident proneness will reflect these biases, and that membership in racially, sexually, wealth- and age-defined categories may be linked to riskiness in driving.[156] In that case, the admirable attempt to bar such classifications, by itself, will only result in the use of surrogates to define and surcharge the same categories by other means. It will cause us to move from insurance classifications that discriminate on the basis of race, sex or age, to classifications which have a disproportionate negative impact on those of the previously disfavored race, sex, or age.

Thus a major effect of such laws is to hide from ourselves the fact that much of the burden will still be placed on those we supposedly did not wish to burden. There are some advantages to this, especially if the insurance companies do not intentionally use the surrogates to circumvent the ban on discrimination, but use them only because the substitute categories are the optimal actuarial classifications permitted and available. Perhaps it is good for the law to forbid us from assessing rates and limiting driving on the basis of race, sex, and so on, while still allowing it to happen indirectly. There may be an advantage to denying our racism and sexism at the formal, legalistic level because it may help the whole society become, in time, less racist and sexist.[157] Such societally created categories would then become insignificant, people's behavior would no longer correlate with membership in them, and the surrogate categories would themselves fall out of use.[158]

In the interim, however, the effect may be far from good. The members of the accident prone category, who have been assured that they are no longer being made to pay more, are apt to conclude (on seeing that their premiums are still higher than those charged to other groups) that the assurances were all just a trick. They may resent a society that promises non-discrimination in certain activities, but still charges them more to participate in them. The subtle, and important, legal distinction between discriminatory rules and rules that have a disproportionate negative impact on a group is apt to be lost on individuals who are still bearing what they consider to be an unfair burden. Inner city blacks do not need my analysis to tell them that insurance rates based on place of residence or occupation make a mockery of the claim that race is irrelevant to what one must pay to drive. They may even be more angry for the subterfuge, especially those who doubt that the prohibition of discriminatory classifications will, in time, lead to a non-racist society. To such individuals the whole exercise may seem to be a maleficent attempt to perpetuate discriminations which if made openly would be too shocking to survive. In addition, the occasional 50-year-old rock-and-rollers who will be charged more because the surrogate puts them in a high risk category, are also likely to be resentful. Somehow, people like that "know" they are *not* accident prone and bitterly attack any system that discriminates against them on the basis of irrelevant characteristics like preferring a certain type of music.[159] They will sense that they are bearing a disproportionate part of the cost of prohibiting racial, sexual or age classifications, and they will demand to know why that should be the case.

At this point, inevitably, comes the suggestion much favored by all right thinking people like the editorial writers of the New York *Times*. Why not require that insurance categories be based *not* on outside characteristics but rather on previous driving records?[160] Surely that way, the editorial pundits tediously intone, the problem could be solved.[161] But charging drivers on the basis of past accident records may instead be of very limited use if the object is *not* to discriminate against certain groups. It can readily be shown that such "record based" rates will, on quite probable assumptions, do little to assure unfettered participation by accident prone minorities, and in fact add undesirable elements of scapegoatism and risk to the exclusion process.

The key question is whether past accidents are good predictors of future accidents. To the extent they are, then one would have expected that insurance companies would have used them heavily in establishing categories and in setting rates, without being prodded by newspapers or obliged to do so by law. To the extent that they are not, having an accident essentially is a random event which will happen to an unlucky few (the victims of the evil deity). If, however, there are other characteristics—like age, sex, marital status, or ethnic background—which are highly linked to accident proneness, then many more of the unlucky few will be concentrated among members of the high risk group. Of these, not that many will have accidents, but far more of them will than those who are not in accident prone categories. The effect of a record based insurance categorization is to concentrate the bulk of the costs of accidents on those—predominantly in the disadvantaged groups—who are unlucky enough to have an accident. They—the unlucky and disadvantaged—become the ones who, in practice, pay the subsidy for the societal desire to give equal access.[162]

If one thinks about it a bit more, even the equal access that such an approach seems to give becomes more illusory than real. All those in the high risk group are allowed to drive at the same rate as anyone else. When they do so, however, they bear the significant uninsurable risk of having an accident and then being made to pay very large premiums for future participation. This risk is much greater for those in accident prone categories than for those in relatively safe categories *precisely* because such categories are accident prone and give rise to a far larger number of people who will have accidents. In the traditional common law system that risk is insured, it is paid for by *all* members of the high risk pool. All of these pay somewhat higher premiums than other categories because more of them will turn up unlucky. Under the accident involvement approach, this risk cannot be insured against. Each driver in a high risk category must drive bearing the risk of having to pay much higher premiums if he or she turns up unlucky. In the end then, all this approach does is concentrate *actual* losses among a smaller group within the high risk categories and increase risk for all in such groups by forbidding insurance for one consequence of having an accident. Coincidentally, it also lets society off the hook because now those (again predominantly within the high risk racial and sexual groups) who will bear the financial burden are nominally selected not on account of membership in the group, but on account of their own (by hypothesis largely irrelevant) individual behavior.[163]

A fine result then, the evil deity would say. The disadvantaged, as a group, are made to bear a larger risk—and hence a larger burden —when they participate in the societally central activity. Individual members of those groups find themselves disproportionately charged with the financial burden of accidents, and are—unnecessarily, if past accidents are poor predictors of future ones—kept from future participation. In addition, society tells them that they have no one to blame but themselves, for the standard is one which even the *Times* finds unbiased.[164] Any desire among these to divide the risk of such future exclusionary burdens with others (as likely to bear them as they are) is barred, because to permit insurance against such increases in future premiums based on past accidents would simply convert the system into the old (by hypothesis forbidden) common law one. Insurance rates would once again be determined by the actuarial likelihood of future accidents, and hence would overcharge disadvantaged groups!

Let me repeat that I do not conclude from all this that we should stay with insurance rates based on race, sex, or age.[165] Rather, I conclude that the kind of cosmetic solutions newspapers and legislators have come up with are to be criticized precisely because they make it appear as though our only choice is between openly offensive classifications and surrogates which still surcharge disadvantaged groups. My point, instead, is that we are not *obliged* to choose a lesser among these evils. We make such choices, as a society, not out of necessity but out of ambivalence. If we *mean* access to certain activities to be unfettered for members of groups that, for reasons of culture, age, or past societal mistreatment, are accident prone, we can do it, but we must do more than "bar" the relevant categorization. We must, as a society, take on the burden ourselves. We must subsidize directly (from government funds or government structured pools) the insurance rates offered to people who fall into high risk categories on account of race, sex, age or anything else we wish to treat as irrelevant. If we did this — to the extent necessary to counter the accident proneness of the group — one can be quite sure that insurance companies would quite quickly and happily jump in and exploit (that is, sell to) this now "equally" attractive group of customers.[166]

Such a subsidy is quite easy to imagine when the high risk group is defined by characteristics such as physical handicap or great age. It even may be possible when the group is defined by characteristics — like youth — which are linked to driving habits we dislike, but which we have all gone through. In all these cases society may be willing to pay the cost of that group's equal participation. It is far more difficult to imagine such a subsidy when it would have to be paid to a group which, for cultural reasons or for reasons arising out of past mistreatment, drives too fast or badly.

Let me give a catastrophic hypothetical situation which I have reason to believe may be a true one. On occasion I have gotten insurance executives rather drunk and they have "confided" in me that accident involvement statistics "show" that low-income blacks have many more auto accidents than low-income whites and many, many more than middle-income whites. They then add, almost as an afterthought, that middle-income blacks have the fewest accidents of all, considerably fewer than middle-income whites. Let us for the moment accept these doubtful statements as true, though they obviously present problems for those like myself who don't believe in race, and don't understand what the concept means except as a nasty societal construct. [167]

The only way I can understand the statements by the insurance executives is in pseudo-sociological terms. As I said before, if a group is *defined* by a society as being of a race or category and is treated worse on account of that definition, then, however fictitious, fanciful, and absurd the basis of the definition is, it is not unlikely that members of the group will react to their mistreatment, to their separate classification, in their general behavior. Thus, if we *are* a racist society and treat some differently than others, it is possible that those we have chosen to stigmatize and separate will behave in many circumstances differently from those we have not. If this makes any sense to you, it should not surprise you if low-income blacks might (justifiably) feel put upon and perhaps unconsciously express their resentment by (for example) driving more aggressively. It might follow that they have more accidents than, say, less put upon low-income whites.

Conversely, the same way of looking at things could explain the alleged "safe driving" by middle-income blacks. If you were part of a group that a racist society chose to stigmatize, and, by work and good fortune had managed to lift yourself up to the point where you lived decently, you might be especially wary of anything that could push you back to where the racist society seemed to wish to place you. Caution, leading to careful, more defensive driving, and fewer accidents, might become the order of the day. I am not a sociologist or a psychologist and so do not offer these suggestions *at all* as explanations. They are mentioned only as ways which have helped me to accept as *possibly* true the comments of the drunken insurance executives, despite my lack of belief in race and racial characteristics.

Assuming then that the figures are real, what then should such a society do? Charging higher insurance rates on the basis of race combined with low income is surely intolerable and should be prohibited. Should we therefore subsidize insurance companies which insure low-income blacks? Somehow that has been harder for our society to do than subsidizing driving by the aged, the handicapped, or even the young. Perhaps it has smacked of subsidizing insurance rates by those who have more accidents because they think of all driving as automobile racing. Yet if we do not do that, what are we to do? We surely will not use a lower standard of reasonableness to test members of the group — that would make victims pay the subsidy and still not avoid the problems which open subsidization immediately brings to mind. Can we give a hidden subsidy by putting *all* high risk drivers (whatever the source of the high risk) into one "assigned risk pool" which then is subsidized? We sometimes do just that, but by doing it we subsidize risky driving by some whose participation we do *not* wish to encourage.[168] We encourage driving by those whose riskiness is *not* based on attitudes derived from the way society has treated them, but simply from the fact that they drive badly![169] In other words, we accept too much of the gift of the evil deity and not just what is needed to assure equal access to core societal activities regardless of race.

Too often, as I said before, we give a hidden *non-subsidy*. We forbid racial classifications, but allow surrogates such as occupational, geographic, or even accident record classifications. This is a non-subsidy and a non-solution. It still treats the disfavored group worse than others, but hides the fact that this is being done on the basis of race. Perhaps most often we use this hidden non-subsidy with a twist, putting some of the burden on victims, and the majority of it on the most responsible members of the disfavored group. We do this by not requiring insurance, or requiring very low insurance, for drivers.[170] In this way, some of the low income blacks in my hypothetical example avoid any of the burden. They do not insure and have no assets, with the result that accident losses are borne by victims.[171] However, those low income blacks who feel they should insure in order to be able to compensate anyone who is injured would usually still be in high risk categories (through the use of surrogate classifications). These people would, along with victims, be the ones who are most burdened. Like the "solution" of accident record based classifications, this very common approach ends up not being very nice!

The problem remains, and for precisely the reasons it is a problem — namely that we are unwilling to admit openly that some groups in our flawed society may have attributes which are *undesirable and even dangerous*. However, because *we* are in a deep sense responsible for the existence of these attitudes, we would like both to deny their existence and to avoid hindering or excluding further those who have such attitudes. We would like to do this without in any way suggesting that the attitudes themselves are to be tolerated, let alone encouraged. It is this ambivalence that so often pushes us into subterfuges and wishful thinking.

Of course the whole hypothetical example may be false. The drunken executives may have been mistaken or lying through their teeth. If that were so, there would be all sorts of nice liberal ways out. When I put this case to my class there are always some who hopefully suggest solutions which would work, but only if the hypothetical example is false — if we are not in fact a racist society. There is always a white liberal who says that if we discriminated further (distinguished further, he or she quickly adds), made insurance groups smaller, we would find no difference between poor blacks and whites. This would be fine, wonderful even, because it would indicate that our society is not racist and did not discriminate against blacks in all sorts of ways which affect how people drive. There also is always a self-declared radical (inevitably white) who comes up with the idea that if we had some insurance companies owned only by blacks, the problem would disappear. I never need to answer that suggestion, since, before I can, a black student seems to beat me to it by saying that would suit him or her just fine. He or she would love to have such a company and then, under anti-discrimination laws, sell insurance only to middle income blacks, and make a fortune. The sarcasm of the reply is not infrequently lost on the original proponent of the idea.[172]

In the end, of course, whether the specific hypothetical example turns out to be true is less important than what it demonstrates about our ambivalence with respect to some risk related attitudes. With this behind us, I can quickly summarize how our law treats, and fails to treat, a variety of attitudes and attributes that are idiosyncratic, but not based specifically on religion. Where risky, cost causing behavior is due to physical attributes, or to age, or to handicap in a victim, or even to attitudes arising from these, it is generally considered "reasonable" and does not bar recovery by the victim. Where instead, the same attributes exist in an injurer, they are usually, in common law, unreasonable and the basis of liability. Sometimes, however, through legislation, subsidization occurs in such situations so that the whole society takes the burden from the injurer category. Where cost causing behavior derives from attitudes linked to ethnic or racial status it is generally deemed to be unreasonable at common law, whether in victims or in injurers. I cannot say for sure whether the same applies to *attitudes* (as against physical attributes) that are linked to sexual differences. That is not so clear, but my *impression* from reading many cases is that the reasonably prudent man has, in the past, been a *man* and not a person. As a result, I think, attitudes which stereotypically are female and are linked to accidents received no more protection, at common law, than those which stereotypically were Italian or black.

Despite this, we have, by statute and judicial decision,[173] acted to forbid the use of race, sex, and ethnic background as the basis of insurance classification. In this way we have tried to deny that we were penalizing attitudes which our racist and sexist society has developed in, or assigned to, certain ethnic, racial, and sexual groups. This could be taken to mean that we wish to treat such attitudes as reasonable and as an inappropriate basis for liability when they appear in such groups, even if they are still deemed undesirable or unreasonable in those not of such groups. Despite such statutes and decisions, however, very often the burden of accidents linked to these attitudes still gets put predominantly on such ethnic, racial, and sexual categories — or on some part of them — usually through a complex combination of subterfuges. All this indicates an extraordinary degree of ambivalence in our legal system with respect to these attitudes, especially when they are linked to ethnic, racial, and sexual stereotypes for which we all feel in part responsible.

3

The Beliefs of a Reasonable Person

THERE IS CONSIDERABLY LESS AMBIVALENCE in the law of torts when what is at issue is behavior (peculiar or unreasonable in most people) that is justified by those who acted that way on the ground that their actions were required by their religious beliefs. If the background for the last chapter required a few comments on tort law, the premises for this chapter can be found in some constitutional notions. Since, however, I am not a constitutional lawyer, I will spend even less time discussing these than I did discussing torts in the last chapter. And this is bound to be inadequate. Nevertheless it is all the space I can give to it.

We are a society constitutionally committed to the ideal that there shall be no establishment of religion, whatever that means.[174] Similarly, we are bound to the notion that church and state shall be separate and that there also shall be a free exercise of religion, whatever these mean.[175] What they do mean, and how the threads of their meanings intertwine and apply to small and to large "cultish" sects as well as to nonreligious beliefs, make up this chapter's yarn. The point of mentioning constitutional notions is not, however, to imply that we will be discussing what the Constitution *requires* of tort law. I am not dealing with constitutional law as much as with constitutional premises or notions. Thus I am not concerned with what the Constitution mandates as treatment for idiosyncratic religions and beliefs.[176] I am, rather, focusing on what the effect of the gravitational pull of these constitutional notions is on tort cases which involve religious beliefs.

I am not suggesting that tort law must respond to these as *rules,* or be in some sense unconstitutional. I am saying, instead, that our *definitions* of reasonable are profoundly influenced by the fact that we have a Constitution which says something about non-establishment of religion, separation of church and state, and free exercise of religion. All law responds somewhat to the gravitational pull of legal notions extraneous to the particular area of concern.[177] Inevitably, "ordinary" law such as torts responds especially strongly to the gravitational force that is our Constitution.[178] All this can best be seen by looking at some cases.

I would like to start with a 1930s Connecticut case called *Lange* v. *Hoyt* or, popularly, "the case of Minelda's pelvis."[179] I will simplify the case for purposes of this discussion — and in so doing misstate it — but in ways that are not relevant to the issues immediately at hand. There was an accident in which a driver was negligent. As a result of that accident, a young woman named Minelda suffered a shattered pelvis. Her injury became far more serious than normally would have been the case because Minelda delayed greatly in going to a doctor. She did this, she said, because going to a doctor violated her belief as a Christian Scientist.[180]

Leave aside whether it was true that she was a Christian Scientist, whether the damage to her pelvis was made greater because of her delay, and even whether she did, in fact, delay in getting medical assistance. All these factual questions were raised in the case, along with the question of whether, assuming she was a Christian Scientist, her faith, as she reasonably understood it, barred her from going to a doctor.[181] All these, as I say, were raised and properly put to the jury to decide. Nevertheless, we can ignore them all because the Connecticut court assumed (as it must for purposes of the case) that she was in fact a Christian Scientist, that she behaved as a reasonable Christian Scientist would have, and that the injury was made worse because she did not go to a doctor as soon as a reasonable non-Christian Scientist would have done.[182]

The question the court asked itself, as a result, was simply: "Is this a case of a negligent injurer taking a victim as he found her, that is with a belief (Christian Science) which made her subject to greater damages than others, or is this a case of a victim assuming the risk of her belief or acting unreasonably in not mitigating damages (because the reasonable prudent man would have gone to a doctor immediately)?" Both of these last would mean leaving the loss on the victim in order to lead her (and those like her) to decide how much of the evil deity's boon — in this case the greatest boon of all, faith — she wanted to risk taking. The first approach would instead put the loss on the injurers in order to induce potential injurers to consider, when they engage in risky activities, that the risk is greater than they might otherwise think because sometimes their actions will harm people, like Christian Scientists, who will suffer much greater losses than the ordinary victim. In deciding whether to act, which roulette wheel to buy and so forth, the injurer category is thus reminded that the presence of people like Minelda makes the deity's boon more costly than one might have thought.

This last approach, in effect, treats the existence of Christian Scientists in the same way tort law treats the existence of people with thin skulls. If the injurer had hit someone with an unusually thin skull, instead of an unusual belief he surely would have been liable for the unexpected harm that ensued. For, typically, as I mentioned in the last chapter, it is not the thin skulled person's obligation to wear a football helmet or a steel yarmulke wherever he or she goes, and the negligent injurer must pay for the extra harm that injuries to thin skulled people occasionally cause.[183] Conversely, the first approaches would treat Minelda's belief like the extra value of a violinist's hand, were he or she injured in a steel mill.[184] It would be her responsibility to decide whether the risk of the belief was worth its harm.

Not surprisingly, the Connecticut trial court ducked the issue and the Connecticut Supreme Court (of Errors as it then was) affirmed the ducking.[185] The court ducked it by sending the case to the jury and charging the jury in the following way: In deciding whether the victim acted with reasonable prudence in mitigating damages, you *may* consider that Christian Science is a widely held belief.[186] In a sense, the court answered Pilate's celebrated question "What is truth?" with a facile reply, "A popularity contest."[187] The jury in such a case gives results, not reasons. It does not tell us why it decides as it does, nor does it spell out which of many possible reasons it found compelling. It can apply the unspoken, and sometimes unspeakable, values of a society without having to give utterance to them and thus, once it has the case, can conclude that beliefs like Minelda's are reasonable or not, without telling us much about what motivated it.[188] Since the court permitted the jury to rule *against* Minelda (if they chose to ignore her belief as a justifiable ground for her behavior), had the jury found against Minelda, it would have been hard to know whether the jury had deemed the belief "unreasonable" or whether it had ruled against her on other grounds. As it happened, however, the jury ruled for Minelda and (since she won) the higher court was asked by the injurer whether merely *allowing* the jury to consider her belief, if it chose to, was permissible. The Connecticut Supreme Court answered that it was permissible and affirmed the lower court judgment.[189]

My students, when they read this case, are almost uniformly offended. "Why," they used to thunder — and now, in more genteel times, ask, — "protect beliefs like Minelda's in a polity in which church and state are separate?" Why not have the costs occasioned by idiosyncratic beliefs be a burden on those who hold them? Beliefs are different from thin skulls, and physical damages. It is only as to these last that the rule, that the injurer takes the victim as he or she finds him or her, should hold. Perhaps that rule should be a bit broader and apply to difficulties, attitudes, and idiosyncrasies that derive from physical differences or handicaps, but it should certainly not give protection to victims with "thin skull" religious beliefs.

If, however, one starts to consider the consequences of the position my students take, things begin to look far less clear than they suspected. Consider, for example, another case, this time hypothetical. I call it my Catholic case. Assume that Minelda, instead of being a Christian Scientist, was a devout Catholic who took the pope's encyclical, *Humanae Vitae,* rather more seriously than many Catholics do.[190] She genuinely believed, as the encyclical teaches, that it is a sin of the highest order to use what are called unnatural or artificial methods of contraception.[191] Assume also that the injury to her pelvis made pregnancy extraordinarily dangerous for her.

My Catholic Minelda would then be faced with three possibilities, none of them attractive. She could abstain from sexual intercourse. This would be very costly to the injurer, because the law normally gives very high damages to a victim and her husband who are kept from normal sexual relations as a result of an injury.[192] She could violate her conscience and use "artificial" contraceptives. (We shall put to one side what damages, if any, accrue to someone who is led to violate his or her conscience on account of an injury. The pains of hell surely are costly, but it is not clear that they are cognizable in a court of law.)[193] Or, finally, she could take a chance and use the rhythm method of contraception. The issue my hypothetical example raises is whether the third approach would be a reasonable one under the circumstances.[194]

Let us assume my Catholic Minelda opted for the rhythm method. Let us further assume she became pregnant and now had the terrible choice of either violating her conscience even further by having an abortion, or risking the dangerous pregnancy.[195] Let us finally assume she stayed true to her beliefs and all sorts of awful things happened to her in her pregnancy because of her shattered pelvis. Ultimately, of course, she — or her heirs — if death ensued — sue the injurer whose negligence had caused the shattered pelvis in the first place, demanding damages not just for the original injury, but for all the disastrous consequences that followed.[196] The injurer would, naturally, claim that would be insane. "If Minelda had used modern methods of contraception, I would, of course, be liable for some things: for the shattered pelvis, for her inability to have more children, had she wished them, and so on," he would say. "There would not, however, have been further catastrophic effects — like those brought on by the pregnancy — so why should I be liable for these? If Minelda had acted like reasonable people who do not follow *Humanae Vitae* do, the damages would have been much more limited. She failed," he would conclude, "to act reasonably to mitigate the damages that my admitted negligence caused."

Minelda's reply would, of course, be, "But following my belief *was* reasonable. It is in fact costlier to give up a cherished belief than to take the risks entailed by adherence to it. Hence, under standard cost-benefit definitions of reasonableness, I acted reasonably."[197] "Nor," she would add, "does the fact that the consequences of following the belief turned out to be catastrophic make any difference, so long as taking the chance of such consequences was reasonable to begin with." On this she is clearly correct. Suppose that, through your negligence, I suffer a minor injury to my arm and, reasonably, choose to have an operation to repair the injury because the injury affects my teaching (since it impedes my waving my arms about). The anesthesia in the operation, however, tragically leaves me a paraplegic. There is no doubt I can successfully sue you for all the damages because having the operation was reasonable, even though the consequences of the operation were far worse than if I had left bad enough alone.[198] Thus, Minelda is quite right that if using the rhythm method was reasonable originally—because violating her conscience or abstaining would have been worse—it was not rendered unreasonable simply because it led to still worse results and damages. For these too, she could recover from the negligent injurer.

We can put the issue more precisely, under the dominant test for reasonableness propounded by Learned Hand (actually taken by him from Professor Terry).[199] Reasonableness requires that one weigh the costs and benefits of behavior against the costs and benefits of behaving differently. One must weigh the benefits and harms that would occur from doing one thing against the benefits and harms that would occur from doing the other, each discounted by the likelihood of the harms and benefits occurring.[200] If on striking that balance a given behavior is reasonable, it is not rendered unreasonable merely because an unwanted result chanced to come about.

The further and deeper issue, however, is whether in striking this balance (Learned Hand was forever urging us to strike impossible balances)[201] one is or is not permitted to include one's beliefs, and the damages to them, on one side of the scale. If the harm entailed in violating one's beliefs counts as a weight on the balance, then what both the Catholic and the Christian Scientist Mineldas did was reasonable and all that followed was recoverable. If it does not count then what they did was unreasonable and they must put up with the consequences.[202]

This helps some of my students, but it does not help others. Many of them say, "There you are. You see, the issue was not one of mistreating Christian Scientists because Christian Science is an idiosyncratic belief. Surely Catholicism is not idiosyncratic in Connecticut. About 40% of the population of the state is Roman Catholic.[203] What is at stake, therefore, is not whether odd beliefs are to be accorded the same protection as established ones. It is, rather, that the reasonably prudent man/person is, and must be, a 'scientific' person, devoid of beliefs. One must act scientifically [whatever *that* means] to reduce damages. One is bound to do what, apart from any beliefs, would mitigate injuries. If one does not, the loss stays on him or her."

Others of my students are understandably skeptical of the possibility or desirability of such a "scientific" reasonable prudent person (about whom I will talk shortly). They also are more direct and say, "No, it is not a question of science or of being devoid of beliefs at all. It was really a question of *oddness* of beliefs. An odd belief is an odd belief. Orthodox Roman Catholicism is as odd, when it takes a position against contraception, as Christian Science is in keeping people from going to doctors. That's the end of it. We all know what is reasonable and what is unreasonable, and it's all fairly simple. Popularity doesn't enter into it at all; it is just a matter of common sense."[204]

At this point I usually give my class yet another case — a real case — which I call my Jewish case. The case is *Friedman* v. *New York* and is relatively recent (1967).[205] A 16-year-old woman, now married and named Ruth Eider — but then single and named Friedman — went to look at the view from a ski lift in the Catskills one fine summer afternoon with a 19-year-old man, Jack Katz. Toward the end of the afternoon the State of New York (or better, its agents) which operated the ski lift negligently closed it down, wrongly believing that everyone had gotten off. That left the two teen-agers dangling in midair.

Unfortunately for the State of New York, it turned out Ms. Friedman had been taught it was a violation of Jewish law for an unmarried woman to be with a man after dark in a place where she could not readily be reached. And, as the sun sank slowly in the Catskills, Ms. Friedman jumped from the ski lift. Perhaps, more accurately, one should say she dove, because the case reports her most significant injuries were facial lacerations. I must interject that I have never understood why Jack Katz did not jump, or, for that matter, why she did not push him. I have no evidence that the religious tenet could not have been met by having him jump rather than her, and so I have to think that Katz was something of a cad or was applying a sexual double standard based on the ground that it was no sin for him to be there. But there it is; unfair and sexist or not, she was the one who jumped and sued.

There is good reason to think she was incorrect in her belief and that in her situation — even under the most orthodox of Jewish doctrines — she would not have been required to risk her life by jumping.[206] But the accuracy of her belief was not really relevant. The question was whether she reasonably could believe what she had been taught.[207] She had, in fact, been taught by a rabbi whom she could reasonably believe, that the rule was an absolute prohibition. (The rabbi, I will assume, was impecunious so that even if he taught her incorrectly and negligently it would do her no good to sue him. Indeed, it may be that *all* teachers are rendered immune from the consequences of their wrong teaching not so much by law as by the paucity of their take home pay.)[208] The court, in any event, had no doubt that if one conceded that her belief could be taken into account, then her behavior was reasonable.[209] She in fact recovered financially as well as physically, having lived up to the law as she understood it.

The case is important not especially because it adds another belief to the list, but because the question of reasonableness was decided explicitly by a court rather than by a jury. Since the suit involved a claim against the State of New York, it had to be brought before the Court of Claims rather than an ordinary court, and this particular court decides such cases without a jury.[210] The result is that we have, in *Friedman* v. *New York,* a full judicial statement (rather than just a Delphic jury verdict) that beliefs, however unorthodox in their orthodoxality, are part of what constitutes reasonable prudence. There could be no hedging. The reasonable victim in this case was reasonable simply because she did something on account of her belief which, if done by most of us, would be considered plain silly by a court, jury, or anyone else.

My class reacts to this case in a rather odd way. Some start to worry—too many different kinds of odd beliefs seem to turn up winners. This leads a few students to have second thoughts about bucking what they always—and usually uselessly—seek: a general rule of law.[211] Others, instead, stick to their guns and reiterate either that the reasonable prudent man should act scientifically and apart from all beliefs to avoid harm, or that orthodox Judaism is as odd as orthodox Catholicism or Christian Science. I then give them my last case in this series, a case I call my WASP case, even though I have no idea whether white Anglo-Saxon Protestant parties were actually involved. I call it that, however, because, the beliefs at stake are widely accepted among "ordinary" Americans, like mainstream white Anglo-Saxon Protestants.

The case is called *Troppi* v. *Scarf,* and was decided in 1971.[212] It involves a married couple who had had several children and wished to have no more because they could afford no more. The evidence on this point is quite clear and we can take it as given that the cost of more children was what motivated them. They went to a doctor who prescribed birth control pills. When they took the prescription to a pharmacist, however, he negligently gave them tranquillizers instead. As calmly as can be, they made love and in due course the woman became pregnant. Not as calmly, one imagines, they sued the pharmacist for the cost of bringing up the child they could not afford to have. The case in court involved many fascinating and complicated issues about "wrongful" life, "the compensating joys of having children," and so forth, which we must put to one side.[213] The key issue on which I would like to focus here was the defense claim that the tranquil couple had failed to act reasonably to mitigate damages once the child was conceived.

The defendant may be liable for the pregnancy, the argument ran, but not for the costs of bringing up the child because the couple could have lessened damages by having an abortion or putting the child, once born, up for adoption. Abortion was possible, and there were no lack of people eager to adopt such children.[214] The woman chose to bring the pregnancy to term. It was claimed, therefore, that it was the couple's beliefs—their reluctance to have an abortion or to have the baby adopted—which gave rise to the costs they sought to recover. Needless to say, the couple's answer was that, while their beliefs were involved, people in this position should not be induced to violate such reasonable beliefs by threats of huge financial burdens. The law, they claimed, should not lead them and others like them to do something that offensive.

The court reacted sternly to the injurer's argument. It refused to let the question even go to a jury and said that *as a matter of law,* this pharmacist took his victims as he found them, with their beliefs.[215] The couple believed neither abortion nor adoption was the right thing to do and they had a perfect right to this belief. Others may believe otherwise and those who are negligent to them are lucky, just as are those who negligently hit a thick skulled person on the head. But this in no way means that a negligent injurer is not liable if he or she chances to hurt someone with a thin skull or with beliefs against abortion or adoption. A reasonable person is not, as a matter of law, required to have an abortion or to give up a child for adoption, however much these may be acceptable alternatives for other reasonable people. The defendant may not, by claiming failure to mitigate damages, induce people to act against beliefs such as these. In effect, then, the court held it irrelevant that damages would have been less in the absence of ideals or beliefs. It held, clearly and powerfully, that the reasonably prudent person *can* act upon beliefs.

Strangely enough, virtually everyone in my class agrees with this case and thinks it is a perfectly sensible result even though it makes shreds of the previously argued "scientific" approach to reasonable prudence and damages. The issue, if one accepts *Troppi* v. *Scarf,* no longer can be whether beliefs are part of the reasonable person, but only which beliefs are reasonable. The reasonable person is not the "scientific" person who is bound to reduce damage costs regardless of the harm it does to faith, beliefs or ideals. Or, to put it in terms of the Learned Hand test, at least some beliefs count in the balance of harms and benefits which define reasonable prudence, and some (like those in *Troppi* v. *Scarf*) not only count but, as a matter of law, tip the scales almost regardless of what is on the other side.[216] But if *some* moralisms, sentiments, attitudes, and beliefs are to be given weight, the question inevitably becomes: Which ones? Such an approach seems to require that we distinguish between reasonable and unreasonable (or odd) beliefs — even among religious ones.

This, of course, presents us with a terrible problem because of the establishment clause of the Constitution. "No establishment of religion" more than suggests that our law ought not distinguish and favor some religious beliefs over others.[217] If we did this we would, in a way, create an *establishment* made up not of one religion, but of that group of "acceptable" religions and beliefs which are sufficiently alright so that their tenets may be part of reasonable prudence. Similarly we would be treating as "non-conforming" those religions whose tenets are unreasonable and outside the pale of "common" sense (which, clearly, is not a value free term).[218]

In practice, it is not hard to tell what tenets would be deemed reasonable in our society in order to define what parts of which religions would form our "establishment." They are what I call our "banquet" religious beliefs. To identify them, one only has to start with those religions whose ministers, rabbis, or priests are commonly invited to give the invocations and benedictions at large public, nonsectarian, banquets. One then must exclude those beliefs of these ministers, etc., which they cannot give voice to, even by implication, in such invocations. What is left is what is "acceptable," what represents reasonable, moderate faith. Even my more aggressive students would recognize such beliefs as alright, although they often would not share them. To define such an establishment, however, is not to justify it. Indeed, the "no establishment" clause was put in the Constitution because many of our dominant religions had, in England, been nonconformist and "not acceptable."[219] The idea was to free from special burdens future, as well as present, "non-banquet" tenets. That certainly suggests that it will not do for tort law to hold "banquet" tenets part of reasonable prudence, while placing accident costs on those who, by their faith, assume the risk of "non-banquet" beliefs.

There is another way, however, to try to explain *Troppi* v. *Scarf* and to distinguish it from my earlier cases. At first glance this may seem promising, though in the end I believe it also will not do. The difference between *Troppi* and the other cases is that the other cases involved religious beliefs, while Troppi only involved secular ones. The notion that we should not be penalized for failing to have an abortion or giving our child up for adoption is not a religious notion. Reasonable prudence includes (and the reasonable person is permitted to have and weigh) non-religious beliefs. They must be common or widely held beliefs in order to be reasonable. This is not a problem with respect to non-religious beliefs since there is no Constitutional clause that bars an establishment of secular beliefs. As a result we can distinguish in law between "crazy" and "common sense" secular attitudes or "moralisms" because that does not favor one religion over another.[220] This approach would, however, conclude that the reasonable prudent person may not have or give weight to beliefs based on religion, whether or not these are widely held, since these are what can get us into trouble with the no establishment clause.

There is an obvious problem with this approach in that it inevitably favors non-religious beliefs over religious ones. That, secularists to the contrary notwithstanding, is a troublesome way of defining what the constitutional notions of separation of church and state and free exercise of religion are about.[221] Passing that, however, the approach has a deeper problem. What are, after all, these secular beliefs and where do they come from? What is the origin of notions that one should not be penalized for not having an abortion or for not giving up a child for adoption? Most of the time such beliefs derive from earlier religious tenets. They are secularized versions of those religions that were dominant in this society in the past. To the extent that we accept only these non-religious beliefs as reasonable, what we are doing is accepting white Anglo-Saxon and core Protestant morality and excluding all others. That is why I called *Troppi* v. *Scarf* my "WASP case," though I should have emphasized that the "P" included only the traditionally "alright" American Protestant sects and not those on the fringes. To take this seemingly secular approach is to say that reasonable prudence permits us to respond to those beliefs which were part of the morality propounded by the religions and groups that founded this land, but requires us to exclude those of the immigrants, of the parvenus. These last must bear the burden by assuming the risks of their faiths.

There is some support for this last, utterly absurd and even despicable, position in Constitutional law. The Supreme Court has upheld laws which require shops to close on Sundays.[222] It has done this, essentially, by saying that Sunday closing laws are not based on religion. States have a right (admittedly) to require a day of rest each week, and if in doing so they happen to pick Sunday, what is the harm? It is after all a "secular" habit to take Sunday off. Where, however, does that habit come from if not from the founding banquet religions? A distinguished former dean of a distinguished law school answered that question when I put it to him by saying only a foreigner would not understand that Sunday closing was not derived from religion, but was simply a part of the American way of life because "*we* are a Christian Society in origin." I cannot say his comment did much to reassure this first generation American.

Similarly, the Supreme Court has refused to permit "partial" conscientious objection.[223] It has denied freedom from military service to those whose consciences do not forbid them from participating in *all* wars, but only in *some* which their faiths define as "unjust." The Court did this partly on the grounds of administrative convenience, as weak a reed here as it was in the Sunday closing cases. One can readily devise a system which meets the nation's needs and treats the consciences of those who object only to some wars and those whose faiths lead them to oppose all wars, equally.[224] Here, as in the Sunday closing cases, the Court seemed to go beyond convenience, however, and suggest that somehow total conscientious objection (despite the clear language of the statute establishing the right to it) was not a matter of religious belief at all.[225] It seemed to imply that *total* conscientious objection was, in those who held to that tenet, almost a secular and, therefore, "acceptable," belief, while partial objection was either a fraud, or based on idiosyncratic religious beliefs.[226] One way or another, our nonestablishment land can favor those whose beliefs forbid all wartime service over those whose beliefs are more discriminating.

The fact remains, however, tha: partial conscientious objection and doctrines of "just and unjust" wars derive from religions (and especially Catholicism) which were *not* "acceptable" when this country was founded and when the admirable notion was developed that, on the basis of faith, some should be exempt from military service. It is more than possible that a country, whose religious traditions held firmly to the doctrine of "just wars," might be more likely than ours to permit selective conscientious objection to wars which were plausibly unjust.[227] Such a country would probably also describe its doctrine as "secular," but that would no more hide the fact that the origins of the doctrine lay firmly in the tenets of the previously dominant religion than does the analogous pap given us by the Supreme Court with respect to the American notion of objections of conscience.

Some Protestant religions which were early and very influential in this country firmly believed in the right of total objection of conscience.[228] That was, understandably, the starting point of American law on the matter. In time that approach, like Sunday closing, became part of the American way of life. This sufficed for the Supreme Court to permit the continued dominance of laws which give advantage to—in a sense *establish*—those whose consciences and beliefs reflect these once dominant faiths.[229]

The trouble with this is that it leads to the danger I mentioned in the last chapter when I spoke of women being led to conform to male stereotypes.[230] It highlights the ugly side of the melting pot. It declares in profoundly practical terms—terms of financial and military burdens—that newcomers, new believers, new religions may indeed have equality in this land, but only if they give up those tenets of their faiths that do not fit; ones that are somehow not of the "banquet" variety. Even if one is to accept the inevitability of the melting pot with respect to many cultural traits of the newly arrived, one may well question if the same can be accepted with respect to their religious beliefs. One could wonder what, if anything, the no establishment clause of the Constitution is about if not to protect from discriminatory pressures the religious beliefs of immigrant groups.[231] These, at least, might be protected from being melted down and consumed in the great pot of American conformism.

One may understand, then, why states like Connecticut in *Lange* v. *Hoyt* and New York in *Friedman* v. *New York* chose to protect the immigrant belief and refused to burden Minelda or Mrs. Eider. Perhaps the courts of these states, while not necessarily bound by the "no establishment" clause to do what they did, were trying to respond properly to the force, to the gravitational pull, of that clause, and to make local tort law and reasonable prudence consistent with the values the clause embodies. If to avoid favoring some faiths over others means treating as reasonable some religious beliefs most people would deem odd, these cases seem to say, "So be it."

But the consequences of such a point of view are also not without difficulties. To say that religious beliefs, no matter how unusual, strange, or idiosyncratic, are reasonable or are to be taken into account in deciding reasonableness, inevitably raises the question of idiosyncratic non-religious beliefs. After all, we are not supposed to favor religion any more than we are to disfavor it.[232] If we have to protect the odd religious belief, then shouldn't we also protect the non-religious belief?

Indeed, that is what the Supreme Court ultimately did in the area of objections of conscience. In *Welsh* v. *United States,* the Court held that objections of conscience not based on religion but grounded in religion-like, philosophical, beliefs were as protected as those based on religion.[233] Passing for the moment the problem of defining such non-religious, philosophical beliefs (an issue which gave the Court some, but apparently not insuperable, difficulties) and the fact that, as to these philosophical beliefs, objection of conscience was also recognized only for those whose conscience was repelled by all wars, the Court's conclusion seemed almost inescapable.[234] Any other conclusion would either abolish all objections based on conscience or discriminate against non-religious objections. As a result, the statute defining conscientious objection had to cover these last as well.

The same step is not as easy for tort law, however. If that were done it would dramatically undermine the notion, fundamental to tort law for centuries, that reasonableness is an objective matter and does not depend on whether someone behaves "in good faith" according to his or her belief.[235] Suppose a person is walking across the street and a cab is coming at him or her. The person could avoid the cab by jumping backwards, but this person does not believe in jumping backwards. The person believes in progress and thinks one must always move ahead and never retreat. This is not a religious belief; it is simply a deeply held philosophical viewpoint that going backwards is wrong. Because of this belief the person jumps forward, gets hit by the cab, and sues for damages. Are we prepared to say that, because we wish to protect Christian Scientists who don't go to doctors, this person behaved reasonably and can recover?

Suppose, to make the analogy even closer, there is a person who, having been injured, refuses to go to a doctor because he or she has a deep hatred or distrust of doctors. Suppose this distrust is based on a coherent — but quite idiosyncratic — philosophy about healing and how it takes place. Do we wish to encourage the added harm which comes about as a result of following such beliefs which are both highly unusual and have nothing to do with religion? Historically, tort law has not been willing to do so. It has held for centuries that victims must live up to some average, community defined, standard of rea- sonableness. The fact that such a standard does include beliefs (like the fact that some unusual religious beliefs are also given weight in determining that standard) has not been taken to justify or to require stretching the standard further to protect "forward jumpers" or idio- syncratic doctor haters.[236]

Actually, tort law is even more complicated, because there are many non-idiosyncratic, non-religious, beliefs that it refuses to pro- tect. Some of these, which deal with what are called fanciful or emo- tional damages, I will discuss in the next chapter. Others, instead, are germane to this one. For example, suppose the accident victim we have been postulating is a white racist. Suppose he or she is an ordinary, run-of-the mill white racist whose views are reflected in the bulk of the society of which he or she was a part at the time of the injury. This victim, having been injured, is brought to a hospital and is told either one of two things: he or she must have a transfusion, but the blood available might come from a black donor, or the only doctor who can treat him or her happens to be black. Whereupon, the victim says, "I'd rather die", and does. Did that person act reasonably?

I believe the law would say no, even though the person was not really idiosyncratic. Evidence that the victim's prejudice was widely held likely would not be admitted. The court would make noises at the jury about the reasonable man not being limited by the juror's own prejudices, but instead representing the greater accident cost avoid- ance ideals and aspirations of the society.[237] The Court might with- hold the issue from the jury altogether and find lack of reasonable- ness as a matter of law.[238]

This situation suggests the gravitational force of the Constitution also can draw in the opposite direction from that which we noted in the religion cases. In those, the Constitution seemed to pull us to say beliefs which would usually seem idiosyncratic should, nevertheless, be protected in order to avoid distinguishing between "acceptable" and "non-acceptable" religions. Here the Constitution seems to lead us to treat as idiosyncratic beliefs which in fact are, or were, much too commonly held.

Once again, I am not saying the Constitution *requires* such a result; I am only saying the presence of constitutional norms and values is a significant factor in determining that which is deemed reasonable in tort law and that which is not. The fact that tort law tends to state its conclusions (even when they are influenced by the Constitution) as though they were matters of relative idiosyncrasy of belief, is more because it wishes to defend the general dominance of commonly held notions in most areas (where the Constitution is neutral) than because idiosyncracy has much effect where constitutional values and norms are significant. It is almost as if tort law had arrived at the conclusion that, unless it used the rubric of idiosyncracy, it would be pushed too readily to give up the notion of an "objective" standard of reasonableness. This would mean individuals would be able to accept—"free of charge"—gifts of the evil deity which the society as a whole would rather have rejected. By responding to constitutional values in defining the concept of reasonableness while at the same time, emphasizing the language of idiosyncracy versus widely-held beliefs, tort law reaffirms the right of the society as a whole to have some say in what individuals must pay if they wish to accept gifts of the evil deity.

As a result, in victim cases in torts we do, in practice, favor religion and religious beliefs. We do this (because of the force of the no establishment clause) by protecting some beliefs which would be deemed idiosyncratic were they not of religious origin. We probably, however, would deny protection even to beliefs based on religion if they could be described as deriving from "cults" rather than "religions."[239]

There may be some beliefs which are considered *so* outlandish that they do not count as religious at all, even for purposes of the establishment clause. In fact that is a subterfuge—for no principled distinction can be made between cults and religions. It may, nonetheless, be a useful—if dangerous—lie, like the statement that there are absolute first amendment rights to freedom of speech and that, what is (at times) "properly" restricted, is simply not speech.[240] The distinction between a cult and a religion and the analogous distinction, often made by courts, between religious beliefs, which are inviolate, and religious practices, which can be regulated by the state, are also subterfuges and myths. They may, nonetheless, help to keep us from expanding too far those narrow exceptions to our constitutional aspirations which we simply cannot avoid making.[241] By denying that some cults are religions at all, we may be able to give full protection in the face of majoritarian pressures to any number of other religions which are *not* "acceptable," but which could not be termed non-religions under any reasonable definition of religion.

There are both dangers and costs to this approach or strategy. When we use it we do create an establishment that is far broader than even the loose establishment of "acceptable" religions which it seeks to avoid. However, it is an establishment which excludes those faiths that are beyond the pale even more thoroughly than would the narrower establishment it replaces. Members of these groups are totally emarginated, and told their beliefs are not even faiths or religions within the meaning of the words. Some beliefs are totally excluded from the polity. To say *that,* of course, is almost to call the holders of such faiths outlaws and to invite them to revolt. This — though it may be highly unfair and unjust — may not be terribly dangerous when the so-called cult is truly small. If the same tactic is applied to a significant belief, however, the emargination and call to revolution it implies can be highly destructive. A society which feels compelled to use the tactic with respect to a belief which is widely held is bound to suffer serious consequences.

To summarize: tort law seeks to avoid emarginating most unusual religions, and therefore grants protection to religious beliefs held by victims even when these are quite idiosyncratic. When, instead, the belief is not based on religion, tort law is "neutral" and generally accords protection to a victim who holds a belief only if the victim's attitude is widely held. Thus, if most people in a society believed that progress required them to jump forward and never to jump backward, the forward jumping victim discussed earlier would probably recover damages. He or she would be deemed to have acted reasonably. The same would be true of a doctor hater in a society in which most people distrusted doctors and only went to them in extreme cases. So long as the belief was in fact sufficiently common, it would not matter that we could show that the belief was "scientifically" wrong (that damages

were demonstrably greater if people failed to go to doctors). Nonetheless, some common — non-idiosyncratic non-religious — beliefs are considered unreasonable in victims. This will be so if the Constitution
(or for that matter significant statutes) exert a gravitational pull against
the belief, as was the case with the racist belief.[242] Finally some types
of beliefs and attitudes which are widely held and which violate no
constitutional norms are, nonetheless, considered unreal, unreasonable, or fanciful.[243]

Before I turn to these latter beliefs however, we must deal with
the fact that in this chapter I have concentrated on what I called easy
cases — that is, situations in which the holder of the odd belief was
the victim. In all these cases the believer was injured by somebody
who was at fault, who hadn't behaved reasonably, who in some sense
"deserved" to pay damages. Minelda, Mrs. Eider, and the tranquil couple in *Troppi* v. *Scarf* were all people who were injured by somebody
who had been negligent. For reasons I discussed in the last chapter,
it is relatively easy to say that if the injurer — the defendant — was unreasonable, he or she ought to pay what is needed to help society give
parity between widely held and idiosyncratic beliefs.

The defendant has no right to complain if society makes him
or her pay the cost of achieving the societal goal of having no established religions. (In a sense there is an analogue between this attitude
and that which has made relatively easy those cases in which the burden of redressing the societal effects of past racial discrimination is
placed on people or institutions which had previously been guilty of
discrimination, as against those which, in the name of such redress,
burden innocent parties.)[244] One may, of course, ask why a wrongful
defendant in torts should only compensate victims of idiosyncratic
religious beliefs, rather than all victims who acted in good faith (like
the forward jumper). One may go further and question whether the
rule of contributory negligence makes any sense at all.[245] But this is
somewhat to the side of the current discussion. It in no way denies
the fact that the problem of protecting beliefs is a much harder one
when the believer is the injurer who, on account of his or her religious
belief, has acted in a way that has damaged an innocent victim.

Suppose Mrs. Eider was born Rothschild, or carried liability
insurance — that is, was able to pay damages. Suppose further that there
either was no negligence on the part of the State of New York in stop-
ping the ski lift, or that because of particular legal doctrines, like "sov-

ereign immunity," the state could not be sued for damages.[246] Suppose finally that Mrs. Eider, because of her belief, jumps or dives and, instead of injuring herself, hits me — as I am walking around picking daisies, or, better (since she could have seen me and waited a moment to dive) jumps into a bush — in which, unfortunately and unbeknownst to her, there is a perfectly reasonable tranquil couple whom she grievously mangles. The tranquil couple naturally sues Mrs. Eider. She, equally naturally, defends by claiming she acted reasonably given her belief, and (if my hypothetical example occurred recently) cites *Friedman* v. *New York*, in support of her position. What does tort law do then; and is what it does correct?

We first should distinguish some special situations. For example, we can put to the side those cases in which the believer has special relationships and owes special duties to the victim. Thus, where the injured party is a child and the believer is a parent, broader considerations come into play which may support damages and even permit society to force the parent to act against his or her belief or to let society care for the child.[247] Similarly, we can set aside cases of intentional or certain harm. Thus Mrs. Eider might readily be liable if she intentionally jumped on a plump passer-by (to break her fall), and caused that victim grave harm, or (following on my earlier suggestion) if she tossed Jack Katz out of the ski lift. Intentional wrongs are, for many reasons which I have not time to discuss, treated differently than accidental ones in which the party involved at worst was careless or negligent.[248] The hard case on which I would like to concentrate is the one in which belief leads to acts which are negligent, acts which only increase the *chances* of injuries to other, innocent, people. When these injuries come about, who should bear the burden — the believer, the victim, or someone else? If belief is the evil deity's gift, and if parity among beliefs is also such a gift, who should pay the price of these gifts?

In such cases tort law has tended to put the burden on the believer, but only if the belief is idiosyncratic. Thus, in a *Troppi* v. *Scarf* situation, if the unwanted child were later to claim psychological scars from being kept "unwanted" and sue the parents because they didn't put him or her up for adoption, the child would almost certainly lose. It may be that the child would lose because it is hard to prove that there was psychological scarring or that the scarring would have been avoided had the child been adopted. But it may also be that this unmeetable requirement of causation is there because it enables us to hide the fact that we want to allow parents to keep unwanted children.[249] To wish to keep unwanted children is an "acceptable" belief, and so we let the loss lie on the victim rather than on the holder of the belief.[250]

My own view is that the last description is the correct one and that our law does distinguish between "acceptable" and "odd" beliefs whenever the victim who suffers as a result of the belief is both innocent and identifiable. In these situations the loss is likely to be put on the injurer if he or she holds "odd" beliefs, but is likely to be left on the victim if the injurer's belief is not-idiosyncratic or when the belief, though idiosyncratic, is part of our establishment.[251] The right to be a conscientious objector is an example of this last point though in a non-tort area. Because some are exempted on the basis of conscience, others must serve and perhaps die. One could argue that this burden is sufficiently diffuse so that there is no identifiable individual who must pay the price of society's desire to protect the objector's conscience. If that were true — if one could say the whole of society bore the burden of accepting this particular gift of the deity — the case would be relatively easy. In many instances, however, one can identify the very person who must serve because someone else claims exemption on account of conscience. This would be true whenever there is a draft lottery, for then one can identify those whom lot would have excluded, but who, because they were the next numbers to come up, are called to take the place of those excluded on account of conscience.

When that happens the person who must serve suffers because of someone else's belief. He is, moreover, as identifiable a victim as if he were damaged in tort by someone whose act is only deemed reasonable, and permitted, on account of belief. The holder of the belief is allowed to put *all* the cost of the belief on the victim and to make the victim bear the whole burden of protecting the belief. Like the desire to keep one's children, even if unwanted, conscientious objection to all wars is an "acceptable" belief. Because it *is* "acceptable," not even the fact that it is unusual — if not quite idiosyncratic — deprives the holder of his entitlement to act on that belief to the disadvantage of specific and innocent others.

How then, in a society which seeks to exclude an establishment of religion, can one justify the placement of losses on injurers who hold idiosyncratic religious beliefs which are not "acceptable"? Why doesn't the same logic which led the courts to protect Minelda and Mrs. Eider as victims — given that the tranquil couple was to be protected — also lead us to protect Minelda and Mrs. Eider as injurers? The answer — which in the end will prove unsatisfactory — lies in the other possibilities the courts think they have for assigning the loss. If it is not assigned to the holder of the odd belief, the courts seem bound to burden the innocent victim. The desire to give parity among beliefs does not seem to extend that far.

This is odd because the traditional (nineteenth century) view of tort law was precisely that innocent victims should bear the burden of accidents which did not result from someone else's fault. These were treated as "Acts of God" and the loss for them lay on the unlucky victim.[252] As a great English judge, Baron Bramwell, put it (when asked by the victim's lawyer "If somebody must suffer, why should it be the innocent plaintiff, instead of the defendant, who chose to exercise his horses in the public streets?"), "For the convenience of mankind . . . [victims] people as they go along roads must expect, or put up with, such mischief as reasonable care on the part of others cannot avoid."[253] In other words, once the society decides to accept a gift of the evil deity ("for the convenience of mankind"), the whole burden of that decision stays with the unlucky victim on whom it chances to fall. If the gift we accept is the notion that all religious beliefs should be treated equally, then it would seem to follow that the unlucky victim is the person who properly bears the cost of that decision, just as he or she bears the cost of society's decision to permit motor cars.

This nineteenth century answer, however, does not seem acceptable today. To return to the discussion in the first chapter, the relict's plea — "My spouse was picked as the evil deity's victim; society got most of the benefits from accepting the deity's gift, why should we bear the bulk of the burden rather than society itself?" — rings true today.[254] To put it another way, when I am hit by Mrs. Eider because she decides to jump from the ski lift, I have only a minimal interest in protecting her right to have her idiosyncratic belief treated on a par with other beliefs. Society has a much greater interest in this equal treatment. *It* says we should have no establishment and we should not distinguish between "acceptable" and "odd" religions. I may agree, or even take some of the benefit of that decision, but my gain remains only a very small portion of society's gain. Why, then, shouldn't society create a special fund to compensate victims of those who would be at fault if their actions were not due to idiosyncratic beliefs?

In practice, of course, such a fund does not exist. Courts are torn between burdening the victim or reneging on the notion of equal treatment for all religious beliefs. In these circumstances it is not surprising that they tend to renege, and burden the victims only when the injurer's behavior derives from beliefs we would readily accept as reasonable. Just as we are not inclined to say individual innocent victims should suffer because someone is young, aged, handicapped, or disadvantaged, so we are not likely to let the innocent victim of Minelda or Mrs. Eider go uncompensated.[255] We would *like* to grant equal access to these groups, but not enough to allow identifiable innocent victims to pay the price. We are of two minds about odd beliefs and are torn between the pull of the no establishment clause and the desire to compensate all innocent victims of idiosyncratic behavior. We grant recovery to *victims* despite their odd beliefs, but burden injurers if, but only if, their beliefs are idiosyncratic.

The result is an unhappy compromise, deriving more from the limits courts face in deciding who should bear the burden of accidents and from the unwillingness of legislatures to face such issues, than from any inherent difficulty in the problem.[256] Just as we can, and sometimes do, subsidize the young, the handicapped, and the aged, in order to create equal access without burdening innocent victims, we could create an accident compensation system which would not lead us to favor "acceptable" beliefs over "odd" ones.[257] Assume, for example, we had a fund from which all victims of evil deity gifts could be compensated, and to which all activities would contribute according to their proneness to create such victims.[258] Thus, cars, drivers, ski lifts, and ski lift riders, would be taxed to make up the compensation fund according to their propensity to cause accidents which would give rise to claims against the fund.[259] Would we then tax more highly those whose greater accident proneness was due to religious beliefs, handicap, age, sex, disadvantage, or attitudes deriving from these? Or would we instead decide that, whatever we did about the others, we would tax "acceptable" and "not-acceptable" beliefs equally?

I have little doubt that, if we had such a scheme, we would not treat "acceptable" and "odd" beliefs differently from each other. The burden would be sufficiently spread across society so that no single individual would suffer much in order to preserve our wish to avoid an establishment of religion.[260] (Of course, if we were a country which had an established religion, or a tradition of establishment, the line might well be drawn in a totally different way.) We would, in effect, again be pulled by our constitution to treat idiosyncratic religious beliefs like common religious beliefs and like common secular ones. There would be no countervailing pull from the desire to compensate innocent victims which could block the force of the no-establishment norm. In practice we would probably fund this part of the compensation fund from general taxes, not through a special tax on the holders of those beliefs which made them more prone to serious injury.[261] We would, I expect, do the same with respect to the extra risk of injury arising from handicap, sex, age, or disadvantage. In each case we would have judged that equal access, or equal treatment, was an acceptable evil deity gift so long as no single identifiable relict had to pay the bulk of the price of our accepting the gift.

The fact that such a solution is feasible, even though we have not chosen to avail ourselves of it, means that the cases we have been discussing are not likely to be searing ones for our society. We can, if we wish, preserve our egalitarian and non-establishment ideals without depriving individual victims of compensation. We can avoid burdening injurers on account of age, sex, race, handicap, or oddness of religious belief, without thereby making unlucky victims pay the financial price of our egalitarian aspirations. We who collectively benefit from these ideals can collectively pay for them. It is not, of course, as easy when what is involved is not amenable to financial compensation. To some extent this is always the case when there are physical injuries involved, but is especially so when the injuries are to a belief![262] The hardest case, and therefore the one I shall put aside until the last chapter, is the one in which beliefs or ideals clash.

When giving weight to your beliefs offends mine, financial compensation is likely to be meaningless. Those situations are not viewed by people as raising issues of who should bear the costs of beliefs, but rather of who can impose beliefs on whom. The struggle to make sure that one's own beliefs are, in such circumstances, deemed acceptable and not outlandish, is apt to be a searing one; it will determine whether whole groups will come to feel emarginated from society (like the "cults" we discussed earlier) or whether contrasting beliefs can survive as part of one polity.

Before I turn to this issue, though, I would like to spend some time considering why some attitudes and beliefs which are not at all idiosyncratic and indeed are very widely held, are so disfavored in law that the costs to which they give rise are left on innocent victims, even when faulty injurers are available. What determines when injuries to emotions and to moralisms count as compensable damages and when they do not? We must discuss this problem both for its own interest and for the insights it can give us into the hardest case, the case in which beliefs clash.

4

Should Moralisms and Emotions Count?

O NE CAN CONCLUDE from the earlier chapters that what is deemed unreasonable behavior, no less than who is the cheapest avoider of a cost, depends on the valuations put on acts, activities, and beliefs by the whole of our law and not on some objective or scientific notion. That is why beliefs do count in the calculus—at least sometimes. One equally can conclude that concepts, like reasonableness, also depend on whom our law wishes to burden. That is why beliefs of injurers and victims are treated differently—at least in the absence of a general social insurance fund. One finally can conclude that what is reasonable in an area such as torts reflects judgments and norms found in our constitution and our law as a whole and does not respond only to the narrow needs of accident law. That is why widely held and idiosyncratic beliefs are treated differently when religious faiths or attitudes of racism are involved. In other words, what is efficient, or passes a cost-benefit test, is not a "scientific" notion separated from beliefs and attitudes, and always must respond to the question of whom we wish to make richer or poorer. It will almost invariably reflect views on these which derive from areas of law far removed from torts.

In this chapter, I would like to examine some beliefs and attitudes whose costs are left on the holders of the beliefs even though they are common attitudes and are not (like racism) disfavored in our fundamental norms. In torts these attitudes give rise to what are called fanciful damages, purely psychic damages, and emotional damages, and include some, but not all, of what I have elsewhere termed moralisms—my mental anguish, pain, or disgust which stems from something you do. The terms themselves are conclusory. They simply signify that those who are injured will not be compensated. They do not explain why this should be so, nor even what the terms include.

In practice, two large categories of damages are excluded from recovery by these terms. At first glance, such exclusion seems hard to defend. First, if someone destroys my watch—which has special value to me because it was given to me by my aged Aunt Amnesia—that special value will not be taken into account if I sue for damages. Yet, why should not the potential injurer be made financially aware that one of the costs which he or she should consider in deciding whether or not to engage in activities which endanger my watch is the special value the watch has? If we make injurers (or their insurance rates) take damages to religious belief into account, why not do as much for such widely held emotions as those that I happen to attach to my watch? Second, if I suffer pangs, feel sick to my stomach, because I see an accident in which people have been killed, I cannot recover damages for that suffering. Yet why should not the "costs" of that accident include my pangs? Why not give people recovery when they drive past a bloody accident and feel the worse for it? That my feelings are for others, rather than for myself, does not make my feelings any less real, or any less a reason why the behavior, which led to the accident and to my feeling ill, should be discouraged. That is—if we were to do a full societal cost-benefit analysis—one of the costs of accepting the deity's gifts of motor cars is surely my feeling ill when I see an accident, and another is my special sense of loss if Aunt Amnesia's watch is destroyed.

Yet, traditionally, neither of these two cases has given rise to damages in torts law.[263] There are exceptions, of course, and they have been growing. Intentional emotional harms, for example, have always been sources of recovery.[264] Also, if someone very close—a spouse or child—is killed, purely emotional damages to the bereaved relative may be available, especially if he or she saw or was near the accident site.[265] In Hawaii, a family named Rex was even able to collect emotional damages for the death of their dog, Princess.[266] The exceptions, however, remain just that, and emotional damages—especially for harm to others—are treated with great suspicion in torts.

My sometime colleague, Professor Ronald Dworkin of Oxford, has tried to explain this by attempting to show that, in a utilitarian calculus, counting moralisms or our feelings for others is "double-counting."[267] I must say that while I usually find Dworkin (even when wrong) to be extraordinarily lucid, this argument seems unintelligible. In the end, I am forced to conclude that, as a matter of pure theory, another former colleague, Judge Robert Bork, was correct when he stated that psychic harm was as real as — and in principle indistinguishable from — physical harms.[268] It may be that there are *practical* reasons on the basis of which harms that are psychic, or based on our feelings for others, should be left on victims more often than physical harms. But that pragmatic possibility is far different from an argument that would suggest the two should be treated differently as a matter of principle.

We already have seen that harm to some emotions, like harm to religious beliefs, are counted. Other emotional harms, like the sense of disgust I may feel at knowing that you read pornography, and then, in the privacy of your room masturbate, by and large are not counted today. The "cost" of these is left on the one who suffers the attitudinal harm. It is as surely a "cost," however, as if what you had done was to make noise, break my glasses, blow smoke in my face, or for that matter masturbate in public.[269] This last suggests that the line drawn is not between emotive harm and physical harm. It also indicates that the line is not drawn so as always to burden the holders of such moralisms, those who feel disgust as a result of other people's behavior.

In practice, we prohibit the sale of "live" hearts or kidneys even among consenting parties.[270] (Leave aside the laws prohibiting sex among consenting adults though their existence demonstrates that moralisms are at times protected. Such laws are under substantial attack, and I would rather make my point with cases that most would find acceptable.)[271] On what basis do we do this? (Let me emphasize that I am not speaking of someone selling a heart for delivery after he or she has died, but rather of someone who, because he or she is tired of living or wants to leave a large estate, offers to sell a heart for immediate delivery to someone who needs a transplant, now.) People sometimes say that the objection is due to the financial harm such a sale would cause to third parties — like the seller's children who would lose a "breadwinner." But that is rarely an adequate answer. Indeed, if one looks at the cases in which people have tried to sell vital organs, the common theme is that the would-be sellers are very poor and are suggesting the sale because they think it would benefit those closest to them, like their children.[272] Yet such sales are not allowed. The most plausible explanation remains that permitting the sale would offend the rest of us. It even offends many who would permit suicide and, since enough of us are sufficiently offended, we act to forbid such sales, even though doing this burdens the would-be seller and buyer.[273]

When we do this we are, of course, doing something analogous to placing the emotional costs that a passerby feels from seeing an accident on those who wished to engage in the accident prone activity. We are doing something like putting the special value I attach to Amnesia's watch on the one who damages it. And so the question becomes, again: "On what practical basis can we distinguish the cases in which the burdens of emotional losses are placed on the holder of the emotions from those in which they are instead put on those who damage other people's feelings? On what basis do we choose between public and private masturbation, between the emotional harm one feels at seeing one's child be killed and the pangs one has when one sees a gruesome (but anonymous) accident, between appropriately recoverable pain and suffering and the 'fanciful' damages which result from injuries to Amnesia's watch?" In all these cases the event, the accident, does not affect or harm only the immediate parties involved, but also makes a variety of third parties feel "worse." When do these feelings "matter" and when, instead, do they get described as though they were not real and, as a result, get left on the emotional victim?[274]

Let us look at what tort law calls "fanciful" damages, the injury to Amnesia's watch, first. Let us admit that such emotions—the feelings I have for my aunt's watch—are common, are widely held. There are very few of us who do not have *some* items which we value way beyond their market price on account of some special emotional attachment. Most of us would say it is good that people have such attachments. There is a positive societal benefit, many would argue, in encouraging this kind of moralism as a result of which not everything is for sale at a standard, market price.[275] Thus such feelings are quite different from other widely held attitudes, like racism, which we should like to discourage, even through tort law.

Yet we do not give recoveries for them. The reason for this seems to lie in the fact that, though common and desirable, such feelings attach to specific goods in a highly individualized, particularistic way. *I* am specially hurt by harm to my watch because Amnesia gave it to me. *Your* watch is entirely fungible. But let anyone harm the ancient car left to you by your distant cousin, Euthanasia, or the fedora you inherited from your Uncle Grandiloquent, and you suffer the pains of hell. In each case you and I know far better than the potential injurer which items are especially valuable to us, and which, though perhaps special to others, are purely "market priced" as far as we are concerned.

This difference in "knowledge" explains a lot. It would give rise to dangers of fraud if damages routinely were awarded for such emotional damages.[276] (But these—like most administrative reasons—though often mentioned, are rarely the ultimate grounds for inclusion or exclusion of damage items.)[277] More important, it gives rise to very significant differences in the capacity of injurers and victims to avoid serious harm—differences in what could be called cost-avoidance potential.[278]

If the injurer were to take into account what we call "fanciful damages," he or she would have to decrease activities (accept less of the deity's boon) to give extra protection to your watch (which has no special value for you) and my fedora (which is, for me, an ordinary hat). Because the injurer lacks the information which would allow him or her to distinguish among those items which are "special" and those which are not, the only incentive the injurer has is to protect all possible sources of fanciful damages equally. As a result, putting the burden of fanciful damages on the injurer adds a very slight, and usually unnecessary, extra protection to many things (watches and hats in general), but gives insufficient added protection to those specific objects which have special value. My watch would still be treated as yours is, even though it is, in fact, because of the extra value I give to it, more valuable.

Instead, you and I, the owners of the old car, watch, and fedora, because we know that extra value attaches to the object in question, are much better placed than even a *negligent* injurer to give extra protection to those things we value specially. The situation is like that of the violinist who goes to work in a steel mill which we discussed earlier. Though he or she was perfectly reasonable in going to work there, the *extra* value of his or her hand was not normally compensable, even if the mill owners were negligent. (The artist, we should recall, could not inform the mill owners of his/her special status and value, for to do so would interfere with the object of employment: the writing of a great proletarian symphony.) In such a case, to charge the mill more than the cost of an injury to an ordinary worker's hand would not create significant incentives to greater safety for the violinist's hand, it would only (and by hypothesis unnecessarily) raise the safety standards with respect to all employees whose hands did not have special value or warrant special care. Only the violinist knows enough to be able to give his or her hand the extra protection it deserves and so, traditionally, the *extra* loss is left on him or her.[279]

It is quite different, of course, if protection of the valuable hand by the violinist requires doing something that would remove the artist from society in general. In such cases, a little added protection to all people is the best we can do — consistent with our desire to maintain full societal participation by all its members. Recovery for auto accidents does extend to the extra value of a violinist's hand, to people with thin skulls, and to holders of unusual religions. But for me to be a part of society does not mean that I have to carry Amnesia's watch on the freeway. Nor need you do the same with your fedora or ancient motor car. We can leave the special items home, or, in the rare trips we have to make with them, make sure that extra safety and protection are available. Since we know better than negligent injurers what needs to be done, the incentive to do it is placed on us.[280]

In a sense, though the attitudes which give rise to fanciful damages are not idiosyncratic, the damages themselves — and their loci — are. As with most idiosyncratic behavior, the doer of it may be in the best position to evaluate how much is worth spending to minimize the harm. He or she has the knowledge to decide for or against taking a risk, for or against accepting a gift from the evil deity. I say *may*, because knowledge (knowing the most about the risks involved) is only one factor. The others are: capacity to do something with the knowledge (are there realistic, safer options among which the person can choose, or is the situation one, like driving, in which no feasible alternative to accepting the deity's gift exists), and our own willingness, on distributional grounds, to burden that person as against some other party who has less knowledge.

On all these grounds, burdening those who give a special, emotional value to a particular item seems reasonable. They have the greater knowledge, "safer" alternatives do exist, and therefore, they (unlike the persons with thin skulls) can opt for safety without excluding themselves from ordinary life. There are no special wealth distribution reasons for suggesting that they should be spared this burden which they are best placed to minimize.

The decision to leave fanciful damages on the injured party turns out to be based on the same kinds of factors that determine who bears accident losses in other areas of tort law. This book is not the place to go into a long disquisition on products liability. However, I would suggest that analogous factors determine when we tend to say a defect exists and liability should be placed on the product manufacturer, and when, instead, we deny the existence of a defect and leave the loss on the user. Take, for example, the case of contraceptives. There is no contraceptive which is not defective in terms of definitions used in other products cases (cases in which even user negligence has been no defense). All contraceptives have side effects (risks of illnesses, pregnancy, or diminution of spontaneity or pleasure). If one were talking about a wide variety of other goods, one would very likely say contraceptives all have serious design defects.[281] Yet, no such law suits succeed (provided the knowledge of the side effects of each contraceptive type is made sufficiently available to the users).[282] Once again avoidance of fraud is certainly a factor, but the other factors seem at least as, if not more, significant.[283] Principal among these is the greater knowledge the users have as to which of the many widely different side effects are most harmful and costly for them. To some, pregnancy only is a timing inconvenience and the risk of it a minor defect; to others, it would be a catastrophe. For some, loss of spontaneity or reduction of pleasure is a minor issue; for others, it would destroy the relationship. Finally, some know they are in a high risk category for illness as a side effect, while others know they are virtually safe. In effect, the users are like me with respect to Amnesia's watch and you with respect to the fedora and the motor car. As a result, concepts like "warning," "defect" or "fanciful damages," are manipulated to allow the losses to be put where it seems most sensible to place them.

Idiosyncrasy is frequently linked to knowledge, to a capacity to choose safer options, and sometimes, even, to burden worthiness (to distributional considerations). For these reasons it often is used in torts as if it were the telltale for liability. Where, however, as in the case of the thin skull or the "odd" religion, idiosyncrasy does not correlate well with these factors, tort law ignores the idiosyncrasy or ordinariness of the belief or the attribute and finds a way to assign losses differently. It is one important indicium of the underlying factors. As such it is given much weight both in creating presumptions of what the law should be and in explaining (even if incorrectly) why a particular result was reached. In the area of beliefs and attitudes, it must be used with great care for often it misleads. Properly understood, however, it can even help to explain why so-called fanciful damages, though the product of widely held attitudes, are nonetheless frequently left on those who suffer them.

The explanations just given with respect to fanciful damages do not, however, explain the fact that emotional harm from seeing an accident is generally not compensable. Such harm is in no way idiosyncratic; we all feel it to some extent, and we all feel it in essentially the same kinds of situations, and as to the same kinds of things. In this last respect it is not at all like my affection for Amnesia's watch. If injurers were made to pay for such emotional damages, those activities which give rise to the kinds of accidents that are particularly disturbing to passers-by would be given significant incentives to be more careful.

It is, of course, true that different people feel such emotions to different degrees. Some feel them more than others — some much, much less than others. (The same is true of other psychic damages, like pain and suffering, which generally are recoverable. But as we shall see soon enough, recoveries for pain and suffering may be explainable on other, rather special grounds. That is, they may be an exception, which can be justified, rather than the rule, deviations from which need explanation.) Still, if the problem were that the *degree* of harm felt is idiosyncratic, there would be rather easy ways of dealing with it, without going to the length of barring recoveries altogether.

The most obvious of these would be to give scheduled or average damages. In a sense, that is equivalent to charging injurers for the market value of Amnesia's watch and then letting the victim who is unusually sensitive or affected worry about the difference. It also is the equivalent of the predetermined figure in many workmen's compensation damage schedules for losses of members and limbs, which take into account some psychic harms but do not compensate for special or unusual ones, or for violinists' hands.[284] Scheduled damages would eliminate many of the administrative cost arguments that are made against recoveries for such damages as well. They even would, to some extent, meet the argument that such damages are prone to fraudulent padding, though one would still have to worry about excluding recoveries by those who went out of their way to see an accident in order to be able to claim the scheduled damages. But this too could be dealt with, if we cared enough about granting recoveries.[285] As a result, I conclude that there must be some more fundamental reason we do not recognize such damages. The reason I would suggest is relevant both to what has already been discussed in this book, and, perhaps even more, to the discussion of abortion in the next chapter.

The rule against awarding purely emotional damages can be justified by the plausible, and perhaps correct, fear that awarding such damages will increase actual suffering. This happens not because people lie about feeling hurt (though that is a possibility), but because the very fact of focusing on these items, as is necessary in order to bring a claim, makes the hurt last. Unlike altruism — which is destroyed if purchased — emotional pain, if converted into money terms, often is increased.[286] To put the same thing in a slightly different way, the very fact that someone is given a *right*, and *entitlement*, to something (vindicable in court and in money) makes the destruction of that right or entitlement harmful. The cost of the insult is added to the cost of the injury. This may be inevitable or even desirable when there is an injury to an underlying entitlement which we are determined to protect. (We do not worry too much about the fact that giving people property rights makes them feel almost violated, and hence more injured, by theft than would be justified by the value of what was stolen.) It is far from clearly desirable when the entitlement under consideration is to be free from the insult itself.

If I see an accident in which people are injured and know that I have no right to recover for my emotional upset (that I am not entitled in a legal sense to feel anguish), I may feel sick for a time, but then I go home and after a while forget about it. The only ones who don't forget about it are those who are idiosyncratic with respect to such emotional damages. They are treated with respect to these damages like "forward-jumpers," "doctor-haters," or as I was with respect to Amnesia's watch. Most people, however, who see such an accident may feel some emotion, but they get over it, and that is the end of it. If, instead, they had a right to recover for their emotion, that passing pang would surely *not* be the end of it. At least until the recovery came in, and perhaps longer, they would be quite likely to focus on the horrible scene they had witnessed and continue to feel some of the anguish it had first induced. Again, this is not because of dishonesty (indeed, it would likely be so even with scheduled damages which would not increase, *in the individual case,* as a result of persistence of anguish),[287] but because the law told them they had been violated, had been hurt, and induced them to pay attention to that hurt.

That individual emotional response is affected by changes in the law can scarcely be doubted. Consider the effect of the easier availability of divorce on the ordinary person's response to spousal desertion. There was a time when spousal desertion was assumed to be a source of catastrophic hurt and resentment. Any reader of novels of that time well knows the sense of personal violation to which such an occurrence gave rise.[288] Desertion remains a very painful event, of course. Nevertheless, it is hard to doubt that we have become more callous about such things.

The fate of the alienation of affection action is one indication of this. There was a time when money damages could be won from someone who ran off with one's spouse. The spouse's affection — to which one had an entitlement — had been stolen and one had the right to get redress from the thief. Such causes of action have now been abolished in many states and fallen into desuetude in most others.[289] This change is in significant part an acknowledgement that the deserted parties are no longer injured in the way they once were by spousal desertions. The sense of loss may still be there but the sense of theft and violation has been diminished. It is harder to feel robbed when the "theft" happens so frequently and usually through the entirely legal process of divorce.[290]

Also consider pornography and one's feeling of offense at someone else reading or seeing it. Not so many years ago people were deeply offended by it. One could hardly hear of nudity, or of suggestive or vulgar language appearing in scurrilous magazines without all sorts of people saying: "My God, what has the world come to?" So long as the law gave them the right to be offended by these things and to have these barred (even if it didn't give a right to personal damages), such people continued to be offended. Today what used to be seen only in the pages of the then equivalents of *Penthouse,* appears in staid newspapers, in PG films shown on airplanes, and on the common stage — and most people don't bat an eyelash. Only relatively few people like myself (though I have no interest in censorship) say, "Isn't it remarkable to read *that* in the good, gray *Times,* or to see *such* a movie on an airplane flight, where one can avoid buying ear phones, but can hardly avoid seeing the screen and getting the point?"[291]

Once again, one may ask whether the change in law followed or brought about the change in attitudes. And once again, it probably was a case of a little of both. Here, as with alienation of affection, it is hard to deny that changes in law had at least something to do with making what was highly offensive to many become less so for most, and innocuous for some. To that extent the question can properly be put: "Does leaving the burden of being offended on the person who feels it in the first instance lessen the offense? Does this allocation of emotional costs lessen the burden to society as a whole, given that the 'injurer' will continue to bear the same costs if he or she is burdened?"

If the costs of *avoiding* a grisly accident remain about the same whether those who suffer third party emotional damages recover for them, while the extent of those damages is less in the absence of recovery, then *an* argument exists for allocating the burden to the one who suffers the emotional damages. Similarly, if the desire to read pornography or see nudity remains about the same whether pornography or nudity is barred or not, while the offense caused by it is diminished when such things are permitted, then *an* argument exists for allocating the burden to the one who feels the offense.[292] Strangely enough, the fee charged by the evil deity for giving the "injurer" pleasure may well be smaller if the burden of it is placed on the victim.

We shall see, soon enough, that this argument by no means ends the matter. But, before we do, we should look at some situations in which tort law does give damages for emotional suffering, to see whether they can be explained. The first, of course, is the case of the damages that are awarded when one sees a close relative mangled in an accident.[293] This, on the whole, is an easy one. In such cases the award of damages does not increase the pain much, if at all. The deep anguish is there anyway and all that allowing recovery does is give injuring activities a somewhat bigger incentive to be careful, to take those damages into account. It is not like the previous cases in which, by giving the injurer a greater incentive for safety, we also increase the injury and the harm done.[294]

Pain and suffering damages are, at first glance, rather more difficult to justify. In tort law if someone has an accident and suffers physical injuries, that person can recover all pain and suffering which results from that injury.[295] Would not these "emotional damages," like those we feel at seeing an accident, also be reduced if they were not cognizable at law? I think the answer is surely that many of them would. Some would not, but much pain and suffering now genuinely felt would be reduced if the victim were not entitled to recover for it. But pain and suffering damages, in most accident cases involving physical injuries, are not given only, or even primarily, to compensate victims for their suffering. They are given at least in part to pay for lawyers' fees under a contingent fee system.

The customary—American—way to sue in torts is one in which the lawyer virtually is not paid if the injured party loses. If the injured party recovers, the lawyer gets a percentage of the recovery. This amount presumably compensates the lawyer not only for the time spent on the winning case, but also that spent on all the losing cases for which he or she got virtually nothing.[296] While this system has been severely attacked, not only by those who are committed partisans of injurers in accident cases but by some scholars as well, it has much to be said for it.[297] It is, essentially, a system of mutual insurance among accident victims. Short of a highly expensive, universal system of legal aid, such a private insurance-type device — though also expensive — is probably as effective as any for giving people access to justice in this kind of civil litigation.[298]

If, however, lawyer's fees are to be recovered from cases won and if such recoveries must compensate the lawyer not just for the time spent on the successful cases but also for the time spent on cases lost, then somehow damages must be allowed which will yield recoveries greater than the actual damages suffered in the cases won.[299] Pain and suffering damages, because they have no set definition, and hence can be expanded beyond the requirements of the specific case, have come to serve that function. I do not mean that juries do not consider the actual suffering which a particular injury caused. I mean that victims and juries alike are aware that lawyers will be paid contingent fees and that this fact affects the way they react to the award of pain and suffering damages. So, for that matter, does the law itself. Thus, in virtually all reform proposals which would result in automatic recoveries for victims, pain and suffering damages, as such, have been eliminated. Often, what the reform proposals term "reasonable" lawyer's fees in the particular case are provided for instead.[300] Since the chance of spending time on a losing case would be substantially done away with, the need for the expandable pain and suffering damages to cover that risk also can be abolished.[301]

Pain and suffering damages are tolerated in their current form in the American system[302] because they are necessary to the success of valid suits for physical or economic damages. If one believes the injurer is best suited to bear the burden of such economic and physical injuries (as, by hypothesis, our law does in such cases), then the extra "injury" which occurs as a result of allowing pain and suffering damages may be worth bearing. It becomes, in fact, just another expense of what is a highly expensive way of assuring that victims can recover for their economic and physical injuries in some cases.[303]

It is quite another matter to give emotional damages when no economic or physical injury exists. The justification of meeting lawyer's fees is no longer valid. Such damages must then be justified on their own terms—as were the emotional damages awarded for seeing the death of a close relative—and not in instrumental terms. To say this is not to say such a justification cannot be made. As I said earlier, the fact that awarding emotional damages may increase the hurt is only one argument against such awards, and by no means a conclusive one. I must now turn to the reasons we often do create entitlements which increase such hurts and costs.

Is it not the case that if we permitted people to sell their hearts or kidneys, many of us would become accustomed to such sales and no longer find them to be shocking or offensive? If we could become callous to such sales, could one not make the same argument that I made with respect to pornography,[304] and emotional harm, and suggest that permitting the sales of body parts would reduce the injury? Once again, those who originally were offended would, over time, be much less troubled, while those who wanted the sales would have gotten what they wanted.

Some would deny that we, as a society, ever would become callous to sales of hearts, and hence of life. I am far less sanguine. Some individuals would continue to object, but, *as a society,* I fear we would "adapt" all too well. If, in the nineteenth century, someone had said, "Don't worry about divorce and alienation of affection; permit such things and in time people will feel the pain less," most sensible sorts would have thought the person mad and answered that they would never get used to such a world. Not all that many years ago, a distinguished playwright said at an academic-liberal dinner party I at-tended, that: "In a few years there would be 'screwing' on stage and screen." Everyone among the "open-minded" guests was shocked (and not only by the language, which was stronger than I care to use); they denied that people would ever accept such a development. Within three years, most of those present had attended plays or movies in which sexual intercourse was explicitly depicted, and had not batted an eye-lash. One of the extraordinary things about the human species is that it is so adaptable. It is at once a great strength, because it has permit-ted survival in widely different circumstances, and a terrible moral danger.

If you had asked people in Germany in 1933—I mean the ordi-nary people, not the die-hard Nazis—whether racial laws then being enacted would, *in less than ten years,* lead to extermination camps, they would have thought you to be insane. They might have admitted that some things would happen to some Jews, that their economic and so-cial situation would be substantially worsened. But, as to the calcu-lated killing of millions of people, they would have said, "It can't hap-pen. We will never allow it or become callous to it." And yet they—or quite a lot of them—did. I have little doubt that our society also could become used to the free sale of hearts and body parts, in less time than one might imagine.[305]

Let me repeat that such adaptability—this capacity to become callous to what previously seemed deeply wrong—also can be a strength. The current attitude toward alienation of affection or toward nudity and sex on stage and screen may be a good thing. Many certainly would say so. Or it may be controversial, with some decrying the adaptability and others hailing it. This may be the current situation with respect to abortion. Twenty-five or 30 years ago, most people would have been shocked at the notion that abortion might be taken as a matter of course by large parts of the population.[306] Yet today, polls suggest that about 70 percent of the people in America, includ-ing Roman Catholics, say abortion should not be against the law.[307] The issue still is highly controversial, to put it mildly, and many are as offended as ever. Perhaps, for reasons I shall discuss in the next chapter, some are more offended than they were years ago. They would—and do—vehemently decry the callousness that has taken hold. But they would not deny that there has been a high degree of accep-tance of abortion by society and that, here too, many people have adapted to something which, not long ago, they would have found appalling.

For good or for bad — or at times for both good *and* bad — if one permits some people to do certain things and gives them the *right* to do them, other people will get used to the things being done. If instead, one denies people the right to such things and gives others the right to *be offended, shocked and appalled* by these things, these others will continue to view the things as terribly offensive, hurtful, and even abominable. If, therefore, the test were that which I gave earlier, namely that we should place the burden of beliefs and attitudes so as to lower the harm (the cost of being offended) derived from such attitudes, we would rarely, if ever, let moralisms or emotions count. We would deny the right to emotional damages, and at the same time permit the sale of hearts, because to do so would encourage the callousness which would diminish any emotional costs felt.

The difference we make between the emotional costs we protect and those we discourage is derived I would suggest, from a deeper, longer run view of costs and harms. At the same time we make the decision of whom to burden, we also are deciding whether we *want to get accustomed, whether we wish to become callous, or whether, instead, we think that as a society we would be better off if we continued to view some things as shocking, offensive, and even abominable.*

If we, as a society, think it really is not a bad thing to be relatively callous with respect to auto accidents in which other people are hurt, then a denial of the financial entitlement to be offended by such accidents makes sense. It reduces the harm in the short run and is not undesirable in the long run. If we think there are long run gains from callousness which counter some long run losses, we are likely, once again, to let short run cost reduction win out and allocate rights so as diminish the costs of being offended. Thus, while sexual license on stage and screen readily tends to pornographic exploitation and to a cheapening of humans, such license may be needed if (what many view as desirable) sexual freedom and avoidance of sexual repression is to be achieved.[308] Similarly, while easy divorce and permissiveness toward alienation of affection undesirably may have produced less stable families, it also undermined the wretched notion that people had ownership rights to other people. In such situations, there is a kind of long run stalemate. Since the society cannot decide one way or the other on the basis of deeper long run values, it is likely to drift toward that allocation which diminishes the moralism, or emotional cost, and deny people the right to be offended.

If, instead, we think that a society which does not share these moralisms — which does not have these tastes and is not offended — is a bad society, we will do all we can to assign entitlements so as to keep such emotions real and alive. We will avoid those allocations which diminish and undermine attitudes and beliefs to which we wish to cleave because we are not bound to reduce the cost of the evil deity's offer. We want the boon to remain not worth having.

Law, unlike economics, is not concerned only, or even primarily, with reduction of costs, "given tastes." It is fundamentally concerned with *shaping* tastes.[309] Legal rules which further altrusim survive because, though altruism cannot be purchased or coerced, we nonetheless want to increase the amount of it in society.[310] We, at great peril only, drift into legal rules which diminish the taste for beauty or for the unspoiled. We always must be on guard that those allocations which lessen short run costs by reducing moralisms or offense do not *mindlessly* lead us, in the long run, to tastes and values which today we would find appalling.

Our society does not want people to become callous about seeing their children or spouses killed. Therefore, if denial of damages in such cases led to callousness, we would especially want damages to be awarded. Our society seems to want people to remain shocked that some might wish to sell their hearts to better themselves or their families financially and so we make such sales impossible. The majority of us may, increasingly, wish people to be somewhat more sensitive and conscious of the purely emotional harm certain physical risks entail. If so, tort law may (as it has) increase, somewhat, the area of recovery for purely psychic damages.[311] We make these rules of law because we know our tastes are in part shaped by our laws. We therefore try to pick rules of law which will help us become the society most of us wish to be years hence, even though they may seem more costly today.

Let me repeat that not all such moralisms are, by any means, worthy in the long run. We may wish our law to shape our tastes so that some attitudes and beliefs are undermined. Our Constitution demands that racism — even if it is a widely held belief — be reduced, and so we deny recovery to the racist who refuses the blood transfusion. We define our law, even our ordinary run-of-the-mill tort law, so those emotions and moralisms that are somehow unworthy in the long run will be undercut. We would do it even if this did not have short run offense-reducing potential.

Only when we do not care about the long run or, more often, when the long run is in stalemate, is short run cost avoidance the determining factor in shaping our laws. This last may be more frequent than one thinks and may help explain the popularity of some schools of economic analysis of law.[312] Nevertheless, one always should remember that the situation in which the short run mattered came about only as a result of a stalemate, and hence after a long run type argument about values, tastes, ideals, beliefs, and attitudes.

Not surprisingly, then, when there is an argument among people about whether moralisms or emotions should count, the discussion does not concern itself with the short run or with what allocation would reduce the sense of offense. One rarely hears a debate about whether, if we put the loss of a given accident on those who see it, the total cost of the accident will be reduced. The argument turns, rather, on what the society should look like in the long run. It almost always concerns itself with whether we should encourage some emotions or become callous toward them. Is it good if people feel troubled by commonplace sexual depictions and bad if they become callous to them? Or is it desirable for people to get used to sexuality as an ordinary thing and not feel repressed in this regard? Is a society in which people are free to sell their body parts a good one or a bad one? These are the issues which always are in debate. The issues of short run cost avoidance (as to emotions) tend to arise only later, in more technical contexts, and only after the broader debate has worked itself out, implicitly or explicitly, one way or another or into a stalemate.[313]

Thus, to return to religious beliefs and attitudes arising out of disadvantage or age, we may protect them for either short- or long-term reasons. We may decide, for example, that the holders of a belief would continue to adhere to it even if made to bear damages, and conclude, therefore, that there is little cost avoidance potential in burdening such believers. Or, more importantly, we may feel that, even though they would abandon their beliefs (and so, in a short run sense, reduce costs), such a reduction would injure our long run aspirations as stated in the Constitution. We may not wish to be a society which discourages non-establishment beliefs. The melting pot society, we may believe, should not melt or homogenize all sorts of different faiths into one set of innocuous semisecular established attitudes. Conversely, as we have seen in this chapter, we are quite ready to burden the holders of other widely held attitudes because we think this allocation will result in a reduction in short-term emotional costs, without making the society as a whole worse for having such beliefs diminished.

❧ 5 ❧

When Ideals Clash

S O FAR we have been pitting emotions, moralisms, and beliefs against
ordinary costs. We have been treating the issue as one of deciding whether and when to compensate financially, someone who is injured as a result of the existence of beliefs or moralisms. The hardest
issue, however, is a different one. It arises when beliefs and moralisms
of like sorts clash. In such a situation, all of the hard problems we
have been discussing so far combine.

When beliefs on both sides clash, financial compensation is often
not enough because compensation does not make up for the violation
of one's beliefs. What is at stake is not whether one has a right to impose the *cost* of one's belief on someone else (which is hard enough),
but rather whether one has the right, in some sense, to impose the
belief on the other. If my doing what I believe violates your beliefs,
and vice versa, then compensation is likely to be less than useless and
may make matters worse. Not all conflicts of beliefs, of course, rise
to these proportions. Some beliefs have to do with relatively trivial
matters and the loser in that clash is likely to accept the loss with more
or less grace. When, however, the conflict involves beliefs which attach to fundamental values, the fact that others are given the right
to impose their beliefs on me becomes close to intolerable. This is especially so when the values at play are those like equal status or sanc-
tity of life — that is, values to which we ideally would like to hold
absolutely even when we know we cannot. Indeed, the very fact that
we cannot hold to them as absolutely, as sacredly, as we would like,

87

makes us all the more vehement in rejecting any stated deviation from them. Such open rejections destroy the fragile balance between aspiration and practice that characterizes how humans cope with impossible, but fundamental, ideals.[314] They are anathema.

In such situations the holders of the belief will deny that they will ever get accustomed to — or be less offended by — the dominance of the contrasting belief. More important, however, they assert that if they, or if the society as a whole, did adapt to the change, this very fact would signal the deep moral decay of that polity. If people did get used to the sale of hearts, if people came to accept slavery, if the Nazi "final solution to the Jewish question" became a matter of little concern, then that society would be cursed. If you, who had opposed these, lessened in your opposition or came to tolerate what had become common, you would be cursed with it. Rebellion, flight, or martyrdom might be acceptable possibilities — conformity never would.[315]

In an earlier book I said that such conflicts are the essence of what I there called "tragic choices."[316] To cope with such tragic conflicts, we often resort to subterfuges. We look for solutions which seek to cover the difficulty and thereby permit us to assert that we are cleaving to both beliefs in conflict. We do this when the irreconcilable conflict is internal (each of us would deeply like to hold to inconsistent faiths). We do it when the clash of beliefs is external (two or more significant groups in a society adhere to irreconcilable faiths). We also do it when the difficulty arises from some of each (there are two or more conflicting beliefs in the society with significant groups clashing over which should be dominant, but at bottom many in each group yearn to be able to hold to all of them).

The "solution" our society has reached with respect to euthanasia represents one such subterfuge; that which dominates accident law is another, different one. Our law says mercy killing is wrong and is no defense to murder charges.[317] But our jury system permits us to let mercy killers go free without ever forcing us to admit they were acquitted because what they did was euthanasia.[318] We use the fact that juries can give us results without reasons or explanations, and rely on them to be sensitive to the tragedy involved in mercy killings and reflect the society's desire to paper it over.[319] The conflict with respect to euthanasia may arise because some believe in euthanasia and think it would be appalling to jail or execute a mercy killer, while others think the willful taking of any life is terribly wrong and society should never condone or encourage it. It may arise because many feel both ways about it and fear that to permit mercy killing openly would result in more of it (and abuses of it) than is justified, but, nevertheless, do not wish to jail those who, despite laws against it, are driven to it.[320] Finally it may arise because even some of those who are sure that euthanasia is morally right or wrong, sympathize with, and long to be able to give weight to, the feelings of those who disagree with them.

We therefore send such cases to juries — which regularly acquit. In any given case the acquittal may be explainable on the basis of temporary insanity or some other "accepted" defense (*e.g.,* the defendant's action was not the actual cause of death).[321] It need not have been because the defendant acted out of "mercy," and the jury does not tell us. As a result we can have it both ways by both forbidding euthanasia and freeing mercy killers. It is, of course, a lie because we want, and get, what formally we deny we wanted. But it is a lie that works reasonably well because juries work reasonably well.

In accidents we use another kind of subterfuge, which also works reasonably well. We want people (drivers, manufacturers of dangerous products, road builders) to take into account the lives that would be saved if they choose a more expensive, but safer way, approach, or device. But we do not want to *price* lives. Heaven forbid we should openly say that device X is worth installing because it costs Y dollars and that is less than a life is worth, while device Z is not worth installing because it costs Y + 10 dollars, which is more than a life is worth.[322] Yet by requiring (in many cases) that victims be compensated financially, we introduce into the system monetary values which create just such limited incentives for safety, without requiring an open pricing of lives. Again, for reasons I need not go into here, this subterfuge, which relies on market prices and incentives — like the subterfuge used in euthanasia, which depends on a state agency, the jury — seems to work acceptably and avoids a searing societal conflict.

Some subterfuges work, while others — though very similar in structure — do not. For me, an example of a subterfuge which did not work was the one that Justice Powell used in the *Bakke* case.[323] The conflict there was between the belief in affirmative action — that there ought to be positive reparations toward members of groups that had been deeply discriminated against in the past on racial grounds — and the notion that the Constitution should be color blind and should not permit favor or disfavor based on race or on similar "attributes." Justice Powell, writing for the Supreme Court, used a subterfuge which structurally was a close analogue of the euthanasia one. He said, in effect, you cannot admit people to a medical school on the basis of race (mercy killing is illegal).[324] On the other hand, diversity is a perfectly acceptable ground for selecting a class and its use is almost constitutionally protected (like the insanity defense to murder).[325] Admissions decisions are to be made by faculty committees which need not tell us the basis of their decisions (like juries in criminal cases).[326] So long as such committees do not tell us what they are doing or why, he seemed to imply, we can nominally adhere to the standard of a color blind constitution and yet achieve desirable affirmative action admissions.

Unfortunately, the euthanasia and affirmative action cases are not the same either in substance or in form. As a result, what may be a desirable or effective subterfuge in one context may be neither in the other. Diversity does not have the same history as the insanity defense, and was, in fact, malignantly used in the past by universities to discriminate against people on the basis of race and religion.[327] Furthermore, an admissions committee is not composed in the same way as a jury. A jury (or at least a series of juries) is a relatively representative body, the unspoken values it imposes tend to be those of the society.[328] A university admissions committee since it represents hardly anyone — except perhaps the university administration — is a very dangerous group to which to give the power of hidden, subterfuge-based decisions. Indeed, it was just such committees that in the past used diversity for clearly malignant, discriminatory purposes.[329] For these and other reasons, I criticized the *Bakke* subterfuge and suggested that it was both wrong and likely to be — as it has been — ineffective.[330]

Whenever possible, of course, one should look for a solution to such tragic conflicts which does not rely on subterfuge, and the availability of such a possible "honest" solution is bound to affect our view of whether a given subterfuge is a good one. Usually such an honest solution relies on the fact that many people on both sides of the conflict are themselves torn and would like to have it both ways. It then seeks to recognize the conflict, give some weight to both beliefs, but mediate the clash by limiting the extent of each belief's dominance.[331] Such an approach may work because partial dominance may be acceptable if each side has (even if only subconsciously) some sympathy for the other's position. The law sometimes has the function of trying to hide a basic conflict and, through subterfuges, to allow us to hold to conflicting aspirations. At other times, in other conflict situations, it must try to set up structures which permit us openly to give less than full weight to our own deeply held beliefs, in recognition of those of others (which, incidentally, we also partly share). This last is especially desirable if that structure also looks to possible future changes or inventions which may permit us *in fact* to reconcile the conflict — to give full weight to both beliefs — in the future.

With this in mind I would like to take a few pages to approach the thorniest "belief conflict" extant in America today: the abortion issue. I would like to see whether some of the things discussed earlier in this book (as well as in *Tragic Choices*) can be helpful to us, in considering how to deal with it. That it involves a conflict of beliefs of the deepest sort should be obvious. The very fact that the partisans of each side spend so much of their time calling each other bigots makes that clear. It suggests that both the self-defined "pro-choice" and "pro-life" groups have some justification when they claim that the other is seeking to impose its world view — its deeply held beliefs — to the detriment of their beliefs and world view.[332] Both want to do something which, apart from any physical harm it may cause, deeply offends beliefs and values of the other.

One thing that might follow from our previous discussion is that this kind of name calling is misplaced. It is neither wrong nor unusual for people to wish to have their beliefs protected, accepted, or at least recognized as reasonable and valid. The fact that the belief is or is not religion-based is not of great consequence. If anything our law tends in the direction of treating as "reasonable" beliefs which, if they were not based on religion, might not be so protected. That is one of the things which I think the treatment accorded Minelda, Mrs. Eider, and even the tranquil couple suggests.[333] Thus, the fact that someone argues for abortion because he or she believes — as a matter of faith — that life begins at parturition, or against abortion because — equally as a matter of faith — he or she believes that it occurs at conception, should neither validate nor invalidate the argument.[334]

Similarly, it should be clear from the last chapter that even if support for abortion or opposition to it were based solely on moralisms, the positions would be neither validated nor invalidated. Thus, someone who supports abortion — not because of any physical harm that pregnancy may do to a woman, but because he or she is offended at any laws which make participation in sex unequally burdensome on men and women — has an argument that is not *ipso facto* dismissable. Equally, someone who opposes abortion — not because of the harm it does to a fetus, but because he or she is offended by the very notion of abortion — also cannot be dismissed out of hand. Moralisms often are the bases of our laws, and remain so even if the holders of them would in the future become callous or less offended if the legal system allowed that which today would violate those moralisms. That is what we can learn from the fact that sales of body parts are not permitted.

Indeed, the last chapter suggests that sometimes the best way of dealing with a clash of moralisms is to find a way which *maintains* the offense and, in a sense, preserves the moralisms which lose out in the conflict. That is, the loser may be more willing to accept the loss if losing does not mean that society will become callous to the values he or she held. If, in as many other contexts as possible, these values are upheld and reaffirmed, the loss in the specific context may be more tolerable. What may be intolerable is for the loss to mean that the society will come to regard as insignificant or valueless those ideals the loser cherishes as fundamental.

For these reasons, and some others discussed earlier, we also can conclude that whatever one thinks of the *result* in *Roe* v. *Wade* (which held most anti-abortion laws to be unconstitutional), the Supreme Court *opinion* in that case was highly unfortunate.[335] One can view the opinion as an attempt to resolve the deep value conflict by subterfuges, simple or complex. And while I cannot say there necessarily is anything wrong with that,[336] the subterfuges attempted in the case are, at best, ineffective at papering over the conflict and, at worst, likely to exacerbate it wildly.

The simple subterfuge (which really does not do justice to the Court's opinion) would urge us to regard that which is not seen (the fetus) as nonexistent. That move cannot succeed; it is simply not convincing. If a subterfuge is to paper over a deep value conflict it must be sufficiently complex, have sufficient verisimilitude, so that it cannot readily be exposed as a sham by anyone who wishes to preserve the conflict. There must be some truth to it, even if it is not *fully* truthful. The jury works in euthanasia cases because there are many reasons juries are used, selected as they are, and permitted to give results without reasons, that have nothing to do with our desire to use juries to blunt the conflict of values inherent in mercy killings. Compensation of victims works to price safety in accident cases without forcing us to accept that life is being priced because we also want to compensate accident victims. The fact that, were compensation our only goal, we would not use our existing system makes our insistence that our goal is compensation a subterfuge. The fact that we truly do mean to compensate makes it a feasible one.[337]

In the abortion case the simple subterfuge is too transparent. It becomes an incitement to conflict by inducing people opposed to abortion to try to show it up as a sham. Thus, laws gets passed which would require a woman who is about to have an abortion to view color photographs of a fetus, as if what was needed was to convince her or the society that that which was not seen could in fact be extraordinarily life-like.[338] The subsequent striking down of these laws — though understandable given the original decision in *Roe* v. *Wade* — neither preserves the subterfuge nor eases the underlying conflict.[339] Thus, the same "what is not seen does not exist" approach leads opponents of abortion to walk around carrying fetuses, to demonstrate that they really look like neonates.[340] In other words, it leads to behavior (designed to expose the subterfuge) which in itself is provocative and hardly helps to push toward a cohesive societal solution.[341]

The Court, in fact, used a more complex — but even more unfortunate — method of trying to duck the underlying conflict. The Court did not say that a fetus is not alive, and did not suggest that the metaphysics of those who believe that life occurs at conception are not true. It avoided the issue of when life begins, saying that this issue was something on which it could not speak. But the Court then went on to say that for purposes of our Constitution, a fetus (at least until independently viable) is not a person.[342] This last statement is a deeply troublesome one in a legal system like ours.

In the first place, from the standpoint of constitutional law in most other legal contexts, the statement was probably incorrect. That is to say, the statement completely ignored the gravitational pull of other areas of the law. Our law has for centuries given a fetus substantial kinds of recognition and protection. It is quite doubtful, for example, whether (before *Roe* v. *Wade*) a state law which denied an unborn fetus the right to inherit from its parents would have been constitutional. More likely, such a law would have violated the equal protection clause of the Fourteenth Amendment.[343] (Once again, I am not concerned here with the result in *Roe* v. *Wade*; I am concerned with the specific statement made by the Court in that case that a fetus is not protected under our Constitution.)

The protection traditionally given to fetuses, like many of our constitutional notions, goes back to early English law. It dates from the time when, in English property law, a family would lose its estate (its ownership of land) if there were a gap in the ownership, if there were any time when no heir was in being to take over the property. Under such circumstances the land would revert to other, distant, relatives or to the Crown.[344] The question then arose: What would happen if a male property owner died while his wife was pregnant? It would appear that there was a gap in the ownership (the seizin) and the land should revert to others. At the end of the 17th century this would have seemed the logical result, as described some hundred years later in Charles Fearne's celebrated treatise on this field of law.[345] Nevertheless Baron Turton, a great English judge, held that the fetus was alive for these purposes and, so long as it did not subsequently die without heirs (*i.e.,* was born alive and survived long enough to have sons), the property would not be lost.[346] This led to the celebrated toast, once known to most law students, "Let's fill the cup to Baron Turton, who though the law was clear and certain, would rather help a little fetus, than round our Charlie Fearne's dull treatise."[347]

From Baron Turton's time on, the gravitational pull of the law has been in the direction of saying that (at least for some purposes) a fetus is accorded the protection of our law. Thus, as tort law slowly became less injurer oriented and victim recoveries expanded, damages started being given to parents for the tortious killing of fetuses. Prenatal injuries to a child also came to be recognized as a source of damages.[348] The ironic thing, of course, is that though *Roe* v. *Wade* ignored this gravitational pull when it made its misguided (and, in terms of results, quite unnecessary) statement, the fact that such a statement was made inevitably exerted gravitational pull and so has tended to *undercut* these tort cases in which, in a non-abortion context, fetuses did have rights. It has done so even though from the perspective of modern tort law these cases make a great deal of sense.

So although the abortion decision should have been quite irrelevant to these cases, the Court's statement in *Roe* v. *Wade* that fetuses are not persons for purposes of due process has made recovery of damages for injuries and killing of fetuses considerably more difficult.[349] It also has led — in a context totally removed from that of voluntary abortions—to a decision that someone who killed a fetus could not be guilty of murder or of manslaughter.[350] The Court's statement, moreover, is likely to continue to muddle the law in these areas. Because the Court chose to ignore the established gravitational pull—which said that for some purposes a fetus was surely protected by our law—in order to make a statement that it believed would help it duck the hard conflict actually involved in abortion, it fostered bad law in other areas. The Court, absurdly, acted as if the right of a woman to have a voluntary abortion depended on our law's willingness: (a) to deny damages to would-be parents when their unborn child was killed by a negligent driver, and (b) to let a thug off lightly for shooting a pregnant woman in the stomach, because "nothing had been killed." Baron Turton, at least, knew better!

In this way the Court, instead of writing an opinion that would, in other areas of law, strengthen and reaffirm the values it ruled against in the abortion context, chose a way of reaching its result that seemed almost designed to weaken those values. What the Court did, however, was far worse than this muddling of the law—this willful ignoring and undermining of what had seemed to be a sound and growing tendency in the law. The Court, when it said that fetuses are not persons for purposes of due process, said to a large and politically active group: "*Your* metaphysics are not part of *our* constitution." This is far worse (and more dangerous) in a pluralistic society than the statement the Court sought to avoid making, namely, "Sorry, but your metaphysics are wrong. A fetus is not alive." The Court said it does not matter whether a fetus is alive (whether *your* metaphysics are correct). A fetus still is not protected by *our* Constitution.

Such a statement is about as bad as can be made by the Supreme Court of the United States in the area of conflicting beliefs. One can argue about the truth of one's beliefs; if the Court had simply denied that fetuses were alive, unpleasant arguments on metaphysics would have followed. The question of whether fetuses are alive would have been debated acrimoniously (as they have been in any event),[351] but they would have been debated within the Constitution. The argument would have been between people in the same polity, under the same *acceptable* Constitution, seeking to convince each other about an unprovable, metaphysical issue—whether a fetus is alive.

When, instead, the Court proclaimed that the truth of the beliefs did not matter—that anti-abortion beliefs as to commencement of life, *whether true or not,* are not part of our Constitution, of our legal system—it immediately made that Constitution unacceptable to the holders of these beliefs. It said to highly defensive groups comprised in significant part of recent immigrants that their highest beliefs, their metaphysics, are not part of *our* law as represented by its most fundamental statement, the Constitution.[352] In effect, it told these groups that their beliefs are not acceptable, that they are not a part of our establishment, whether or not they happen to be true. It told them, in as dramatic a way as one can through a legal opinion, that even now, even after all their other assimilations, they could not be true Americans so long as they held to their beliefs. This was catastrophic because it reinforced doubts which the holders of anti-abortion beliefs already had about their full acceptance in American society. It reminded them, moreover, of how many of their values and their cultural traditions the melting pot had required them to give up in order to be accepted.[353]

Such a statement almost always is wrong even if it is only made to Minelda or to Mrs. Eider, even if the group excluded from the establishment is small. It has the effect of emarginating the holders of the belief, of putting them outside of the protection of the no-establishment clause. It treats their beliefs as if they were "unreasonable regardless of their truth," as if they were those of an "outlandish cult" and not even a religion. It is, as I said earlier, an invitation to revolt, to demand that the Constitution be changed to incorporate the beliefs or be burned as a pact with the devil.[354] If the group is small enough, the invitation may result in outlawry for its members, and in the ultimate destruction of the group.[355] Or it may result in the group yielding and (in practice) giving up the outlawed beliefs (as happened with the bulk of the Mormons).[356] Both should be troubling in a pluralistic society, to say the least. If the group is large, such a statement almost always ushers in a period of profound unrest as the excluded group tries desperately to redefine the Constitution so that it no longer excludes its beliefs, but excludes the contrasting beliefs instead.

This is, of course, what happened after *Dred Scott,* and it seems to be happening in the conflict over abortions.[357] The time for compromise is over. If the choice is between my beliefs or yours being recognized as acceptable by our law, I will fight to have it be mine and to exclude yours from those that are acceptable in the polity. It is an interesting fact that, before the Supreme Court's decision in *Roe*

v. *Wade,* legislature after legislature moved toward permitting abortions. Some state laws went as far as *Roe* v. *Wade.* Although there was powerful opposition to these changes, there was not a sense of desperate embattlement in the debate.[358] After *Roe* v. *Wade* everything shifted and the legislative history has been one of almost fanatical pressure to forbid abortion, even in situations where, before the case, abortion was virtually universally permitted by the law.[359]

It is as if at least some of those opposed to abortion could reluctantly accept *results* which did not coincide with their beliefs, but could not accept the statement that the beliefs themselves were valueless and beyond the pale. Once *that* statement was made, the only way to affirm the fact that the belief—and its holders—were part of the polity seemed to be to enshrine the belief and its practical consequences *absolutely* in the law. For these reasons, then, far from being a successful subterfuge or ducking, the Court's opinion in *Roe* v. *Wade* was a disaster. It opened wounds one wishes were closed. The decision made it impossible for the opposing views to live with each other, and created a situation in which one side seemed to need to *win out* over the other. And, while that may be the side the Court supported,[360] the losers will not quickly forget their exclusion (just as they have not forgotten their treatment as recent immigrants) to the detriment of our pluralistic society.[361]

And yet, the issue on which the Court spoke *was* a Constitutional one. To have failed to act in *Roe* v. *Wade* would have been to risk emarginating another previously mistreated group—women. Women bore the brunt of anti-abortion laws which not only limited their access to sex, but also placed on them the often catastrophic consequences of illegal abortions. And women have traditionally been discriminated against in our society.[362] The issue of abortion is one which involves a deep conflict of beliefs among groups that view themselves as historically mistreated. As such, it did—and does—involve a tragic conflict of ideals that would not be dissipated by inaction. To have acted as though *our* Constitution was unconcerned with the effect of anti-abortion laws on women would have been about as bad as to make the statement the Court made.

In such situations it is far better to accept our complex and conflicting metaphysics for what they are. It is essential to recognize that *all* of them are part of our fundamental law and significant to it. Since they are in conflict, one must seek solutions in which—though one set of ideals and beliefs will win in the particular case (that cannot be avoided)[363] — the victory will not reject as invalid or outside our law the ideals, beliefs, and values (yes, even the metaphysics) of the losing group. Because such solutions respect both the winning and the losing metaphysics, they look to a time when it may be possible to accommodate both sets of beliefs. Even if such a time never comes to be, they serve to place the burden of the immediate result on all of us rather than just on the losers. They tell the losers that society does not wish to become callous, or indifferent to their faith.

We must admit that what needs to be done is something that we wish not to do, but cannot avoid doing. We must regret deeply, that given the existing, irremediable conflict between two fundamental sets of values, we must inevitably give more weight to one than the other, much as we hate to weaken either. Only in this way are we *all*, to some extent, shouldering the responsibility. When, instead, we deny that anything of value is being sacrificed and say that the losing belief is one to which our polity gives no weight, we are adding significantly to the loss of the losers. We are not merely saying that we do not care to try, with a different technology or under different conditions, to reconcile the values in the future; we are, by our very statement, undermining the losing value more than is needed, and thereby increasing the offense to the losers. By denying that we have qualms or regrets at the loss of something of value in our law, we are also concentrating that sense of loss on those whose views and values did not prevail.

Solutions which recognize the existence of a conflict among fundamental values are rarely acceptable to the pure holders of a metaphysic and belief. But, even to these, such solutions are likely to be less hurtful than a statement that their values do not matter. That is to say, a statement such as, "Your views matter, and are worthy. They are part of our law and on many occasions they will be upheld. On *this* occasion, however, they do not prevail," is much less emarginating, and more hopeful for the future of the society, than a statement that our law excludes your metaphysics as worthless.

Moreover, if the fact that we are a pluralistic society means that most believers of one metaphysic feel strong tugs toward other sets of beliefs, such solutions are likely to be particularly successful. The recognition of the different values in conflict, then, mirrors our own internal conflict. Like the society, we want to have it both ways. We would like to hold to both ideals, though we know that we cannot. It is easy to see why people who feel that way can be sympathetic to a result which, while it may end up striking the balance differently from the way they would have done, discloses the same anguish they feel in having to give up or lessen an ideal to which they would like to adhere. Under those circumstances they may accept results which they deeply regret.

Let me be more specific about how such an approach might have been used in the abortion situation. Suppose that, instead of viewing the issue as a conflict between a belief that life (or legal protection of life) begins at parturition or at independent viability, and a belief that it begins at conception, we viewed it in a quite different way. Suppose we described the clash, more accurately, as one between values and beliefs which would give primacy to equality (among men and women as to participation in sex) even occasionally at the cost of life-values, and values and beliefs which would give primacy to life-preservation (even of not fully developed life) over equality. If we did view it in this way, would most of us feel that, if we could, we would hold to both sets of values, or would we lightheartedly negate the worth of one set and deny that it should have any legal weight? I believe that most of us would give some weight and recognition to each set of values.

But is that an accurate way of describing the abortion conflict? I think it is. First, it is fair to say that most of those who would give primacy to fetal life do recognize (or at least did before *Roe* v. *Wade*) that fetuses are not quite the same as fully developed people or even neonates. That is, before the abortion cases there was no great fuss over the laws (which existed in virtually every state) permitting abortions to save a woman's life. These laws allowed such abortions even extremely late in pregnancy and, though from the standpoint of pure anti-abortion metaphysics they had to be unacceptable, they were accepted without any major conflicts.[364] The woman's life was universally treated as more important than fetal life in law if not in morals. Since no equivalent preference existed between women and neonates (I know of no American law allowing the killing of a neonate for the sake of the mother's health) it seems fair to extrapolate and say that our law did make some relatively uncontroversial distinction between neonates and unborn.[365]

Conversely, I would suggest that most of those who give primacy to equality of access to sex over the life values associated with fetuses recognize that there is more to a fetus—and more to a more fully developed fetus—than to an egg or a sperm. Again, there is no great fuss over the facts that contraception is much more desirable than abortion, that early abortions are much to be preferred to late ones, and that abortion used indiscriminately as a contraceptive device is a bad idea.[366] Moreover, these points of view seem to be based on more than what is preferable for the woman involved. In other words, there seems to be some recognition (even by those who often would not give them primacy) that there are some values attached to fetal life.

Admittedly there are purists on both sides of the issue—those who hold that a fetus is nothing at all, and those who would ban first-month abortions even when pregnancy endangers a woman's life.[367] But there are enough indications, both in past law and practice, that permit me to say with a fair amount of confidence that most people in our pluralistic society would like to have it both ways. At least before *Roe* v. *Wade* drew the battle lines—and probably still today—most of us would like to hold to values that would make abortions undesirable and values that also would make some effects of its prohibition undesirable. Most would like women to have equal, and equally unburdened, access to sex as men, and most would like to protect the life of the fetus—if they could have both at the same time.

Some may question whether the countervailing value to fetal life is equality. Other values, such as privacy and rights to one's own body, have been mentioned. I think most statements of the issue in terms of those rights alone tend to be misleading. We have not in our law had any consistent pattern of constitutional rights to our own bodies or to privacy in sexual matters that seems to exclude governmental regulations. Where any substantial countervailing interest exists and where the regulation applies in a nondiscriminatory fashion, rights to our own bodies and rights to privacy in sexual matters regularly lose. Indeed, even when that countervailing interest is based purely on moralisms, it seems to be upheld. Sales of hearts and body parts are not allowed.[368] Laws against homosexual practices among consenting adults are, absurdly but regularly, held constitutional (even though they are clearly based on moralisms alone).[369] When these last are attacked, the attack seems to be as much focused on their discriminatory nature as on anything else.[370] I do not say one could not—or should not—have a jurisprudence of sexual privacy which would support abortion rights in those terms. I do not even say that one could not have an equivalent jurisprudence of body parts. I simply say that we do not have it, and certainly did not have it at the time of *Roe* v. *Wade*.[371] We do, instead, have a highly developed jurisprudence of equality, and that jurisprudence readily attaches itself to fundamental interests — like sex and control of one's own body — to require that the state not discriminate invidiously with respect to these. In this respect the constitutional issue concerning abortion mirrors the general framework of our Constitution. Of the many rights that philosophers would deem fundamental only relatively few are accorded direct constitutional protection. Most are subject to regulation through laws enacted by duly elected representatives of the people. Almost all of these rights, however, are accorded constitutional protection against legislative actions that would limit them in an invidiously discriminatory fashion. When groups that do not have full access to the legislative process are made to bear most of the burden of a law limiting such rights, the Constitution frequently intervenes to bar the unequal burden.[372]

For me, the essence of the argument in favor of abortion is an equality argument. It is an equal protection rather than a due process argument. It is a women's rights versus fetal life debate. It is based on the notion that without a right to abortion women are not equal to men in the law. They are not equal to men with respect to unburdened access to sex — with respect, that is, to sexual freedom. It assumes that what makes anti-abortion laws suspect is the fact that they put the burden of fetal life saving (given sexual freedom) solely on women, and that if men bore an equal burden such laws would be constitutional. It is, of course, no argument against my position to say that, were *that* the case, few such laws would be passed by legislatures. Quite the contrary, for that is *precisely* what Constitutional notions of equal protection are about. Such clauses are there to strike down laws enacted by a dominant group which disproportionately burden a disfavored group — laws which frequently would not be passed if their burden were equally shared by all.[373]

Not only do I believe it correct in terms of the cases to view the abortion debate in terms of equality, but I also think that viewing it that way may help us to cope better with the values in conflict. It helps explain decisions by courts which would otherwise seem peculiar and gives guidance for future cases. More importantly, it also puts the argument in terms that most of us can understand and sympathize with. Life values and equality among men and women are ideals to which most of us can respond, and hence which we can respect even when they ultimately are balanced in ways with which we would not agree.

There is a catch, however. Both the life and equality values are presented in a somewhat weakened form in the abortion debate. What is at stake on one side is not general equality among men and women, but rather equality of access to sex — equality in *sexual freedom* among men and women. What is at stake on the other side is not life in general, but fetal life. Those who do not respond to one of these attenuated values will obviously find the conflict one-sided. I shall later argue that, far from undercutting my position, this fact helps to explain the abortion debate today, and even tells us why some pro-abortion laws seem to be less controversial than others.

One may ask, however, whether putting the argument that way tilts the scales unfairly against abortion. Do we not always give primacy to life over other values in our law? In view of the discussion of the evil deity's gift in Chapter I, the answer I would give, not surprisingly, is: far from it. While it may seem queer to suggest that in our law any value is greater than life, the fact is that, though we wish to hold to life (at least nominally) as a pearl beyond price, we do not infrequently value other things more. We rarely do this openly because we are uncomfortable when we do it, but we do it all too often. At times what we call freedom is the value we prefer to life. At other times we let people die to preserve individual autonomy. Still other times (as in car accidents) we allow lives to be lost because we wish to cut costs, or to further convenience — to get where are going faster or more easily. In different situations and for any of these and other reasons, we do, in fact, sacrifice lives.[374] When, moreover, the burden of saving lives would be unfairly or discriminatorily borne by a disadvantaged group, we may require the sacrifice of lives as a constitutional imperative.

There is in American law no general duty to be a good samaritan, to save lives. If I see someone drowning and I can save him or her at little or no cost to myself, there is no general requirement that I do so.[375] I happen to think that strange and wrong. And it is different in many other advanced countries such as Italy.[376] Judge Richard Posner, when he was a professor at Chicago, disagreed with me and went so far as to suggest that jurisdictions which imposed good samaritan duties tended to be either fascistic or communistic. (He "explained" an analogous duty in Vermont, by pointing to the fact that it had the third highest tax rate of any American state.)[377] I never understood Posner's argument, and even less his comments about fascism, etc.[378] Be that as it may, he was correct in saying that our legal system would rather let some people die unnecessarily than impose duties on others to save them!

I suppose the reason is that we do not wish to interfere with individual autonomy or freedom, even in order to save lives. If that is it, I do not like the rule. I would prefer a rule which would require us all to be good samaritans. But consider for a moment a different rule, one that required only women, or only blacks, to save people who are drowning. Such a rule would not only be offensive, but would surely be unconstitutional.[379] That might, of course, be because the choice of the group burdened is entirely arbitrary. Others, it might be said, could save drowning people as well, and so the choice of blacks or women would be unfair. That, however, may be too quick a reply. Consider a law that would require women (they being the only ones who could) to have fetal implants and to bring fetuses to term whenever a pregnant woman could not. The choice of category would no longer be arbitrary. The *individual* "samaritan" might or might not be chosen by lot. She might be picked because of similarity of blood type. Would such a law be valid? It seems unlikely.

Contrast such a law with one in which the category of compelled good samaritans did not itself involve a classification (like women or blacks) that our Constitutional Law calls "suspect" or "near suspect," and makes subject to very close scrutiny.[380] Think about the validity of a law which said that every time someone needed a kidney or bone marrow transplant, the best donor (the one with the closest tissue match) had to contribute the kidney or bone marrow, had to suffer to save another's life. Would that be valid? Perhaps, because no invidious discrimination is involved. More important, no such law has been passed and none is likely to be passed, precisely because it *is not* discriminatory.[381] Since all of us would bear the burden, we have preferred to let others die, rather than to compel life saving. Compelled life saving is easier to enact (and for that very reason constitutionally suspect) when disfavored groups are forced to do the life saving.

Consider the same law requiring organ donors to contribute to those in need if it turned out that those who had recessive sickle cell anemia genes were far and away the best donors.[382] Let us assume that, by some strange quirk, those who would be compelled to donate organs were almost universally those people whom our society calls black. Let us further assume that without such transplants those who needed the organs would surely die. Would a law which required blacks to donate organs to save identifiable lives be constitutional? It surely would be invalid.

It would be void, not because we do not value the life of the donee, but because we sometimes value other things more than life. We uphold these other values (like autonomy) for themselves, and we uphold them especially (constitutionally even) when those who would be made to give them up are members of a group which has been traditionally discriminated against in our society. As a matter of ordinary law, we often prefer other values to life. Moreover, when saving lives would require both the infringement of significant other values and the burdening primarily of those in disfavored or discriminated against groups, we may be barred by our Constitution from compelling life saving behavior.[383]

A rather dramatic example of choosing other values over life was the case of *Cooper* v. *Aaron* in the 1958 term of the Supreme Court.[384] The public schools in Little Rock, Arkansas were to be desegregated under Court order. The governor of Arkansas had refused to go along. The federal government sent troops to enforce the court order. At this point the School Board sought to prevent integration. The claim made was that public hostility to integration, promoted by state officials and requiring the use of troops, made education in integrated schools impossible.[385] When the case came before the Supreme Court, the solicitor general of the United States, a man named J. Lee Rankin, argued in favor of enforcing the Court order. Rankin was not known for his forensic skills, but he cared deeply about the case and, apparently, had strongly urged the reluctant President Dwight D. Eisenhower to send the troops. The Court questioned Rankin about the state's argument (that integration enforced by troops would hurt education in those schools), and asked whether he conceded that to be so. The solicitor general, to his great credit, not only conceded that, but even that the use of troops would likely cost lives. Nevertheless, he argued, the Court must declare to this nation and to the world that there are values, like equality, that are more important to us, even than life!

And so the Court held, in an opinion designed to emphasize the strength and unanimity of its views.[386]

What strikes me as interesting is that most of the examples and hypotheticals I have just given seem strangely easy. The choice to give preference to values other than life (though masked) seemed almost inevitable and not seriously controvertible in those cases. Moreover, only one of the examples (that of fetal implants) involved less than fully developed life. The other concerned people who could by no stretch of the imagination be deemed anything but living human beings. In many instances (people drowning, the transplant donees), the lives at stake were also clearly identifiable and not uncertain or statistical, and in at least one (the desegregation case) commission rather than omission was involved. Yet our law preferred to support some value other than life saving. This was especially true—indeed seemed to be required by our Constitution—when the other value either was equality or when the other value, though not itself equality, was undermined in a discriminatory fashion. What, then, makes the abortion case seem so much harder?

The abortion situation is different—and for some harder—because of its link to free sexual choices. The woman who seeks an abortion is not a random, compelled good samaritan picked from a group which is discriminated against. She freely undertook a line of conduct that made her more likely to be in the position of being the only one who could, by bearing a burden, preserve life values. She was not just conscripted to be a life saver, nor was she chosen by lot or by blood type to be the recipient of a fetal implant.

This is not always true. In rape cases and in most incest cases, the woman did not choose a line of conduct that made her more likely to be the needed good samaritan, in any sense our law would or should recognize.[388] In those cases, it is not just equality of access to sex that is being balanced against life values—it is equal rights in general. It should be no surprise, therefore, that abortions in such rape and incest situations are not nearly as controversial as they are in other contexts.[389] For the true believers in life values over equality values, abortion should be barred in these cases as well.[390] But for most, when *general* equality of treatment and life values come into conflict, equality of treatment as often as not wins easily. The notion that a raped woman can be conscripted to preserve a fetus seems to many to be as wrong, and discriminatory—indeed as constitutionally flawed—as the notion that women could be compelled to accept fetal implants or that blacks could be required to be kidney donors.

Many abortion situations are not, however, of that sort. The equality value at stake is a more complex one. It must attach to the right freely, and without a discriminatory risk, to undertake the very line of conduct which may result in the woman becoming the only available good samaritan. In other words, the right at stake is the right of women to participate equally in sex without bearing burdens not put on men. The argument for abortion must be that discrimination against women in the right to engage in sex is unconstitutional, and remains unconstitutional even when that discrimination would serve to preserve some life values.

It is on this proposition that people's views differ sharply, even bitterly. What makes the abortion case so divisive is that, while fundamental values are at stake on both sides, the values on neither side are presented in their most dramatic, incontrovertible forms. For many, fetal life is not the same as fully developed life. Also for many, equal and nondiscriminatory access to sex is not the same as the generalized right to equality. Under these circumstances, it becomes all too easy for those on each side to give the values on the other side no significance at all. The temptation to say that *our* Constitution does not recognize *your* values can become overwhelming with all the disastrous effects I suggested in my criticism of the Court's opinion in *Roe* v. *Wade.* Yet such devaluation of what the other side would defend does not, I think, reflect our deepest convictions. Even when the issue is described as a conflict between fetal-life values and equality in the right to engage in sex, I believe that many would like to uphold both values. Many are ambivalent because, unless it is impossible to do so, we would like to have it both ways.

Consider the following intentionally unreal hypothetical example. Suppose, in a society as addicted to sexuality as ours seems to be, there were a disease which could be spread among adults only through sexual intercourse. Suppose further that the only people who were carriers of this disease were those who had a genetic trait that had come to be concentrated almost exclusively in a specific ethnic group, for example, Jewish people (say the asymptomatic form of a recessive syndrome like Tay Sachs disease).[391] The disease, though harmless to the carriers, would be 100 percent fatal to those newborn children of the carrier who contracted the disease. The disease could be spread to the carrier's children who were less than two years old without sexual contact, and a certain proportion of these would get the disease and die.[392] Like most venereal diseases, the disease could usually—though not always—be kept from spreading from adult carrier to adult carrier if certain forms of contraceptives (condoms) were used. (In other words, like pregnancy, becoming a carrier could usually be avoided by contraception and always by abstention).

Assume now that there was another way through which someone who had become a carrier could be kept from infecting and killing neonates. The carrier would not infect the neonates if he or she wore a very heavy and clumsy lead tunic for the period of time during which he or she was a carrier, say for nine months. Also assume that the wearing of the lead tunic was inextricably associated in the society with antisemitic discrimination. Bigots commonly refused to hire Jewish people for many jobs and justified the discrimination by saying that one never knew when they would not be able to work for months at a time because they had to wear the tunic. The tunic and those who wore it were described as funny, ugly, and so forth. The sexual link to the need to wear the tunic was the source of all kinds of myths and disparagements with respect to the sexuality of Jewish people. Finally, susceptibility to having to wear the tunic was commonly attributed to all in the group, whether or not they had the Tay Sachs trait or used the appropriate forms of contraception. The bigots argued that they could not know who in the group was in danger of having to wear the tunic and who was not. Hence, all Jewish people were discriminated against because of the occasional need by some of them to wear the tunic.

Would laws requiring those who were carriers to wear such a lead tunic be clearly constitutional? Remember, the problem would not arise if all Jewish people (but only Jewish people) abstained from sexual intercourse. And the problem would not be as common if Jewish people (but again only Jewish people) always used particular contraceptive devices. Others in society could enjoy sex casually and without analogous dangers or impediments. Would a holding that such laws were invalid require, or even suggest, that neonates were not persons? That would have nothing to do with it. Nor would there be any doubt that a harmless cure (should one be developed) permitting the neonates to survive without requiring anyone to wear the lead tunic, or to be otherwise disadvantaged, could be required in order to save the neonates. Since life saving could be accomplished without discrimination, it clearly could be compelled. Similarly, if the carrier came from all groups in society, or only from groups which traditionally dominated the society and which suffered no invidious discrimination, laws requiring the wearing of a lead tunic would surely be upheld. Again constitutionally prohibited discrimination would be absent.[393] Conversely, what if the possible carriers were not Jewish people but an even more discriminated against racial group in that society, blacks, for example? What if they were women? Would the protection given to neonates depend on the degree of discrimination life saving implied?

One can see many differences between my hypothetical example and the abortion cases. These differences make the question of the constitutionality of anti-abortion laws both easier and harder. On the one hand, fetuses are not neonates and have, without much controversy, been recognized in the law as being somewhat less "alive" than neonates. (As I noted earlier, we have had no laws which justified killing a neonate to preserve its mother's health. However, virtually every state in the United States did permit even late abortions to save a woman's life, long before *Roe* v. *Wade.*) On other hand, the harm to the fetus as a result of abortion is obviously more direct, though not necessarily more intended, than the contagion and death of the neonate in my hypothetical example.[394] Moreover, Supreme Court decisions have said that classification and discrimination when based on race or ethnic background are constitutionally more suspect than when based on sex. That is, laws exclusively affecting blacks or Jewish people are more likely to be held invalid than those affecting exclusively women; these are only semi-suspect. I am not, of course, arguing that this last is as it should be. I am simply stating what current constitutional doctrine seems to be. Indeed, that state of things is one reason why the ERA was proposed.[395] Nor am I probing into the deeper question of whether certain groups have been more discriminated against in our society than others, and what effect the *gravity* of the past discrimination should have on laws like the one compelling the wearing of the lead shield. *Indeed, I am not, in this book, even suggesting what the Supreme Court should do in the lead tunic case, or should have done in the abortion cases.*

I am intentionally abstaining from giving my own view of how

the conflicting values of (a) equality in access to sex for a deeply discriminated against group, and (b) the life values associated with the
unborn, should be balanced. I am doing this because my concern is
less with stating a "correct" answer than with defining a way of looking at things that is appropriate to a society that wishes to include
within it highly diverse beliefs, moralisms, and attitudes. Thus, I have
no doubt that my lead shield hypothetical example will not strike all
readers in the same way. Some certainly will think such laws should
be upheld. Others will wish them struck down. Almost all, however,
will deeply wish that both values at stake could be upheld, that equal
access to sex for Jewish people could be achieved (and the concomitant discriminations ended), and that the neonates still could be saved!

Because almost all would like to hold to both values, a decision,
either way, which is made in these terms is likely to be more respectful
of the faith of those who lose — and hence less harmful — than was the
opinion of the court in *Roe* v. *Wade*. A decision which recognizes the
values on the losing side as real and significant tends to keep us from
becoming callous with respect to the moralisms and beliefs that lose
out. Properly written, it can even lead to a strengthening of those values.
It can exert a favorable gravitational pull and create a climate of opinion which will lead courts and legislatures to uphold the losing values
in contexts in which the winning values are not at stake.[396] This gives
the losers hope that the values they cherish will not be ultimately abandoned by the society, and that the society, despite what it chooses to
do now, will not become immoral in the long run. It tells the losers
that, though they lost, they and their values do carry weight and are
recognized in our society, even when they don't win out. In other words,
it treats the believers as citizens of the polity, and not as emarginated
bigots or unassimilated immigrants.

I do not for a moment suggest, however, that we can stem the
current conflict by going back and rewriting the abortion opinion in
terms of a conflict between egalitarian values and life values in which
the egalitarian values won out. Once the issue is put, as it was, in
terms of which beliefs are recognized by our Constitution and which
are not, it is too late to return. The genie is out of the bottle and cannot be put back. Extreme protagonists of both views are out on the
streets and are unlikely to be reconciled by a way of stating the issue
in which, even if correct and respectful to their beliefs, they lose out.
At this point, such a way of putting things is bound to seem no more

than a rationalization for the offensive and emarginating decision which actually was made. Now, the conflict must work itself out — one way or the other — until one set of moralisms becomes sufficiently dominant in the society so that relatively few will hold fast to the losing side, and so that these can be emarginated, unjustly perhaps, but with relatively little social strain. This is hardly a good result in pluralist society!

What I am suggesting is that, had we been more attentive to the variety of beliefs which we purport to encourage, this might have been avoided. The United States might even, like Italy in which Catholicism is the established religion, have permitted abortions without emarginating those who deeply think that abortions are fundamentally wrong.[397] I once had occasion to put the abortion issue in these terms to a senator, who was famous for his anti-abortion stances, and to a Catholic Bishop, who had prided himself on his links to the pro-life movement. (One is now dead and the other is out of office, but at the time they were dominant figures in the anti-abortion movement, and both were active in trying to establish the fact that we really do recognize fetal life as something worth preserving.) Both of them said to me that they would, of course, have strongly opposed *any* holding that permitted abortions. They said fetal life was far more important than equality in sexual participation (even if inequality in access to sex led, as it did, to other discriminations). Nevertheless, they went out of their way to assert that they would not have been *offended* by an opinion which recognized legal value in fetal life, even though it found other, egalitarian, values to be dominant.

They may, of course, have been lying, but I doubt it. I think they said this in part because they wanted to affirm their own adherence to egalitarian values, but more because such a holding did give legal recognition to what they believed. The senator even suggested that he had been an active supporter of a law prohibiting the execution of pregnant women because that law, in a small, almost ironic way, gave legal standing to his belief that fetal life has a value. Even though it had no practical consequences, such a law gave legal recognition to his beliefs, and hence, made him and his faith a part of the polity.[398] When the issue is belief, recognition of its validity — its reasonableness in our law — seems to be almost as important as results.

There are other reasons a holding in *Roe* v. *Wade* that had been firmly based on the dominance of fundamental egalitarian values over fetal life values (also fundamental) would have been preferable to the actual holding. Though these are somewhat to the side of the main thrust of this book, they are not irrelevant and I cannot resist advert- ing to them. Such a holding would have been much more consistent with subsequent, almost inevitable, holdings by the Court. It also would have given better guidance to lower courts in more complicated cases. Most important of all, from the standpoint of this book, it would have encouraged activity—by those who are most committed to preserving the life-values—in constructive directions rather than in divisive ones. It would, obviously, have rendered unnecessary, useless even, laws and actions designed to demonstrate that fetuses are alive or life-like. In- stead, it would have put a premium on support by pro-life groups for technological developments which would have enabled us to uphold both egalitarian and life values.

If an early fetus has no rights in our law (and if *that* was the basis of *Roe* v. *Wade*), then it is hard to see why the male involved cannot demand that an early abortion take place, even though the woman does not wish it. The same is true if abortion simply is an acceptable means of contraception, or if people have the constitutional right to destroy their genes (or offsprings, whatever you wish to call them) rather than letting others bring them up. It would seem equally true if (as some undoubtedly argue) parents have a right to prevent a defective child from being born, even if there are others who are willing to raise such a child.[399] All these rights to destroy the fetus, rather than merely be separated from it (even when separation happens to entail destruc- tion), would seem to run to sperm no less than to egg sources.[400] In- deed, if the issue were rights over one's genes (which had no rights of their own), it is hard to see why the male could not also block an abortion sought by the female.

That the courts have, instead, consistently held that the male involved does *not* have rights in the matter[401] indicates again that the key issue is not one of fetal life, but of women's rights to equality. It is an issue of the constitutionality of being required to wear the lead tunic. It goes to the woman's right to separation from the fetus, even if separation entails the fetus' death, because without that right she would not be equal to men in access to sex. It is in this sense that I believe the approach I have been arguing for is more consistent with the cases that have followed *Roe* v. *Wade,* than is *Roe* v. *Wade* itself.

An equality versus life values approach would also give better guidance in harder cases. Consider, for example, the Massachusetts case (after *Roe* v. *Wade*) in which a relatively late abortion was performed, and in which it was alleged that the fetus lived and was allowed to die by the doctor. In defense, the claim was made that this could not be a crime because the fetus was not a live person until it left the mother's body. Though it may have lingered after being detached from the mother, it was still in the womb and so was not a person when the doctor failed to act.[402] Certainly the doctor involved was led by *Roe* v. *Wade* into thinking that what he allegedly did was legal. Yet the defense that what the state claimed he did could not be a crime is hard to accept and is deeply troublesome. There was at the point he supposedly failed to act no reason not to try to keep the fetus alive and let it be adopted by any number of willing parents. (I am assuming that it was possible for it to be born healthy, because to assume otherwise raises many other deep, fascinating, and immensely troublesome issues with which the court did not really deal.) I do not say, of course, that the doctor should have been convicted in the actual case. The combination of *Roe* v. *Wade* and the Massachusetts statutes on manslaughter were vague enough so that a conviction would have been wrong on that ground alone.[403] What I am saying is that a decision which permits abortions on federal Constitutional grounds ought not to imply that states cannot, if they wish, protect — even through criminal law — aborted fetuses which are, or can be, born alive. In such cases the woman's right to separation has become independent from the need to destroy life values, and only muddled thinking — and a badly reasoned Supreme Court *opinion* — would require us to rejoin them. It is the same kind of muddled thinking that has led some courts to treat the killing of a wanted fetus as of no legal significance, but only as an ordinary battery to the would-be mother.[404]

Moreover, if one views the issue in abortion as being one of equality of treatment, then the cases dealing with the right of welfare recipients to abortions become as hard as most seem to feel they are, and their difficulty becomes understandable. I do not say that the result the Court reached in those cases (allowing the banning of welfare payments for abortions) still could not be reached, although it would be much harder.[405] I only say that if the abortion issue is treated — as I hope to have shown that it should be — as an equal protection issue, then the question of the extension of that right to the poor becomes a significant one, however one comes out on it. If, instead, abortion is only an issue of the right of an individual to do away with an unwanted, inanimate body part (as *Roe* v. *Wade* in a sense treated it to be), then the issue of welfare abortions loses most of its significance. Why should the state be *required* to pay for such a decision? That most people would feel that the issue of welfare abortions is a serious one suggests, once again, that *Roe* v. *Wade* misstated the problem.[406]

Most important, an equality versus life values approach to abortion would look to a time when we could uphold both values, and would urge the current losers (the partisans of life values) to work to speed that time, rather than to try to convince the winners that life values also are at stake. (This last, by hypothesis, would have already been established.) One can imagine a time and a technology in which a woman who wished an abortion could have the fetus removed without pain or risk to her and without necessary harm to it. One also can imagine that *willing* volunteers, women who wished to adopt babies, could have that same fetus implanted in them and brought to term. Why should our Constitution prevent states from requiring *this* form of separation (if truly riskless) rather than another form which entails destruction? What special interest—different from the male interest which has been held by the courts to be of no weight—would the female have which would give her the right to destroy her genes or offspring? Why, in other words, under such a technology, should those who wish to preserve both life values and equality values not be able to legislate so as to achieve both?

The right to separation, because it is necessary to ensure that women have equal and equally unburdened rights to participate in sex without thereby inviting other forms of discrimination, could remain dominant, as the Supreme Court determined it to be. But it would no longer need to undermine life values that others in society deem to be at least as important.

There are, of course, many other issues which are inherent in the abortion debate. I have in passing adverted to some of them—they include questions of population control, what one should do about defective babies, and the alleged right (in whom, female or male?) to determine the sex of one's offspring.[407] I have not gone into these because, if one stops to think about them, most of them would apply as well (or in some cases better) to infanticide as to abortion. Unlike the right to abortion, they concern issues which are separate from the special burden that is put on a woman when she is required to carry to term a fetus she does not wish to bear. Those go to the right to destroy; abortion, as Professor Judith Thompson has so brilliantly argued, goes to the right to separate, even if destruction follows.[408] I do not deny that some in our society, and perhaps many more since *Roe* v. *Wade,* believe in the right to destroy. If so, the conflict underlying abortion has become much deeper than it once was, and bodes worse for the unity of our polity than one, even as pessimistic as I, believes.[409] No matter what can be said for and against those positions, they are, analytically, very different problems from the question of abortion rights in itself, and should be treated separately.

They remain to the side in this book. My object has not been (despite the time spent on it) to discuss fully, let alone to resolve, the abortion issue. For that reason, I do not need to consider all these other elements that surround the abortion question. I have only discussed abortion because I wanted to talk about conflicts of belief in a pluralist society. It would have been cowardly to do so without treating the prime issue in conflict today. The object, and hence the scope, of the discussion was limited to learning something about how such conflicts might be approached. I believe this object was furthered by the discussion of abortion and that from it, and from the analyses of beliefs, ideals, and attitudes in the earlier chapters, we now can draw some conclusions. These are few and may seem obvious, but we can take comfort in this obviousness because we have journeyed long in order to arrive at it.

Conclusion

BELIEFS, IDEALS, AND ATTITUDES are an integral part of our law. Whether based on current creeds, secularized versions of past faiths, or non-religious beliefs, they shape what is expected and what seems reasonable in the most diverse sections of our law. Their role in any given area of law is determined both by the needs and functions of that area and its relationships (the gravitational pulls on it and from it) with the rest of the law. Each part of law must not only achieve relatively specific functions, but also must answer to a key aspect of our sense of justice: the need to be reasonably consistent with the requirements of other parts of the law. I have looked primarily at one area of law—torts or accident law—both because I know it best and can speak about what is likely to happen in it even when past cases are contradictory or ambiguous, and because the interplay it displays between its own needs and its desire to respond to the requirements of the rest of law, is at the same time especially obvious and typical of other areas of law.

At the core of tort law is the need to resolve, to cope with, a fundamental conflict of values—the desire to treat life as sacred and the wish, the need even, to do things which enrich the way we live but which endanger and ultimately take lives. That is the essence of the evil deity's gift. The conflict is made more complex by our desire to reduce the risk to lives as much as possible, but to do so without burdening those whom other areas of law tell us should not be disfavored. Thus our Constitution urges us not to burden or exclude certain classes

115

of people defined by age, sex, race, or handicap from key activities, even if their full participation costs lives. The Constitution presses us not to distinguish between widely held religious beliefs and rarely held religious beliefs despite the fact that such distinctions could help lessen the costs of accidents. It also urges us not to favor religious over non-religious beliefs and vice versa.

These conflicting pulls lead to a series of uneasy compromises. Sometimes these are relatively open (as when victims whose injuries are greater than normal because they hold unusual beliefs are compensated, but injurers holding similar beliefs are made to pay). Sometimes they give lip service to one ideal, while serving other goals (as when we declare that insurance categories based on race, age, or sex are invalid, but then permit surrogate categories that accomplish analogous burdenings). Sometimes they are unresolved or characterized by subterfuge (as when we favor unusual religious beliefs over idiosyncratic non-religious beliefs [in victims], or when we distinguish between religious faiths which get protections, and odd cults or practices which do not). Sometimes they make uncertain judgments between present needs to reduce accident costs and the wish to preserve or develop future moral sensibilities (as when we do or do not compensate for purely emotional damages).

In these compromises—uneasy and unhappy though they may be—certain things stand out. First, moralisms, faiths, and beliefs do matter and must be taken into account in making law. To try to ignore them usually means to give weight only to the beliefs and ideals of those groups which have traditionally been dominant in our society (even, as with abortion, when they are relatively new beliefs of these groups). Second, subterfuges—though often used and often needed—are always dangerous, rarely can be intentionally chosen, and can only work when they are not simply lies. They must have something to commend them apart from the desire to hide that which cannot be resolved. Third, while honest and open solutions are best, they cannot always easily be made to work. They are more apt to succeed (a) if they are respectful of the beliefs of all those in conflict (especially of those who lose out in the particular case), (b) if that respect not only preserves and strengthens the belief—the moralism—of those who lost, but looks to a time when both the winning and losing beliefs can be upheld, and (c) if many of those who prefer, even strongly, one of the beliefs in conflict also share, or have sympathy for, the ideal on the other side. Fourth, and perhaps most important, one must think long and hard before emarginating, or treating as unworthy, beliefs that are deeply held in the society. To declare a belief to be outside the pale, or unrecognized in our law, leads to deep and searing conflict if the holders of the belief are sufficiently numerous or can become so through martyrdom and conversions. More often it leads to the exclusion and ultimate elimination or exile of the believers.

There are some beliefs which our legal system wishes to treat that way, even though to do so reduces pluralism and creates deep conflicts. Racism is clearly one. There are others, including most religious beliefs and many ethnic or cultural attitudes, that our constitutional norms urge us to protect. We are required to go to great lengths to avoid excluding and emarginating them. Conflicts among them are inevitable, but we must not let such conflicts lead us into declaring that some of them are enshrined in our law while others are unrecognized. We can try to hide and obscure the conflicts by subterfuges if we can do no better. However, if at all possible we must honestly and openly find ways that will allow such deeply held convictions to survive in tension with each other, all recognized as part of our law and all looking toward a day (which may never come) when the conflict can be resolved and they all may be consistently upheld. We must do this not because we all should wish to adhere to all of them, but because it is the only way we can be the society our constitutional ideals ask us to be.

Notes

1. Actually, it was my co-author, Philip Bobbitt, and I who called these choices "tragic." I use the pronoun "I" merely because it is more convenient than the pronoun "we" in this context. *Cf.* G. CALABRESI & P. BOBBITT, TRAGIC CHOICES (1978).

2. All the wars fought by the United States in the 20th century have been of this type. To find wars in which American civilian life or even property was widely threatened, one must go back to the Civil War (for the South only) and the Revolutionary War (in which large areas of the south and parts of the north were wracked by guerilla warfare).

3. My interest in the issue of how "tragic choices" are made began when I started to compare automobile accidents with medical experimentation with human beings. Medical experiments typically involve some (often substantial) danger to experimental subjects. Sometimes, the benefits of such experiments to the subjects are low or even nil. Instead, the principal gains from experimentation accrue to future patients. Modern industrial societies frequently employ technologies that are of substantial benefit to most individuals in society but which impose disproportionate costs on certain unfortunates (*e.g.,* the victims of automobile accidents). In Calabresi, *Reflections on Medical Experimentation in Humans,* 98 DAEDALUS 387 (1969), I wondered why disproportionate allocation of burdens and benefits seemed much more morally troublesome in the context of medical experimentation than it did in the context of accidents. In that article, I suggested the major difference might be the sheer blatancy with which these allocations are made in medical experiments. I then outlined some possible solutions to reduce the blatancy. However, by the time Philip Bobbitt and I wrote TRAGIC

CHOICES, *supra* note 1, I realized the issues raised by this type of allocation were far more complex and escaped easy solution.

4. G. CALABRESI, A COMMON LAW FOR THE AGE OF STATUTES (1982) [hereinafter cited as CALABRESI, A COMMON LAW].

5. For example: (1) The California Supreme Court's nullification of a statute severely limiting the liability of car owners to guests who were passengers in their cars after comparable common law limitations on the liability of landowners had been abolished, *cf. id.* at 10–11; or (2) The United States Supreme Court's treatment of statutes governing the liability of railroads and shipping companies to their employees in the face of alterations in the common law doctrine governing the liability of other kinds of injurers, *id.* at 32–33; or (3) The Wisconsin Supreme Court's "interpretation" of a statute allocating losses between negligent victims and negligent injurers in the face of changing common law doctrine and statutes in other states, *id.* at 36–37.

6. A similar strategy was adopted in CALABRESI & BOBBITT, *supra* note 1. See especially, *id.* at 28 and compare the use made of the concepts developed in investigating intractable moral dilemmas in TRAGIC CHOICES to the somewhat more tractable problems raised by the *Bakke* cases, in Calabresi, *Bakke as Pseudo-Tragedy*, 28 CATH. U. L. REV. 427 (1979).

7. Technically, "casuistry" refers to a particular method of inquiry into ethical problems. Broadly defined: Casuistry involves the following elements: (1) A particular (typically ethically complicated or troublesome) situation; (2) Accepted general moral principles; (3) A discussion of how the moral principles may be rationally applied in the particular circumstances. *Cf.* 3 ENCYCLOPEDIA OF RELIGION AND ETHICS, *Casuistry* 239–47 (1911).

Typically, however, the term is used to refer to the use of this method in theological disputation during the Reformation. Although casuistry was used both by Catholics and Protestants, the Jesuits' use of casuistry was notorious. The method fell into disrepute after Pascal's attack on it in LES PROVINCIALES (1657). Pascal and later critics have viewed the method as a particularly noxious type of literary sophistry designed to fulfill the ideological needs of the Roman Catholic Church. This view of the use of casuistical methods to investigate particular ethical dilemmas is exemplified in the 19th-century Protestant theologian Adolf Von Harnack's comment:

> The comprehensive ethical handbooks of the Jesuits are in part "monstra" of abomination and storehouses of execrable sins and filthy habits, the description and treatment of which provoke an outcry of disgust. The most shocking things are here dealt with in brazen-faced way by unwedded priests as men of special knowledge, not with the view of calling down with prophetic power upon the burden of horror a heavier burden of judgment,

but often enough with the view of representing the most disgraceful things as pardonable, and of showing to the most regardless transgressors a way in which they may still always obtain the peace of the Church.

A. VON HARNACK, VII HISTORY OF DOGMA 101ff. (1897–1910) (English translation).

Whether or not one agrees with such characterizations of casuistry, the fact that the method may have been grossly misused in theological debates of the 17th century hardly seems a damning criticism of its use to explore legal and ethical issues in the 20th century. In any event, the common law has a long tradition of proceeding quasi-inductively: by developing limited propositions through the resolution of particular controversies in the light of past solutions of related problems. The results have frequently been impressive. This success suggests that the method of working from the specific to the general has much to recommend it when confronting a particularly tangled controversy. Here, we also wish to confront a series of particularly difficult ethical/legal issues. The similarities in the problems confronted in these two situations suggest the case method can be profitably employed here. If this be casuistry, then let us make the most of it.

8. *See* CALABRESI, A COMMON LAW, *supra* note 4; Coffin, *Book Review,* 91 YALE L.J. 827 (1982). There I also relied on investigation of particular problems in tort law to argue that the increasing volume of statutory law created an increasing number of obsolescent statutes. Chief Judge Frank Coffin, in his thoughtful review, suggested that the problem was less general than I had suggested particularly in federal law. *Id.* at 836–37. I was much relieved later to receive a letter from another federal judge pointing to a "pet hate" of his—the in-state plaintiff diversity jurisdiction statute—as a prime example of an obsolescent statute in federal law. Letter from Judge Henry Friendly (July 7, 1982) (on file, Yale Law Library). One may conclude that investigation of particular cases can illuminate problems that afflict broad areas of the legal system, but only by creating the danger of over-generalization. Or one may conclude only that reasonable people can disagree on how systemic an issue detected by this method really is.

Another danger of excessive reliance on cases is that one is likely to overlook issues not raised in lawsuits. In 1971, Frank Michelman analyzed three alternative rules for allocating the burdens and benefits relating to the right to pollute or be free of pollution. Michelman, *Pollution as a Tort: A Non-Accidental Perspective on Calabresi's* COSTS, 80 YALE L.J. 647 (1971). Because we used a simplistic model rather than a case method, Douglas Melamed and I became convinced there was a fourth solution applicable to pollution cases: that the victim of pollution might be permitted to stop the pollution but only by paying damage (or compensation) to the polluter. Calabresi and

Melamed, *Property Rules, Liability Rules, and Inalienability: One View of the Cathedral,* 85 HARV. L. REV. 1089 (1972). This solution would be impractical for a judge to apply in most lawsuits, but is commonly used in other contexts, such as eminent domain proceedings. *Id.* at 1116. Because it was unlikely to appear in any lawsuit, the rule had been overlooked even by commentators as sophisticated and able as Michelman. Interestingly, the approach was applied in a case involving quite unusual circumstances at about the time our article was published. Spur Industries v. Del. E. Webb Devel. Co., 108 Ariz. 178, 494 P.2d 700 (1972).

9. *Cf.* D. BRAYBROOKE & C. LINDBLOM, A STRATEGY OF DECISIONS: POLICY EVALUATION AS A SOCIAL PROCESS (1963).

10. *Cf.* E. H. LEVI, AN INTRODUCTION TO LEGAL REASONING, 8ff. (1948). *Cf. also* Clardy v. Levi, 545 F.2d 1241 (9th Cir. 1976). In that case, the Ninth Circuit declined to find the Administrative Procedures Act applicable to disciplinary proceedings in federal prisons. The court, after noting the advantages of incremental rule making, explicitly justified this ruling in part because such a holding would allow the continued evolution of standards for such proceedings via adjudication in federal courts.

11. I choose to call the deity evil. Whether he or she is in fact evil, is a highly complex philosophical question.

12. The United States experience with the 18th amendment dramatized the problems involved in prohibiting goods people are accustomed to using. These problems would, however, be minimized in the case of the automobile since driving an automobile is essentially a public act. Of course, the economic dislocation involved in prohibiting the manufacture or use of alcoholic beverages pales into insignificance beside that which would result from banning the use of automobiles. In practice, it is hard to imagine a concatenation of political events that could ever induce Congress to ban the automobile. The point here is not that banning the automobile is in any way a realistic political option. The point is that if *enough* people *really* wanted to ban the automobile, it could be done.

From a social scientific viewpoint, it may be quite correct to say that what is going on is simply that social structure militates against most individuals deciding not to use the automobile. *Cf. infra* note 14. However, the problem addressed here is ethical, not scientific. We are not so much concerned with why Americans failed to refuse this gift of the evil deity, as with the effect this failure has had. The result has been to allocate the benefits provided by the automobile very widely and place a disproportionate share of the concomitant burdens on a relatively few unfortunate victims.

13. It would be almost impossible for citizens of a modern industrial nation to refuse totally the gift of the evil deity. In order to do so, they would have to remove themselves from contact with the modern industrial econ-

omy. Otherwise, they would be forced to use products that have been delivered by truck and whose fabrication depended on the existence of the automobile and truck. This level of withdrawal would exceed that maintained by even such religious groups as the Amish and the Mennonites.

14. The problem is that both the costs and benefits attendant on the use of the automobile have significant external effects. The user of the automobile obtains the benefits resulting from the widespread use of the automobile. A non-user sacrifices these benefits and is forced to rely on the goods and services produced to satisfy the relatively few (and typically poor) non-users.

If a large number of people decided to become non-users, then the benefits of their decision would also be, in part, collective: (a) a variety of goods and services oriented to non-users would become available more cheaply due to economies of scale: (b) the risk of being involved in an automobile accident would decline as there were fewer automobiles. There might be a considerable number of people who would opt to become non-users in return for these benefits. However, most of them might rationally choose not to become non-users when deciding individually since these benefits would not result from such isolated choices. *Cf., eg.,* Bator, *The Anatomy of Market Failure,* 72 Q. JOURNAL ECON. 351 (1958).

15. A tradition has grown up in legal writing of using the term "medical experiment" to refer exclusively to experiments in which the experimental subjects are exposed to possible harm while any results of the experiment are not likely to benefit the subjects. *Cf.* J. KATZ, EXPERIMENTATION WITH HUMAN BEINGS (1972). The term "medical experiment" is used here in the more traditional sense of referring to any medical research which involves direct manipulation of a factor the researcher deems to be causally important and the presence of an (at least, implicit) control group. The first experiment discussed here is a medical experiment only in this less restrictive sense. This experiment directly benefitted the experimental subjects. Consequently, it raised none of the ethical issues raised by the second experiment which was of the type that has concerned legal scholarship. *Cf.* note 16.

16. That is, he thought up an experiment of the type that has troubled and concerned legal scholarship. *See supra* note 15. The experimental subjects are subjected to an identifiable risk but the experimental manipulation is of no significant benefit to the subjects.

17. The logic of the experiment is simple. To vaccinate is to infect with cowpox, a viral disease. A drug that acted as a systemic treatment for viral diseases would prevent one from acquiring cowpox. The purpose of the experiment was to determine if the drug tested was a systemic treatment for viral diseases by seeing if it would prevent experimental subjects from acquiring cowpox, even when put in direct contact with the virus. The pur-

pose of the second administration of the cowpox vaccine was to demonstrate that the apparent immunity of the experimental subjects to cowpox endured only as long as the effects of the drug lasted.

Cowpox has been used as a vaccine against smallpox ever since Edward Jenner discovered in the late 18th century that milkmaids who had almost invariably had cowpox seemed to be immune to smallpox. It is a far less virulent disease than smallpox and consequently an effective vaccine. Nevertheless the subjects in the experiment described in the text had little likelihood of acquiring smallpox so there was little need to vaccinate them. The cowpox induced by the vaccine had a small but not inconsequential probability of making subjects seriously ill. Consequently, it was not in the subject's interest to be vaccinated.

18. In 1966, the Surgeon General of the United States established the policy that the Public Health Service would not award grants to support medical research which was not reviewed by an experimental review committee. Most institutions, including hospitals, that engage in medical research have established such committees. These review committees typically consist not only of doctors but also of researchers in medically related fields and laypersons. Since 1969, the Public Health Service has required that the committee approve only research in which the risks to the subjects involved in research be outweighed by the potential benefits of the research. J. KATZ & A. M. CAPRON, CATASTROPHIC DISEASES: WHO DECIDES WHAT?, 124–29 (1975). The criteria by which the members of these committees are supposed to make such a judgment remain obscure — certainly to observers and quite probably to the participants as well.

19. It has been suggested that individual assent to taking part in potentially dangerous medical research is seldom the result of a rational calculation of the potential costs and benefits of alternative choices. Rather, a potential subject's assent frequently occurs when the subject lacks knowledge of the alternatives proffered and is heavily influenced by external social cues (*e.g.,* others' expectations). *Id.* at 90–108; *cf.* Ofshe & Christman, *A Two-Process Theory of Social Behavior,* in ADVANCES IN SOCIAL PSYCHOLOGY (A. Harris ed. 1985) (forthcoming) for a discussion of contexts in which social behavior will be controlled by external cues rather than the individual's own choice. Whether or not the consent of subjects to participate in a potentially hazardous experiment actually results from psychological processes approximating a rational choice, the mechanics of securing informed consent probably serves a variety of useful purposes. It has the effect of legitimizing the whole process by which subjects are obtained. It forces the physician to explain the research in a comprehensive and comprehensible way, and thereby minimizes the likelihood of fraud and the possibility of the physician merely pressuring the potential subject into compliance. It may also lead

the physician-researcher to reconsider his or her own research in light of its potential risks and benefits. KATZ & CAPRON, *supra* note 18 at 82–90.

20. United States v. Karl Brandt, *et al.,* Nuremberg Military Tribunals, 1 & 2 Trials of War Criminals. The Nuremberg war crime trials were the most important of the trials of German war criminals after World War II. Of the 12 separate trials conducted by the United States at Nuremberg after the war, the so-called doctors trial was only the first and by no means the largest or most famous. It is extensively discussed in A. MITSCHERLICH & F. MIELKE, DOCTORS OF INFAMY: THE STORY OF NAZI MEDICAL CRIMES (1949). For a complete bibliography of the United States military tribunals at Nuremberg *see* J. LEWIS, UNCERTAIN JUDGMENT: A BIBLIOGRAPHY OF WAR CRIME TRIALS, 101–17 (1979).

21. The doctors prosecuted in this trial showed remarkable inventiveness in devising ways to inflict pain under the guise of scientific research. Experiments conducted included the following: (1) high-altitude experiments — experimental subjects were placed in a low-pressure chamber duplicating the atmospheric conditions prevailing at high altitudes (up to 68,000 feet). Many subjects died. (2) Freezing experiments — subjects were forced to remain in a tank of ice water for periods up to 3 hours so that the most effective means of treating persons who had been severely frozen could be investigated. Many subjects died. (3) Malaria experiment — healthy subjects were infected with malaria to determine the relative efficacy of various drugs in treating malaria. Some subjects died. (4) Poison experiments — poison was secretly administered to experimental subjects via their food to determine effects. A few were shot with poisoned bullets. All subjects died. (5) Sterilization experiments — X-ray, surgery, and various drugs were employed to determine the cheapest, most effective ways to conduct mass sterilization of "undesirables." Few subjects died. MITERSCHERLICH & MIELKE, *supra* note 20.

The experiment in which the woman discussed here participated was an extension of the "freezing" experiment. German doctors, putatively interested in the efficacy of "animal heat" in reviving their frozen and all but dead experimental male subjects, had them lie naked with female "volunteers." United States v. Karl Brandt, *et al.,* Nuremberg Military Tribunal, 1 Trial of War Criminals at 68–71 (opening statement by Brigadier General Telford Taylor, Chief Prosecutor).

22. United States v. Karl Brandt, *supra* note 21 at 70–71 (opening statement by Brigadier General Telford Taylor, Chief Prosecutor).

23. Of the 23 defendants 16 were found guilty of war crimes and crimes against humanity; 7 were sentenced to death by hanging and the other 9 to terms of imprisonment varying from 10 years to life.

24. Statutes banning the use or sale of fireworks were a response to the number of injuries they caused. Prior to World War I, no state had laws

restricting the use or sale of fireworks. *Transportation of Fireworks in Interstate Commerce: Hearing on S. 1722 and S. 2245 Before a Subcomm. of the Senate Comm. on the Judiciary,* 83rd Cong., 2nd Sess. 22 (1954) (statement of Henry R. Backes, V.P., M. Backes' Sons, Inc., fireworks manufacturer) [hereinafter cited as *Senate Hearing*]. At that time, the 4th of July created considerable carnage. In 1903, 466 deaths and 3,983 non-fatal injuries were reported by the American Medical Association as connected to the celebration of the Fourth of July. *Id.* at 69 (statement by George F. Lull, M.D., Secretary-General, Manager of the American Medical Association). This number declined in the following years, and records of injuries were not kept from 1917 to 1936. By 1937, however, the total number of injuries had actually increased (20 deaths, 7,205 non-fatal injuries). The interwar period saw the first prohibitions on the use or sale of fireworks. By 1940, 9 states had passed prohibitory statutes, LEGISLATIVE COUNCIL OF MARYLAND, RESEARCH REPORT NO. 1 (1940), at 30. The majority of states passed prohibitory statutes during the 1940s. By 1954, 37 states had passed such statutes (several others had delegated such power to county or municipal officials). *SENATE HEARING, supra* at 5–6 (statement of Congresswoman Marguerite S. Church). The rapidity with which these statutes took hold may be gauged from the fact that by 1946, total deaths and injuries from fireworks had fallen to 909 from a peak of 7,951 in 1938. *Id.* at 69.

    25. The Guardian (Manchester), Feb. 27, 1981, at 5, col. 5. In the United Kingdom, all medical expenses connected with children's illnesses are borne by the National Health Service. Therefore, these accidents were a direct charge on the state.

    26. *Atomic Power Development and Private Enterprise: Hearings before the Joint Committee on Atomic Energy,* 83rd Congress, 1st Sess. (1953).

    27. *Id.* at 32 (Statement of Dr. John C. Burgher, Director of Biology and Medicine, AEC; question by Senator Hickenlooper).

    28. In the Mayaguez incident, 39 seamen were taken off the S.S. Mayaguez by armed Cambodian soldiers. They were rescued, at the cost of 15 lives, 50 wounded, and however many millions of dollars were necessary to deploy the 7th fleet in the Gulf of Siam. The danger that the seamen would have been harmed by the Cambodians, though uncertain, was probably substantial. J. Osborne, *Mayaguez Questions,* 172 NEW REPUBLIC, June 17, 1975 at 7. It is true that this operation was probably mounted by the U.S. government partly to discourage other similar hostage takings in the future, and perhaps partly to shore up President Gerald Ford's domestic popularity. Nevertheless, the approbation with which the rescue was greeted suggests that most Americans believed the Ford Administration had not paid too high a price to protect the seamen.

    29. Statistical lives are more likely to be protected if they come from

a relatively homogeneous group in society. Such groups frequently can form cohesive interest groups capable of exerting political pressure. As an example, consider miners organized by the United Mine Workers (UMW). In fiscal year 1980, the federal government alone spent $143.6 million on the Mine Safety and Health Administration (MSHA). 68 U.S. DEPT. OF LABOR ANN. REP. 172 (1980). Large additional sums were spent by the various states. Private industry also spent substantial sums of money in order to comply with MSHA regulations. The number of lives lost in mine accidents in a given year tends to be around 600. BUREAU OF THE CENSUS, U.S. DEPT. OF COMMERCE, STATISTICAL ABSTRACT OF THE UNITED STATES 1982–83, at 412 (1982). It is of course possible that if this amount of money had not been spent, many many more lives would have been lost. Nevertheless, it is worth noting that if comparable sums were spent per automobile deaths, the federal government alone would be spending around $13 billion annually on automobile safety.

30. CALABRESI & BOBBITT, *supra* note 1, at 38–41; *cf.* also at 137–41.

31. I have limited myself to speaking of only 1,000 lives because this number is much smaller than the actual number of lives currently lost to traffic accidents annually which in recent years has been around 55,000. Consequently, we can safely assume that the cost of using the automobile will match or exceed the hypothetical gift of our evil deity into the foreseeable future.

32. Large construction projects invariably entail a substantial number of deaths and injuries. The Mont Blanc highway tunnel, the longest in the world at 7¼ miles, cost 17 deaths and 800 injuries. *The View From Mont Blanc*, NEWSWEEK, July 19, 1965 at 74. This was somewhat cheaper than the Brooklyn Bridge that cost 26 lives and an unknown number of injuries. D. McCullough, *The Great Bridge and the American Imagination*, N.Y. Times, March 27, 1983 § 6 (Magazine) at 28, 34. H. SHULMAN, F. JAMES & O. GRAY, CASES AND MATERIALS ON TORTS 161, n. 9 (3d ed. 1976).

33. As do we. It is certainly true that bad drivers contribute to accidents. However, people being careful would simply not eliminate all accidents. The very fact of numerous individuals piloting heavy metal vehicles in close proximity to one another at high speeds is certain to create situations that overwhelm individuals' driving ability. U.S. DEPARTMENT OF TRANSPORTATION, DRIVER BEHAVIOR AND ACCIDENT INVOLVEMENT: IMPLICATIONS FOR TORT LIABILITY 123–71 (1970).

34. *Cf.,* CALABRESI & BOBBITT, *supra* note 1, at 73–77.

35. The extent to which such an explicit quantifiable standard would be desirable has been the subject of considerable debate. The use of Baye's theorem to quantify risk of error in identification evidence was advocated in Finkelstein and Fairley, *A Bayesian Approach to Indentification Evidence,* 83

HARV. L. REV. 489 (1970). Professor Tribe attacked the use of such a standard on various grounds, among them that use of a statistical standard required setting an explicit standard of acceptable risk of error and that such an explicit confession that some degree of risk of error is acceptable creates unacceptable problems for the legitimacy of the criminal justice system. Tribe, *Trial by Mathematics: Precision and Ritual in the Legal Process,* 84 HARV. L. REV. 1329, 1374 (1971); *A Further Critique of Mathematical Proof,* 84 HARV. L. REV. 1810, 1818–9 (1971). The debate has continued. Finkelstein published a slightly revised version of his original proposal, M. FINKELSTEIN, QUANTITATIVE METHODS IN LAW, 78–104 (1978), which was attacked on the grounds that the assumptions underlying probability statistics may be inapplicable to most disputed fact situations that arise in litigation. Brilmayer & Kornhauser, *Review: Quantitative Methods and Legal Decisions,* 46 U. CHI. L. REV. 116, 135–148 (1978). This contention has also been hotly disputed. Kaye, *The Laws of Probability and the Law of the Land,* 47 U. CHI. L. REV. 34 (1979).

36. *Cf.* PROCEEDINGS OF THE CONFERENCE ON THE ETHICAL ASPECTS OF EXPERIMENTATION ON HUMAN SUBJECTS, November 3–4, 1967 (Boston, Massachusetts). A later issue of DAEDALUS, devoted entirely to this subject, grew out of this conference and reflected the issues raised there. 98 DAEDALUS, No. 2 (1969). The "flat EEG" standard for death is presented in *A Definition of Irreversible Coma,* 205 J.A.M.A. 337 (1968) (Report of the ad hoc Committee of Harvard Medical School to Examine the Definition of Brain Death).

37. The response to this statement was polite, albeit nervous, laughter.

38. The fact that one can, in theory, employ both types of tests—a precise non-perfectible test and an imprecise but putatively perfectible test— does not mean both types of tests will be employed in practice. It is quite likely that over time people will increasingly rely on the seemingly more "scientific" precise test. *Cf.,* Tribe, *supra* note 35.

39. If one's test is perfectible, in theory, no lives need be sacrificed. The test's administrators may even be able to believe that, if lives are lost, it was the fault of those who died. CALABRESI & BOBBITT, *supra* note 1, at 73–77. Our hypothetical deity is evil precisely because he demands the sacrifice of lives in return for his gift. If a standard is adopted that is realistically perfectible, such a sacrifice need not occur. At that point, our hypothetical deity might no longer seem "evil," only cruelly demanding.

40. During the late 1970s, the U.S. Department of Transportation sponsored construction of two separate Research Safety Vehicles (RSVs). One was built by Minicars and the other by Calspan. Both delivered excellent fuel economy and crash-worthiness. Both were subject to extensive road tests. Both were suitable for mass-production, although their price would probably have been greater than conventional vehicles. Whether because of cost, esthetics, or other reasons. neither has been produced. *Cf.,* DEPARTMENT OF

Transportation, Research Safety Vehicle — Phase II, Comprehensive Technical Results (November 1977); Research Safety Vehicle, RSV (March 1979) (pamphlet); RSV Test Monitoring and Data Publication — Results of European Performance And Handling Tests on the Calspan RSV (July 1979).

41. Calabresi & Bobbitt *supra* note 1, at 73–77.

42. The death rate from cancer in the United States has increased dramatically over the last 40 years. In 1940, death rates (per 1,000 population) from cancer was 1.1 and 1.3, for males and females, respectively. By 1979 these rates had increased to 2.1 and 1.6 respectively. Bureau of the Census, *Supra* note 29, at 79 (1982). It is probably impossible to estimate what proportion of these cancer deaths are environmentally caused. However, it has been asserted that 80% or more of human cancers are due to environmental factors. Tomatis, *The Carcinogenic Risk for Man of Environmental Chemicals* in Recent Advances in Assessment of the Health Effects of Environmental Pollution, International Symposium (1974). Nevertheless, during this period, life expectancy has continued to climb and death rates to decline in the United States. In 1940, life expectancy at birth in the U.S. was 60.8 and 65.2, for males and females, respectively. By 1979, life expectancy had increased to 69.9 and 77.6 years, respectively. Bureau of Census, *supra* at 71. During the same period, the death rate from all causes had declined from 10.8 to 8.7 for males and females, combined; *id.* at 60.

43. The decline in the death rate from diphtheria alone has probably more than compensated for the increase in deaths from traffic accidents during the 20th century. In 1900 the crude death rate (per 100,000) for diphtheria was 40.3. This rate had declined to below .05 by 1957. 1 Bureau of Census, Historical Statistics of the United States, Colonial Times to 1970, at 58 (1975). The crude death rate (per 100,000) for automobile accidents increased from near 0 in 1900 to 24.3 by 1979. Bureau of Census, *supra* note 29 at 76.

44. The debate over whether cars should have air bags has been long, convoluted, and, at the time of this writing, inconclusive. The latest installment in this continuing story saw the Federal Court of Appeals for the D.C. Circuit order the National Highway Traffic Safety Administration to reconsider making installation of air bags or other passive restraints in automobiles mandatory. State Farm Mut. Auto. Ins. Co. v. Dept. of Trans., 680 F.2d 206 (D.C. Cir. 1982), *vacated sub nom,* Motor Vehicles Mfrs. Assn. of U.S. Inc. v. State Farm Mut. Auto Ins. Co., 103 S.Ct. 2856 (1983).

45. It is well within our technical capacity to clean up hazardous wastes. It is also very costly. In 1980 the cost was estimated to be between $28 and $55 billion, nationwide. *Coping With Toxic Waste,* Newsweek, May 19, 1980 at 34. The unwillingness of the Reagan Administration to spend the money

necessary created a political furor in early 1983. In order to cut its losses, the administration forced EPA director Anne Burford to resign and later appointed William Ruckleshaus. *Cf., Mr. Reagan Turns a New (Old) Leaf,* N.Y. Times, March 23, 1983, at A 26, col. 1 (Editorial).

46. There is no need here to commit ourselves to the proposition that gains from any technological advance must benefit the least-advantaged members of society if implementation of that advance is to be just. *Cf.,* J. RAWLS, A THEORY OF JUSTICE 75–83 (1971), for an argument that such a position should be adopted). It is enough to say that we should certainly be concerned by social change that makes the rich richer and the poor poorer.

47. There is clear need for a term that can be used to refer to either male or female survivors of a deceased spouse. The archaic legal term, "relict," was used primarily to refer to widows, not widowers. However, it is etymologically sex-neutral and so we will use it to refer both to widows and widowers.

48. We need not consider here whether judges or legislatures are the appropriate parties to establish a policy of providing compensation for survivors of evil deity victims. It has been argued that judges are limited to implementing but not establishing such policies. Dworkin, *Judicial Discretion,* 60 J. PHIL. 624 (1963); but *cf.* CALABRESI, A COMMON LAW, *supra* note 4, at 92–101.

Answering the relict's plea does not require that all those who gain by accepting the evil deity's gift bear the same burden. We may choose to "tax" beneficiaries progressively, by placing greater burdens on the wealthy. *See* discussion of "spreading" and "deep pockets" in G. CALABRESI, THE COSTS OF ACCIDENTS, Ch. 4 (1970) [hereinafter cited as CALABRESI, COSTS.]; *see also* W. BLUM & H. KALVEN, THE UNEASY CASE FOR PROGRESSIVE TAXATION (1953).

49. OLIVER WENDELL HOLMES, THE COMMON LAW 77–78 (1963). A similar argument was made in W. BLUM & H. KALVEN, PUBLIC LAW PERSPECTIVES ON A PRIVATE LAW PROBLEM — AUTO COMPENSATION PLANS (1965).

50. The Chicago-based "economics of law" fraternity takes a jaundiced view toward paternalism. *See, e.g.,* A. KRONMAN & R. POSNER, THE ECONOMICS OF CONTRACT LAW, 253–67 (1979); *but cf.* Kronman, *Paternalism and the Law of Contract,* 92 YALE L.J. 763 (1983).

51. A widespread recognition that the temptation to maximize consumption in the near term may prevent one from saving adequate funds for retirement may explain the widespread support for Social Security. Many individuals may wish to be forced to invest in a pension by being forced into the Social Security system. Alternatively, this support may be localized demographically; older individuals who have already invested a substantial amount in the Social Security system and who fear the consequences of any weakening of the system may simply form a sufficiently significant voting bloc to

discourage meddling. In any event, the Social Security system has proven extremely resistant to any attempt to cut benefits. *See Congress Acts on Jobs and Social Security,* NEWSWEEK, April 4, 1983 at 22; *Congress Nets Two Big Ones,* TIME, April 4, 1983 at 30; *Social Insecurity,* 188 NEW REPUBLIC, February 7, 1983 at 4; Buckley, *The Peterson Social Security Reform Act of 1983,* NAT'L REV., January 21, 1983 at 72; Machiavelli (pseud.), *The Modern Prince: Social Security,* PSYCHOLOGY TODAY January 1983 at 8.

52. In THE ODYSSEY, Ulysses is reported to have sailed past an island inhabited by two mythological creatures, half bird and half woman, known as the Sirens. The song of the Sirens was so beautiful that it lured men to their deaths on the rock shores of the island. The wily Ulysses countered the Sirens by plugging his men's ears with wax so they could not hear the Sirens' song. Ulysses, however, was determined to hear the Sirens, so he left his ears unplugged. As a precaution, he had himself tied to the mast of his ship and ordered his sailors not to release him. Suffice it to say Ulysses survived the encounter (at some cost to his peace of mind). THE ODYSSEY, Book XII, lines 140–210.

53. By and large, an enforceable contract is not formed if one party knows or has reason to know the other party is intoxicated. *See Restatement (Second) of Contracts* § 16 (1981).

54. The problem here is the same encountered in the situation in which some people wish to smoke and others don't wish to be exposed to smoke. If physical separation of the two groups is feasible (*i.e.,* not too costly), there is a simple solution to the potential conflict of interest. If separation is not feasible, then one group must compel the other to accept their value preferences (*i.e.,* either anybody may smoke and people who don't want to be are exposed to tobacco smoke, or nobody may smoke, and people who wish to are deprived of the opportunity to smoke). The device of separation acts as the analogue of the badge discussed in the text.

55. Representative democracy does not guarantee that the majority's preference always wins. In American politics, a minority may achieve its preference when certain conditions are met, *e.g.,*: (1) the minority cares passionately about the issue and the majority does not; and/or (2) the minority is well organized and the majority is not organized on this particular issue; and/or (3) the minority is in a position to provide critical votes on another issue and will do so in return for support on the issue in question. *Cf.,* A. DOWNS, AN ECONOMIC THEORY OF DEMOCRACY, 55–60 (1957); E. SCHATT-SCHNEIDER, THE SEMISOVEREIGN PEOPLE (1960). A classic example of a minority imposing its preference upon a majority in American politics is gun control. The National Rifle Association has effectively scuttled all attempts at gun control in the U.S., although numerous surveys have shown widespread support for gun control.

The potential power of a minority is not a peculiar characteristic of American democracy. Israeli politics have provided a textbook example of a minority imposing its will. After the 1981 election, the Likud party found itself dependent on three small religious parties in order to maintain its majority in the Knesset. In consequence the Likud agreed to promulgate legislation demanded by the religious parties that did not have wide support in what is primarily a secular society (*e.g.,* closing the port of Haifa on Saturday; closing the national airline, El Al, on Saturday; exempting "newly observant" orthodox Jews who wished to study orthodox theology from military service). *Saved by the Moral Minority,* TIME August 17, 1981 at 38.

56. I am led to this conclusion by the fact that most states make third-party motor vehicle insurance mandatory (albeit at rather minimal levels of coverage, *see infra* note 170). This apparent widespread support for mandatory third-party insurance cannot be explained merely by the fact that voters are potential victims whose interest lies in protecting themselves against judgment-proof injurers. Were this the sole explanation for mandatory insurance statutes, we would expect the statutes to exempt the relatively prosperous who, of course, are not judgment-proof and who could adequately compensate victims whether or not they were insured. Alternatively, people would be permitted to post a bond rather than buy insurance. This possibility would allow such laws to be written in "universal" terms rather than differently for rich and poor. Self-paternalism may represent a better explanation for the widespread success of mandatory insurance statutes. Even though the prosperous or those who would bond themselves are not judgment-proof, compensating a victim in the absence of insurance, may represent a catastrophic loss for them. For such individuals, mandatory insurance coverage does not merely offer protection against judgment-proof injurers. It also provides protection against the catastrophic loss that may result from their failure to purchase third party insurance.

57. There may be, of course, perfectly good paternalistic reasons to favor making such insurance mandatory. For example, we may feel that it is more economically efficient if everyone carries such insurance, that doing so more clearly accords with widely held values, or that failure to carry such insurance results from a judgment that is so clearly mistaken as to be suspect. *Cf.,* Kronman, *infra* note 50. All of these reasons raise complicated problems if one adheres to the view that individuals are rational utility maximizers who, consequently, must be assumed to know what is best for themselves. R. POSNER, ECONOMIC ANALYSIS OF LAW 3-10 (2d ed. 1977). There is no reason to be drawn into this dispute, here. The twin assumptions of rationality and utility maximization undoubtedly have proved useful tools for the analysis of human exchange. It has been argued, however, that the human information-processing capacity is far more limited than economic

analysis assumes. R. Ofshe & K. Christman, *supra* note 19. If this is the case, then there would be little difficulty in understanding why individuals do not always know what is best for themselves.

Social insurance may also be used as a device to distribute income more equally. Social insurance will lead to a more equitable distribution of wealth if wealthier individuals bear a greater proportion of the burden of supporting the social insurance fund than they receive in benefits and if less wealthy individuals receive more than they pay. Use of social insurance for redistributional purposes is likely to be favored both by those who benefit directly from the program (*i.e.,* those who pay less than they receive) and those who will not benefit financially but who believe for ideological reasons that wealth should be more equitably distributed. The latter group can rationally prefer this and other compulsory wealth-redistribution programs to individual action to redistribute wealth (*i.e.,* charitable giving), due to the familiar problem of "large number choices," *cf., supra* note 14. An individual who gives up some amount of money for redistributive purposes incurs the same cost (ideological preferences aside) whether it is voluntarily surrendered through charitable giving or is involuntarily extracted, through taxes or as a compulsory contribution to a social insurance fund. However, the benefits accruing to our hypothetical well-to-do egalitarian are far greater in the second case than the first. In the first case, the actual impact of the individual's gift on the distribution of income in society is quite small — even if he or she is a Rockefeller. In the latter case, because the government forces large numbers to participate in the wealth-redistribution scheme, the impact is likely to be far more substantial. Consequently, a well-to-do egalitarian will favor the latter over the former. *See* Hochman and Rodgers, *Pareto Optimal Redistribution,* 59 AM. ECON. REV. 542 (1969).

58. CALABRESI, COSTS, *supra* note 48, at 39–67 (1970).

59. *See supra* note 25; of course, if government does not bear the cost of making the medicine bottle child proof but does bear the cost of injuries resulting from non-childproof bottles, it is easy to see why the government would require that medicine bottles be made child proof. This will occur even if the cost of making bottles child proof is greater than the costs resulting from medicine bottles not being child proof. Similarly, economic efficiency is unlikely to be advanced by individual choice if individuals who bear the costs of choosing certain alternatives are not the individuals making that choice. It is this problem that makes medical malpractice a particularly intractable area. Calabresi, *The Problem of Malpractice: Trying to Round Out the Circle,* 27 U. TORONTO L.J. 131 (1977).

60. *Cf.,* Calabresi, *Product Liability: Curse or Bulwark of Free Enterprise?,* 27 CLEVE. STATE L. REV. 313 (1978).

61. Actually, taxes raised to support a social insurance fund may be

structured to create incentives for safety. All that is necessary is that accident-prone activities (leaving aside the tricky issue of how to calculate what activities are accident-prone) be taxed proportionately more heavily than safer activities. This will create an incentive to engage in less heavily taxed (*i.e.,* safer) activities. In New Zealand, a social insurance plan has been instituted that follows this strategy to some extent. The social insurance fund is supported by general revenues from a variety of sources: some of which are arguably accident-prone activities (*i.e.,* levies on owners and drivers of motor vehicles, with the potential of assessing different classes of drivers of motor vehicles different rates on the basis of accident experience) and some of which are not (*i.e.,* a levy charged on all employment regardless of type). Palmer, *Compensation for Personal Injury: A Requiem for the Common Law in New Zealand,* 21 AM. J. COMP. LAW 1, 23–31 (1973).

62. POSNER, *Supra* note 50, at 119–23.

63. It is reasonable to believe that individuals will often be more capable of solving problems of unspecified "risk" when the problems are presented in monetary terms. Monetary concepts have the advantage of being familiar, concrete, and easily quantifiable. Consequently, they have some of the characteristics psychologists have found aid individuals in making burdensome individual choices. *Jungermann, Speculations about Decision—Theoretic Aids for Personal Decision-Making,* 45 ACTA PSYCHOLOGICA 7 (1980).

64. *See* CALABRESI, COSTS, *supra* note 48, at Ch. 5; Calabresi, *First Party, Third Party, and Product Liability Systems: Can Economic Analysis of Law Tell Us Anything About Them?,* 69 IOWA L. REV. 833 (1984) [Hereinafter cited as Calabresi, *First Party, Third Party and Product Liability Systems*].

65. Lord Westbury was a prominent member of the Equity bar, a Liberal M.P., and Lord Chancellor of England from 1861 to 1865. For details of his career, *see* 1 & 2, T. A. NASH, THE LIFE OF RICHARD LORD WESTBURY (1888).

66. *Cf.,* CALABRESI, COSTS, *Supra* note 48, at Ch. 6 for a discussion of how government regulation and the legal system may be used to deter accidents. Similarly, Ch. 5 discusses how burdening individuals with the cost of accidents they cause can encourage greater safety.

67. The Pentagon Paper case resulted from the New York Times and other newspapers publishing excerpts from a government study leaked to them by Daniel Ellsberg. The study was a previously secret history of the origins and conduct of the war in Vietnam up until 1968. Although the study did not cover the years after Richard Nixon became President, the Nixon Administration attempted to prevent publication of the material. The issue of whether the government could enjoin publication of the material reached the Supreme Court in New York Times Co. v. United States, 403 U.S. 713 (1971).

68. *Transcript of Oral Argument in Time and Post Cases before the Supreme Court,* N.Y. Times, June 27, 1971, at 25, cols. 4, 5.

69. New York Times Co. v. United States, 403 U.S. 713, 730 (1971) (Stewart, J., concurring).

70. New York Times Co. v. United States, 403 U.S. 713, 714 (1971) (Black, J., concurring).

71. It is not impossible for the American state and legal system quite candidly to sacrifice lives. It does so under unusual circumstances. Wartime is the most obvious example. Nevertheless, courts are very reluctant to sacrifice lives. Given a choice between a life and a value, the courts will certainly choose life if they can do so without completely sacrificing the value. The consequence of this is that over time a value whose preservation requires sacrificing lives will be increasingly circumscribed, perhaps to the point that it ceases to have any practical import.

72. By "all societies" here, I mean only state-level societies. Societies that lack the institution of the state, as most have in human experience, cannot make these decisions at a governmental level since they lack a government.

73. The issue here is what impact the safety decision will have on the legitimacy of the state. We are not at the moment concerned with whether individuals in the market or the state can make these decisions more effectively. The point is that, in certain circumstances, it is very difficult for the state to make a tragic choice because a choice that too blatantly sacrifices lives may be perceived as illegitimate or even as threatening the legitimacy of the state. Of course, tragic choices made by the market are not always less blatantly life-sacrificing than those made by the state. In certain cases, the market may price lives too clearly for us to be comfortable. Imagine, for example, if we allocated access to kidney dialysis machines by market mechanisms alone. This would mean that the cost of preserving certain lives would be "X" dollars a week and those that could not meet this tariff would die. Furthermore, the state has evolved certain institutions, notably juries, that allow it to make tragic choices without, in fact, openly doing so. *See infra* text at notes 317–321. However, in many contexts, including the one discussed here, a tragic choice is made more blatantly life-sacrificing when entrusted to the state.

74. *See supra* note 57.

75. *But cf.* Calabresi, *First Party, Third Party, and Product Liability Systems, supra* note 64 (suggesting that while various liability systems may be equally good at influencing choices against accidents, they may differ widely in their distributional consequences, and concluding that in such situations there may not need to be a significant conflict between the desire to induce people to choose advertently and the desire to ease the relict's plight).

76. The loss does not always lie on what can strictly be called an insurance category. Under certain circumstances the parties held liable (for example, some manufacturers in products liability cases) bear the loss directly. Nevertheless, because such parties often have adequate loss experience and capacity to spread losses, they are often described as "self-insured," and can be considered to approximate insurance categories.

77. I am using the term "strict liability" here to cover situations in which the loss is placed either on injurer or victim categories. The use of the term "strict liability" is frequently restricted to those "non-fault" areas of the law in which the loss is placed on injurer categories only, *e.g.,* Posner, *Strict Liability: A Comment,* 2 J. LEG. STUD. 205, n. 2 (1973). The problem with this more restrictive use of terminology is that then one must find another term to apply to non-fault areas in which the loss is placed on victim categories (*e.g.,* the term "first-party, no-fault plan" applied to the insurance scheme in which owners of automobiles insure themselves against injury suggested in R. KEETON & J. O'CONNELL, BASIC PROTECTION FOR THE TRAFFIC VICTIM [1965]). Consequently, I have chosen to use the term "strict liability" for all non-fault areas of tort law—wherever the loss lies. *See* Calabresi and Hirschoff, *Toward A Test for Strict Liability in Torts,* 81 YALE L. J. 1055 (1972). For a discussion of the significance of non-fault doctrine (*i.e.,* strict liability) as a basis for allocating losses prior to the 20th century, *see* Rabin, *The Historical Development of the Fault Principle: A Reinterpretation,* 15 GEORGIA L. REV. 925 (1981).

78. The choice of whom to burden with the cost of accidents need not be based solely on who is in the best position to choose between safety and convenience. Distributional criteria are also relevant. We may prefer to burden the more well-to-do with the costs of certain kinds of accidents, even though less wealthy individuals can as easily or more easily change their behavior in the direction of increased safety, because we may feel that it should be the more rather than the less wealthy who should be forced to choose between convenience and safety.

79. *Cf., e.g.,* CALABRESI, COSTS *supra* note 48.

80. It is perhaps symptomatic that of the 12 chapters devoted by Prosser in his influential hornback to the bases of torts liability, only one (Chapter 13) is devoted to strict liability. Eleven (Chapters 2–12) are devoted to "unreasonable" (either intentional or negligent) behavior as a basis of liability. W. PROSSER, HANDBOOK OF THE LAW OF TORTS (1971). It is a widely accepted proposition that "fault" became a dominant concept in torts law only during the 19th century and has declined in importance during the 20th. Gregory, *Trespass to Negligence to Absolute Liability,* 37 VA. L. REV. 359 (1951). Recently, writers have questioned both whether fault dominated tort law during the 19th century to the extent commonly assumed, Rabin, *supra* note 77, and the extent to which fault was absent from tort law prior to the 19th

century. S. F. C. Milsom, Historical Foundations of the Common Law, Ch. 11 (2d ed. 1981).

81. Even in the fault system, there is an initial non-fault decision: "Who will bear the loss in the absence of fault?" Traditionally, the "fault" system has allowed such losses to remain on victims, even though they are not at fault. The loss is shifted to injurers only if: (a) the injurer was at fault; and (b) the victim was not also at fault (the details of the system have been somewhat altered by the shift from contributory to comparative negligence; *see infra* note 85). It is possible to conceive of a fault system that decides this initial non-fault question in the opposite way: a system that places the loss on injurers in the absence of fault. Such a system would fully reverse the current system if it shifted losses to victims only if: (a) the victim was at fault; and (b) the injurer was not also at fault. Calabresi, *Optimal Deterrence and Accidents: To Fleming James, Jr.,* 84 Yale L.J. 656, 664–66 (1975).

82. Of course, this question implies an additional question: Do we or do we not wish the burden to lie on the believer for distributional reasons? *See supra* note 78.

83. A major part of tortious conduct, in the fault system, is "negligent" conduct. Negligence is typically described as a failure to observe a "standard of reasonable prudence and foresight." Jarosh v. Van Meter, 171 Neb. 61, 105 N.W.2d 531 (1960); Rea v. Simowitz, 225 N.C. 575, 35 S.E.2d 871 (1945); Crowder v. Vandendeale, 564 S.W.2d 879 (Mo. 1978) ("ordinary care and skill"). Tortious conduct may be more egregious involving either wanton and willful recklessness or intention to harm. Nevertheless, the standard of reasonableness is a kind of minimum standard to which one fails to conform at one's own peril. Thus, tort law, at least in fault areas, is primarily a law of negligence. 2 F. Harper & F. James, The Law of Torts § 12.1, at 744 (1956).

84. This is the doctrine of contributory negligence. The doctrine holds that if the victim's own behavior did not meet the standard of reasonableness required to be considered non-negligent, *see supra* note 83, then this will bar recovery from the injurer. *See* Martin v. George Hyman Const. Co., 395 A.2d 63 (D.C. 1978); Brownsville & Matamoros Bridge Co. v. Null, 578 S.W.2d 774 (Tex. Civ. App. 1978); Keller v. Frank Kull, Inc., 165 N.J. Super. 258, 398 A.2d 106 (1978). *See generally,* Harper & James, *supra* note 83 at § 22.1 1193–99.

85. The classic criticism of contributory negligence is that "It places upon one party the entire burden of a loss for which two are, by hypothesis, responsible." Prosser, The Law of Torts 433 (4th ed. 1971). *See also,* Schwartz, *Contributory and Comparative Negligence: A Reappraisal,* 87 Yale L.J. 697 (1978). In other words, the contributory negligence doctrine simply does not treat equally a victim and an injurer, both of whom are at fault.

As of 1980, 35 states had adopted some variant of the comparative negligence rule. Wade, *Comparative Negligence — Its Development in the United States and its Present Status in Louisiana,* 40 LA. L. REV. 299, 304–05 (1980). Under this rule, the loss is apportioned between victim and injurer using various formulae related to their putative relative fault. For a history of the development of this rule, *see id.* at 299–307. Though comparative negligence is not a new doctrine, its wide acceptance is new. As recently as the late 1960s, only 7 states had adopted some form of comparative negligence, *id.* at 302. Consequently almost all the cases discussed here were decided under the contributory negligence rule. For a general introduction to comparative negligence, *see* J. A. DOOLEY, MODERN TORT LAW, LIABILITY AND LITIGATION, §§ 5.01–.22 (rev. ed. 1982).

86. Lange v. Hoyt, 114 Conn. 590, 159 A. 575, (1932); Jancuna v. Szwed, 176 Conn. 285, 407 A.2d 961 (1978). *See generally* RESTATEMENT (SECOND) OF TORTS, § 918 (1979).

87. Vaughan v. Menlove, 3 Bing. N.C. 468, 132 Eng. Rep. 490 (C.P. 1837); Hover v. Barkhoof, 44 N.Y. 113 (1870). *See generally,* DOOLEY, *supra* note 85, at § 3.04.

88. If one has special talent or abilities, one is required to employ those talents or abilities. The standard of reasonable prudence is a minimum one. A professional is expected to exercise the ordinary skill and competence of a member of that profession (in the case of physicians, of an ordinary physician, normally in that locality), not that of an ordinary non-professional. *See, e.g.,* Sinz v. Owens, 33 C.2d 749, 205 P.2d 3 (1949) (physician's failure to comply with prevailing method of treatment of complex fracture in that locality). *See generally,* HARPER & JAMES, *supra* note 83 at §16.6.

89. A. P. HERBERT, HOLY DEADLOCK (1934).

90. A. P. HERBERT, *Fardell v. Potts, The Reasonable Man,* in MISLEADING CASES IN THE UNCOMMON LAW 1 (2d. ed. 1927).

91. *E.g.,* Casey by Casey v. Russell, 138 Cal. App. 3d 379, 383, 188 Cal. Rptr. 18, 20 (Dist. Ct. App. 1982); Di Cosala v. Kay, 91 N.J. 159, 177, 450 A.2d 508 (1982).

92. Hall v. Brooklands Auto Racing Club, [1933] 1 K.B. 205, 224.

93. "Bonus paterfamileas" or "diligens paterfamileas" are the terms frequently used in Roman texts. F. H. LAWSON, NEGLIGENCE IN THE CIVIL LAW 40, 77 (1950). This concept of "bonus paterfamileas" or its approximate have continued to shape civil law countries' conception of the standard of care owed by the reasonable man. 1 F. H. LAWSON, TORTIOUS LIABILITY FOR UNINTENTIONAL HARM IN THE COMMON LAW AND THE CIVIL LAW 76 (1982). The term "civil law" refers to the modern system of law developed in Continental Europe (notably in France and Germany) on the basis of old Roman law, canon law, and various traditional Germanic legal codes. K. W. RYAN, AN INTRODUCTION TO CIVIL LAW 1 (1962). Civil law countries are those who have

embraced the civil law. Like the Common Law, the Civil Law has spread far beyond its origins in Western Europe. Consequently, the term "civil law countries" includes not only virtually all Continental European states but also such diverse non-European states as Argentina, South Korea, Lebanon, Turkey, Zaire. LAW AND JUDICIAL SYSTEM OF NATIONS 34, 419, 423, 754–55, 859 (3d rev. ed. 1978).

94. Hall v. Brooklands Auto Racing Club, [1933] 1 K.B. 205, 224 (Greer L.J. quoting unnamed "American author"). *See* HARPER & JAMES, *supra* note 83 at 902.

95. This doctrine is called "assumption of risk." A victim is said to have assumed a risk if he or she was aware or should have been aware of a danger inherent in some situation but voluntarily elected to encounter that situation. The victim's willingness to encounter the risk in this situation is not, however, negligent, otherwise, we would invoke the doctrine of contributory negligence. *See* DOOLEY, *supra* note 85 at §§ 6.05–.07. The problem with this definition is that all situations involve some level of risk. If the definition were applied literally, then all victims (except those unconscious or coerced) might be considered to have assumed a risk. Nevertheless, the doctrine retains some appeal. Its attractiveness lies in its focus on the fact that in certain cases, victims have acted in ways that, although not negligent, materially increased the risks the victims ran, that they are, in some sense, in control of the risk they took. And this, of course, raises the central issue: What risks does a potential victim have the right to run in a somewhat dangerous world? (*Cf. infra* note 96.

96. *Cf.*, James, *Assumption of Risk: Unhappy Reincarnation*, 78 YALE L.J. 185 (1968). Individuals may expose themselves voluntarily to certain risks yet not be held to have assumed that risk precisely because they had the "right" to encounter these risks. For example, in Eckert v. Long Island Railroad Co., 43 N.Y. 502, 506 (1871), the victim was killed while attempting to save a child from being hit by a train. The victim undoubtedly was aware of the risk he ran by attempting to save the child. Nevertheless, the court found he had not "assumed the risk" because he had, in effect, a right to attempt to save the child's life. *See generally* HARPER & JAMES *supra* note 83 at § 21.1.

The distinctions necessary to decide whether a risk voluntarily encountered is a risk "assumed" can become extraordinarily refined. Consider the case of Brown v. San Francisco Ball Club, Inc., 99 Cal. App. 2d 484, 222 P.2d 19 (1950). In *Brown*, a 46-year-old woman was struck by a thrown baseball. The court decided that since the woman had voluntarily chosen to sit in an unscreened portion of the stands, she had assumed the risk. However, had there been no screened portion of the stands available to sit in or if tickets to those seats had all been sold, she might not have assumed the risk. Furthermore, had she merely been approaching her seat in the screened portion or had no tickets for screened seats been available for purchase, the court suggests she might also not have assumed the risk.

97. The doctrine of assumption of risk, like contributory negligence (*see supra* note 85), bars all recovery from a negligent injurer. Consequently, a non-negligent victim who had nevertheless assumed the risk would fail to recover even though the injurer might be liable to some other non-negligent victim who was found not to have assumed the risk. In this sense, assumption of risk acted as a non-fault doctrine placing liability on a non-negligent victim because he or she was supposedly in a better position to decide how to act in the situation than an admittedly negligent injurer. For that reason, I have described "assumption of risk" as a strict liability test that places losses on victims. It is, in many ways, the converse of the "ultrahazardous activity" rule that places liability on all injurers (be they negligent or non-negligent) who choose to engage in certain unusually hazardous activities (*e.g.*, blasting with explosives) regardless of the negligence of the victims. Calabresi and Hirschoff, *Toward A Test for Strict Liability in Torts,* 81 YALE L.J. 1055, 1065–66 (1972).

In fact, the assumption of risk doctrine was often used to place the loss on victims not in a good position to choose between alternatives (*e.g.,* employees prior to passage of Workmen's Compensation Statutes). This and the recurrent confusion of assumption of risk with contributory negligence had led to much criticism of the doctrine, *e.g.,* James, *supra* note 96, and has led some jurisdictions to abandon it (*e.g.,* New Jersey in Meistrich v. Casino Arena Attractions, Inc., 31 N.J. 44, 155 A.2d 90 (1959); McGrath v. American Cyanamid Co., 41 N.J. 272, 196 A.2d 238 (1963). Nevertheless, the basic proposition underlying assumption of risk—that victim categories are sometimes better suited to hear a risk than are negligent injurers—persists. *See,* for example, one of the doctrine's harshest critics both attack the doctrine and seek to preserve it under a new name—what he calls a "no-duty" rule, James, *supra* note 96.

98. We are not talking here about situations that the victim simply cannot avoid. Let us limit our discussion to harm the victim need not, in theory, encounter. However, let us assume that, because of the victim's idiosyncratic individual characteristics, the harm is more burdensome for the victim to avoid than it would be for the average competent adult.

99. Asymmetry in treatment of victims and injurers characterizes several tort doctrines, *e.g.,* proximate cause. In Kinderavich v. Palmer, 127 Conn. 85, 15 A.2d 83 (1940), for example, a man, struck by a train, was struck by a second train while he lay unconscious on the tracks to which he had been hurled. The court found that, although the victim may have been barred by his own contributory negligence from recovery for the first accident, he

was not necessarily barred from recovery for the second accident. His contributory negligence for the first accident might not be a proximate cause of the second accident. It is quite likely the victim's actions would have been considered a proximate cause of the second accident as well if the victim had instead been the injurer, had had sufficiently deep pockets and had innocent bystanders been injured. Courts have tended to view causation as running further for injurers' acts than victims'. To illustrate how far proximate cause can run for injurers, consider a similar Connecticut Supreme Court case of about the same vintage. In Squires v. Reynolds, 125 Conn. 366, 5 A.2d 877 (1939), a motorist hit a pedestrian, seriously injuring his leg. About 9 months later, the pedestrian was exercising his leg using a crutch when he slipped and fell. The motorist's action in hitting the pedestrian in the first accident was found to be a proximate cause of the injuries sustained in the second accident a full 9 months (rather than the minutes elapsed in *Kinderavitch*) later.

100. This, the "thin skull" doctrine, is said to have originated in the dictum of Kennedy, J. in Dulieu v. White & Sons, [1901] 2 K.B. 669, 679. For a discussion of English cases, *see* Williams, *The Risk Principle*, 77 L. Q. Rev. 179, 193–97 (1961). For American cases, *see* Dooley, *supra* note 85 at § 10.08, n. 1. The "thin skull" doctrine entails some tension with the doctrine adopted in some jurisdictions that injurers are not responsible for "unforeseeable" consequences of their negligence. *See, e.g.,* Overseas Tankship (U.K.) Ltd. v. Morts Dock & Engineering Co., Ltd., 1961 A.C. 388 (commonly known as "The Wagon Mount # 1"), which is discussed in Williams, *supra*, and Fleming, *The Passing of Polemis*, 39 Can. Bar Rev. 489 (1961). Despite the tension, the "thin skull" rule seems to persist even in those jurisdictions that are relatively reluctant to give damages for unforeseeable consequences. For example, *see* Smith v. Leech Brain & Co., Ltd., [1962] 2 Q.B. 405 (workman in a steel mill was struck on the lip by a drop of molten metal; the burned lip subsequently became cancerous and the workman died; widow recovered).

101. One may certainly argue that failure to impose a legal duty on potentially more susceptible victims to wear cumbersome protective devices of various types constitutes an acceptance of the gift of the Evil Deity. It is a decision to value convenience over safety. The law has decided to place the burden of accepting this gift of the Evil Deity on injurers, not on the class of potential victims who fail to deviate from their accustomed routine to accommodate the injurers.

102. By "reasonable" I mean only that the violinist may reasonably judge that the benefits of acting this way outweigh the potential for harm. The law considers behavior unreasonable if the risk of harm is of greater magnitude than the utility of the behavior. *See* Restatement (Second) of

Torts § 291 (1965). This is called the "Learned Hand Test" as it was first proposed by Judge Hand in Conway v. O'Brien, 111 F.2d 611 (2d Cir. 1940). For a further discussion of the Learned Hand test, *see infra* note 197 and text accompanying notes 199–200.

103. In the workman compensation laws of most states, some standard proportion of current earnings is awarded for injury to a hand whatever the idiosyncratic value of that hand might be. *See, e.g.,* CAL. LAB. CODE §§ 4658, 4660, 4662(b) (West, 1971, Supp. 1983); N.Y. WORK COMP. LAW § 15 (McKinney 1965, Supp. 1982). However, even in the absence of workman compensation laws, it is probable that our hypothetical violinist would only be awarded the value of a "standard" hand, not the unusually valuable hand, he chose to put "at risk." *Cf.* W. PROSSER AND P. KEETON, TORTS, § 68 (5th ed. 1984); RESTATEMENT (SECOND) OF TORTS § 496(C) comment i (1965) (where defendant's conduct may involve more than one risk to plaintiff, plaintiff may assume only some of these risks). *Cf. also* Western Real Estate Trustees v. Hughes, 172 F. 206, (8th Cir. 1909) (plaintiff, having some notice that party wall has been weakened, failed to move groceries from wall's vicinity prior to wall's collapse; court uses contributory negligence language and holds defendant liable only for damage that would have resulted had plaintiff not left groceries there. The victim had chosen to place valuable objects at risk, although not compelled to do so and with some awareness of the dangers courted and therefore should not recover for damages to these).

104. *See* Smith v. London & Southwestern R. Co., 6 L.R.-C.P. 14, 22–23 (Ex. Ch. 1870) (Blackburn, J., *dictum*). *See also* RESTATEMENT (SECOND) OF TORTS § 461, comment b (1965).

105. Cusick v. Clark, 45 ILL. App. 3d 763, 360 N.E.2d 160 (1977). Rios v. Sifuentes, 38 Ill. App. 3d 128, 347 N.E.2d 337 (1976). *See generally,* DOOLEY *supra* note 85 at § 4.08.50; HARPER & JAMES, *supra* note 83 at § 16.8.

106. Hardy v. Smith, 61 Ill. App. 3d 441, 378 N.E.2d 604 (1978); *see generally,* DOOLEY, *supra* note 85 at § 4.08.50; HARPER & JAMES, *supra* note 83 at § 16.8. As the rule of comparative negligence has become increasingly dominant (with the result that victim negligence is no longer an automatic bar to recovery) a growing number of courts have held injured children engaged in adult activities, like driving, to the same adult standard applied when such children are injurers. *See* PROSSER AND KEETON, *supra* note 103 at § 32 (noting trend but not noticing link to growth of comparative negligence). *See also infra* note 131. Whether juries still take the age and maturity of the injured children into account when they apportion damages in such cases, is, of course, another matter. *Cf. infra* text at notes 145–147.

107. There are a small number of cases which have explicitly held aged plaintiffs to a less demanding standard of care. Kitsap County Transp. Co. v. Harvey, 15 F.2d 166 (9th Cir. 1927); Johnson v. St. Paul City Ry. Co.,

67 Minn. 260, 69 N.W. 900 (1897); Daly v. Liverpool Corp., [1939] 2 All Eng. Rep. 142. However, it has been held that it is not old age, *per se,* but disability due to old age, that affects the standard of care required. LaCava v. New Orleans, 159 So.2d 362 (La. Ct. App. 1964).

108. By and large, both the insane and the mentally deficient are held to the standard of the reasonable man for primary negligence. Ragan v. Cox, 210 Ark. 152, 194 S.W.2d 681 (1946); Schumann v. Crofoot, 43 Or. App. 53, 602 P.2d 298 (1979). *See generally,* Comment, *The Tort Liability of Insane Persons for Negligence: A Critique,* 39 TENN. L. REV. 705 (1972). However, insane individuals are universally considered incapable of contributory negligence if they are incompetent to appreciate danger to themselves. De Martini v. Alexander Sanitarium, Inc., 192 Cal. App. 2d 442, 13 Cal. Rptr. 564 (1961). *See generally* Turton, *Hospital Liability for Negligence to Mentally Incompetent Patients,* 23 BAYLOR L. REV. 517 (1971). Putatively retarded plaintiffs, however, bear the burden of demonstrating that they are incapable of meeting the standard of due care. Miller v. Trinity Medical Center, 260 N.W.2d 4 (N.D. 1977); Dickeson v. Baltimore & O.C.T.R. Co., 42 Ill. 2d 103, 245 N.E.2d 762 (1969).

109. *See supra* note 108, *infra* note 145. *See also* Roberts v. Ring, 143 Minn. 151, 173 N.W. 437 (1919) (reversing a charge to the jury to consider the incapacities of a 77-year-old *defendant* automobile driver with defective sight and hearing while approving a requested instruction that a 7-year-old *plaintiff's* conduct was to be judged in the light of his age and mental capacity); PROSSER AND KEETON, *supra* note 103 at § 32.

110. Memorial Hospital of South Bend, Inc. v. Scott, 261 Ind. 27, 300 N.E.2d 50 (1973) (plaintiff — patient with multiple sclerosis — found not contributorily negligent for accidently pushing a hot water knob rather than toilet flusher).

111. This assumption is not meant to imply that such differences are necessary or appropriate or that they are biogenetically rather than socially created, far from it. Gender differences have been found in a multiplicity of activities in American society; from organization of speech order during social interaction, Ofshe, *Social Structure of the Organization of Simultaneous Speech in Homogeneous, Biased, and Mixed-Gender Groups: An Application of Two-Process Theory,* WORKING PAPERS IN TWO-PROCESS THEORY 1 (unpublished manuscript, U.C. Berkeley), to decisions to initiate a divorce. Zeiss, Zeiss & Johnson, *Sex Differences in Initiation and Adjustment to Divorce,* 42 JOURNAL OF DIVORCE, Winter 1980, at 21. Consequently, it is plausible to hypothesize that there may be differences in driving styles associated with sex as well.

112. It's not really that drivers in Italy are terrible. It's just that the rules of the road are different and allow more room for "individual creativity." *See* Schonberg, *La Dolce Vita? Hah!,* N.Y. Times, August 14, 1983, § 10, at 31, col. 1.

113. The term "melting pot" apparently comes from Israel Zangwill's play "The Melting Pot," which opened on Broadway in 1908. N. GLAZER & D. P. MOYNIHAN, BEYOND THE MELTING POT 289 (1963). Strictly speaking, there is no one "theory" of the melting pot. Details of this vision of American Society differed among the beholders. Nevertheless, it is possible to identify four propositions that most proponents of the theory adhered to: (1) American Society operates to assimilate individuals from various European (and sometimes non-European) cultures into a single uniquely American culture; (2) This single culture, however, borrows heavily from the strong points of the various European cultures but, somewhat paradoxically; (3) Borrowing is heavier as one moves north and west in Europe (avoiding, of course, the Irish fringe); (4) Individuals who have adopted the American culture, whatever their ethnic origin, became members in good standing of American civil society. Cf., M. GORDON, ASSIMILATION IN AMERICAN LIFE, Ch. 5 (1964). Basically the theory of the melting pot is a theory of the end of ethnicity in the American Republic. It promises equality to new immigrants after a transition period of typically unspecified length and difficulty.

114. See e.g., I. CHILD, ITALIAN OR AMERICAN: THE SECOND GENERATION IN CONFLICT 39–44 (1943).

115. Therefore, it is no answer to say that the term "lady" is objectionable because it implies that women have certain "incapacities." This argument implies that we have already accepted the superiority of the male stereotype of gentility.

116. Evidence indicates that attitudes towards premarital and extramarital sexual behavior became much more permissive during the 1970s. Glenn and Weaver, Attitudes Toward Premarital, Extramarital, and Homosexual Relationships in the U.S. in the 1970s, 15 J. SEX RESEARCH 108 (1979). However, it seems to be the case that females remain less approving of extramarital and premarital intercourse than males. Weis & Slosnerick, Attitudes Toward Sexual and Nonsexual Extramarital Involvement Among A Sample of College Students, 43 J. MARRIAGE AND THE FAMILY 349 (1981). Bayer, Sexual Permissiveness and Correlates as Determined Through Interaction Analyses, 39 J. MARRIAGE AND THE FAMILY 29 (1977).

117. See The Incredible Hunks: America has a new crop of bodies beautiful to Worship, and they're male, 101 NEWSWEEK 48 (May 23, 1983).

118. I detect some changes in this attitude among my students. Women who previously accepted stereotypically male behavior patterns as appropriate are now beginning to argue for the superiority of stereotypically female standards, particularly in sexual and parenting behavior, and to urge those standards on males.

119. Consumption of wine has now become a status symbol. There is a regular column on wines in the New York Times. Articles appear in

magazines like Vogue, Gourmet, and Glamour on how to choose just the right Beaujolais for the dinner party you're about to give. Enthusiasm has reached the point in the status-conscious American psyche that Fortune Magazine is capable of printing an article depicting executives who become vintners, *Living the Wine Lover's Fantasy,* 102 FORTUNE 100 (November 3, 1980). It is hard to imagine Fortune devoting similar space to executives who become, for example, pig farmers. All this seems rather strange to those Italians for whom wine remains, what it always has been, a fine drink for all in society.

120. *See, e.g.,* Editorial, *Black Nonsense.* 78 CRISIS (MAGAZINE OF THE NAACP 78 (1971); Glazer, *Black English and Reluctant Judges,* 62 SOCIAL POLICY 40, 52–53 (1981).

121. This leads to significant strain as women attempt to reconcile career and family in ways that men still need not do, L. W. HOFFMAN & F. I. NYE, WORKING MOTHERS 209–11 (1974); Zaslow & Pedersen, *Sex Roles Conflicts and the Experience of Childbearing,* 12 PROFESSIONAL PSYCHOLOGY 47 (1981).

122. As is now happening throughout the country, even in "quiet" Connecticut. Howe, *Area disco caters to entertainment trend,* New Haven Journal Courier, Jan. 14, 1980, at 8, col. 1. Understand that I am not advocating censorship or prohibition. People do all sorts of things that we should not forbid simply because some believe them to be tawdry or undesirable. There are far too many things some people like and others find cheap or unseemly. Burlesque has been one of these. I do not believe the case for banning it has been made any more persuasive merely because its audience has expanded. The issue here is different. American society has traditionally had very different expectations for male and female behavior. We are clearly in the (to me desirable) process of developing role expectations that are less gender-specific. I merely suggest that it would be sensible for us to incorporate many traditional female behaviors into the evolving non-gender-specific roles. I believe it would be a tragedy for these roles to be nothing more than traditional male roles expanded to include females.

123. It is widely believed that American fathers spend relatively little time with their children compared to fathers in some other societies. Mackey & Day, *Some Indicators of Fathering Behavior in the United States: A Crosscultural Examination of Adult Male-Child Interaction,* 41 J. MARRIAGE AND THE FAMILY 287, 287–88 (1979). It is also true that there is little empirical support for this belief at least for father-child interaction in public settings. *Id.* In any event, it is clear that in this culture fathers spend less time than mothers with their children. Booth & Edwards, *Fathers: The Invisible Parent,* 6 SEX ROLES 445 (1980). The result of women following men in placing careers ahead of family has been to increase the proportion of young children in day care. Some have argued that this is not a bad thing. There is even "evidence" that

indicates children in day care may be slightly better off than those raised at home. Harris, *Recent Findings on Infant Socialization from North American Research,* 31 INTERNATIONAL SOCIAL SCIENCE J. 415, 424–25 (1979). Unfortunately much research on children in day care has been done on children in high-quality, often university-based, centers. Such day cares are not representative of the substitute care most children of working mothers receive, *id.*

124. My argument is impressionistic. My experience is that there is a significant difference in the interpersonal relationships that characterize Mediterranean and those that are common in Northern European cultures. Despite the large number of immigrants in the United States from Southern Europe, our values remain those of Northern Europe.

125. H. T. Gans, *Symbolic Ethnicity: The Future of Ethnic Groups and Cultures in America,* 2 ETHNIC AND RACIAL STUDIES 1 (1979).

126. I have picked stereotypes that members of these groups would claim as well. *See, e.g.,* L. BARZINI, THE ITALIANS (1964); D. GREENBURG, HOW TO BE A JEWISH MOTHER (1965).

127. The stereotype is that interpersonal relationships in the United Kingdom are extraordinarily distant. A. GLYN, THE BLOOD OF A BRITISHMAN, chs. 11, 13 (1970); G. GORER, EXPLORING ENGLISH CHARACTER, ch. 4 (1955). Nevertheless, England survives, and very well, thank you. That it should bemuses some Southern Europeans, *see, e.g.,* L. BARZINI, THE EUROPEANS, ch. 2 (1983), for a discussion of the peculiar cultural traits of the "imperturbable British."

128. M. J. LEVY, MODERNIZATION AND THE STRUCTURE OF SOCIETIES 187–91 (1952).

129. This is true even if immigrant groups now form, and have long formed, a majority. The assimilated have always acted as a cultural majority whatever their ethnic identity might be.

130. I am not concerned here with the fact that the legal system, like other American institutions, has engaged in gender discrimination. That this is so is undoubtedly true, and has been sufficiently commented on in the past to require little discussion here. The point I wish to make is another one. That is, that in certain areas of tort law, the notion of what constituted reasonable behavior was the behavior of the stereotypical male. For instance, until recently, the law was unwilling to acknowledge that pregnant women might be more susceptible to emotional injury than the stereotypically phlegmatic male. *See* Hay or Bourhill v. Young, 1943 A.C. 92, 109–10 (8-months-pregnant woman, frightened by nearby motorcycle accident, subsequently miscarries), for a discussion of why the law does not recognize the idiosyncratic damages of the "hypersensitive." *See generally* Bernier, *Mothers as Plaintiffs in Prenatal Tort Liability Cases: Recovery for Physical and Emotional Damages,* 4 HARV. WOMEN'S L.J. 43 (1981). *See also,* Chapter 4, *infra.* Similarly, at one

point the law was unwilling to award damages for mere "touching" by a merely negligent "injurer", even though such touching might be peculiarly socially inappropriate when it occurred to a woman. Spade v. Lynn & Boston R.R., 168 Mass. 285, 47 N.E. 88 (1897) (court refuses recovery to woman who suffers nervous shock from watching and being jostled during altercation on train between conductor and drunken passengers). *See generally,* DOOLEY *supra* note 85 at § 15.05–.06.

131. Schumann v. Crofoot, 43 Or. App. 53, 602 P.2d 298 (1979); Dellwo v. Pearson, 259 Minn. 452, 107 N.W.2d 859 (1961); Vaughan v. Menlove, 3 Bing. (N.C.) 468 (C.P. 1837), 132 Eng. Rep. 490. *See generally,* HARPER & JAMES, *supra* note 83 at § 16.7.

The standard of care expected of both victims and injurers who are physically handicapped is usually stated to be "reasonable care" with the handicap being one of the circumstances that determines what constitutes reasonable care. However, in practice, this rule has typically been employed only to aid handicapped victims who might otherwise be considered contributorily negligent. Harper & James state, for example, that "while a subjective treatment of physical characteristics is perfectly consistent with . . . the fault principle, it is highly significant that such treatment actually operates to assure the injured party of compensation rather than to allow the defendant to escape liability," *id.* at 923.

The situations of children who are injurers is somewhat more complex. It seems now generally well established, that when they are engaged in adult activity they are held to the same standard of care as an adult. *See, e.g.,* Dellwo v. Pearson, *supra.* However, as HARPER & JAMES note, "It is less important and more doubtful what rule will emerge as to injuries caused by children at play," *supra* note 83 at 927. What is deemed "play," however, may at times be perplexing, to say the least. *See* Purtle v. Shelton, 251 Ark. 519, 474 S.W.2d 123 (1971) (17-year-old hunter held to subjective standard as hunting is not necessarily an adult activity). *See also,* PROSSER AND KEETON, *supra* note 103 at § 32 (stating that the cases apply the same standard to children who are injurers as to those who are victims, but citing cases that either overwhelmingly involve children engaged in adult activities or, as they note, children as victims).

132. The traditional position in tort law (outside of non-fault areas) is that the loss from an accident lies where it falls unless there is some reason to shift it. O.W. HOLMES, THE COMMON LAW 94 (1881). The principal reason for shifting the loss has been faulty behavior on the part of the injurer. In the absence of negligence or some other wrongdoing by the injurer, the possible unreasonableness of the victim's behavior did not become an issue; *id.* at 94–95.

133. "Deserve" is admittedly a rather queer word to use in putting the

issue of victim compensation. Nevertheless, courts have put it this way; *see, e.g.,* British Columbia Electric Ry. v. Loach, 1915 A.C. 719 (P.C.) (B.C.); Wakelin v. London & S.W. Ry. Co., [1887] 12 App. Cas. 41, 45 (Lord Halsbury, L.C.).

134. Because of the contributory negligence rule, courts need only confront the issue of what criteria to use to evaluate injurer behavior when dealing with innocent victims. If the victim were not innocent, the rule of contributory negligence would bar the victim's recovery in any event. *See,* Malone, *The Formative Era of Contributory Negligence,* 41 ILL. L. REV. 151, 164–69 (1946). There are some exceptions to the rule barring recovery by contributorily negligent victims. If the injurer's behavior is particularly egregious (*e.g.,* was "wanton and willful" or "intentional"), then the contributory negligence of the victim will not bar recovery. *See generally,* HARPER & JAMES, *supra* note 83 at 1211–27. However, behavior motivated by age, handicap, or religious belief is unlikely to be deemed sufficiently egregious to be styled "wanton and willful."

135. "If somebody must suffer, why should it be the innocent plaintiff, instead of the defendant, who chose to exercise his horses in the public streets," was asked poignantly (albeit unsuccessfully) by the plaintiff in a case in which the injurer had been found non-negligent. Holmes v. Mather, 10 L.R.-EX. 261, 267 (1875). If this question is disturbing when the injurer is non-negligent, it is bound to be much more compelling when the injurer is negligent.

136. CALABRESI, COSTS *supra* note 48 at 69–73; R. POSNER, ECONOMIC ANALYSIS OF LAW 142–43 (2d ed. 1977).

137. *See,* HARPER & JAMES, *supra* note 83, at § 11.4. This problem was confronted in Hill Transportation Co. v. Everett, 145 F.2d 746 (1st Cir. 1944) (bus driver under age of 21 in collision with motorcyclist). In that case, the court declined to apply a lower standard of care for minors employed as drivers than would be imposed on adults. This position (now widely adopted) refuses to facilitate the minor's access to the automobile by not excusing any inability to live up to adult standards. *See,* Prosser and Keeton, *supra* note 103 at § 32.

138. Keller v. DeLong, 108 N.H. 212, 231 A.2d 633 (1967); Dellwo v. Pearson, 259 Minn. 452, 107 N.W.2d 859 (1961). The existence of insurance may prevent participation in these activities from being catastrophic to the individual defendant. However, insurance rates are charged according to the insurer's experience of paying out claims against members of actuarial categories. A rule that increases the likelihood that an insurer must pay claims against members of some particular category increases the insurance rates of members of that category. Therefore, the unwillingness of the law to impose lower standards of care on members of some accident-

prone group (*e.g.,* youths, the handicapped, the developmentally disabled) leads to higher insurance rates for members of these groups because this makes them more likely to be found liable in lawsuits.

139. This may be why we distinguish between the violinist on the road and in the steel mill, *supra* note 103. We wish the violinist to participate fully in civil society. He or she can do so only by driving (an American's birthright, after all!). Consequently, we allow him or her to drive even though driving is a risky activity and the potential costs for the violinist are unusually high because his or her life and (especially) limb are unusually valuable. In a sense, the class of potentially liable injurers subsidize the violinist's right to drive and to participate. We may not, however, be willing to subsidize participation in activities that are risky, not necessary for full participation in civil society, and for which alternatives are available. Consequently, we may treat the decision of the great violinist to work in a steel mill as an activity he or she undertakes at his or her own risk, without subsidy. Similarly, we would probably be unwilling to subject someone prone to fainting spells to a lower standard of care than normal should he or she choose to become an airplane pilot.

140. There is some evidence to suggest that physically impaired workers have equivalent accident rates to their unimpaired counterparts. PRESIDENT'S COMMITTEE ON EMPLOYMENT OF THE HANDICAPPED, *Disability and Employment: Facts About Costs and Benefits* (1981); BUREAU OF LABOR STATISTICS, *Work Performance of Physically Impaired Workers,* 66 MONTHLY LABOR REVIEW 31 (1948).

141. This despite the fact that such drivers represent only 22 percent of the licenses in force. NATIONAL HIGHWAY TRAFFIC SAFETY ADMINISTRATION; FACT BOOK: STATISTICAL INFORMATION ON HIGHWAY SAFETY, Table IV 1.3 (1977). The figures are particularly dramatic for young male drivers under the age of 20. They experience a death rate of over 90 per 100,000 license holders. In comparison, females between the ages of 35 and 70 experience a death rate of less than 10. Trunkey, *Trauma,* 249 SCIENTIFIC AMERICAN 28, 33 (graph) (August 1983).

142. This probably is not due to inexperience. Research in Ontario, Canada, indicates that length of time a teenager has had a license has no effect on likelihood of being involved in an accident. Robertson, *The Teenage Driver,* 1983 TRAVEL AND TRAFFIC MEDICINE INTERNATIONAL 22, 23.

143. I do not deny that there are other factors that may well be more directly related to accidents (*e.g.,* drunkenness, showing off, speeding) than drivers' demographic characteristics. But the demographic characteristics of drivers remain the most easily controllable either by prohibitory legislation (*i.e.,* raising the minimum driving age) or by insurance (*i.e.,* by raising premiums for dangerous categories of drivers). Causal factors which, though

theoretically closely linked to harm, are not controllable are worth establishing, because they help explain and because they may in the future become controllable. They are not of immediate practical significance, however. Consequently, when considering ways to reduce accidents, it behooves us to look at causal factors that are manipulable, not factors that, though they may be more directly linked to accidents, are beyond our reach. There is a regrettable tendency to focus on direct causal links at the expense of manipulable factors. The result is a kind of wishful thinking that, in all too many cases, leads to scapegoating. *See,* CALABRESI & BOBBITT, *supra* note 1 at 72–78. A good example of an emphasis on non-manipulable but direct causes of a legal wrong at the expense of a less direct but more manipulable cause is the campaign mounted by the gun lobby to convince us that "Guns don't kill people. People kill people." This is undoubtedly true. It is also largely irrelevant if we are interested in reducing the homicide rate.

144. The problem here is really that there is a class of potential injurers we would like to subsidize. It would seem appropriate then to have the entire class of potential victims provide the subsidy. Unfortunately, courts lack the mechanisms by which all members of this class can be induced to contribute. The structure of common law adjudication generally allows accident costs to be apportioned only between the parties before the court. It is true that the problem of diffuse parties is sometimes circumvented by the class action suit. But in such suits, one faces the much easier problem of inviting members of a plaintiff class to participate in sharing some benefit. Here we are interested in allocating a burden, and potential plaintiffs will not likely step forward voluntarily to claim their share. They would be compelled to bear this share, of course, if the courts could impose mandatory victim insurance. But this too is considered outside the scope of common law making. Consequently, of the entire class of potential victims, only those few unfortunate enough to have an accident with the relevant class of injurers would end up shouldering the entire burden. A similar problem is discussed in Calabresi and Melamed, *Property Rules, Liability Rules, and Inalienability: One View of the Cathedral,* 85 HARV. L. REV. 1089, 1116–24 (1972). *Cf.,* Spur v. Del Webb, 108 Ariz. 178, 494 P.2d 700 (1972) (developer ordered by court to pay slaughterhouse to move from location near residential development).

145. Charbonneau v. MacRury, 84 N.H. 501, 153 A. 457 (1931); *but see* Hill Transp. Co. v. Everett, 145 F.2d 746 (1st Cir. 1944), in which the court refused to expand the rule to the situation in which the minor was an employee.

146. The ability to ignore substantive law is, of course, part of the charm of juries. *See* CALABRESI & BOBBITT, *supra* note 1 at 57–62.

147. Daniels v. Evans, 107 N.H. 407, 224 A.2d 63 (1966).

148. *See, e.g.,* Cal. Ins. Code § 11628 *et seq.* (West 1972, Supp. 1984); Ins. Law, § 40(10) (McKinney 1966). *Cf. also* Arizona Compensation Plan v. Norris, 103 S.Ct. 3492 (1983) (Title VII forbids use of sex-segregated actuarial tables in annuities).

149. This is because members of the more accident-prone categories can no longer be treated separately, but must be lumped together with less accident-prone categories. This raises the accident rates of these latter categories. Old members of the safer categories therefore will pay higher insurance premiums, while former members of the more accident-prone categories will pay lower rates. In this sense, the members of the less accident-prone categories end up subsidizing former members of the more accident-prone categories.

150. *See* A. Allott, The Limits of Law (1980). I am not, incidentally, suggesting that legislators delude themselves about the extent of their power. They may well have a very sophisticated appreciation of what they can and cannot do by statute. This may not deter them from passing ineffective statutes if voters or organized interest groups labor under the delusion these statutes will be effective and are willing to reward (by votes or otherwise) legislators who vote for their passage. *See* A. Downs, An Economic Theory of Democracy, ch. 4 (1957).

151. They also may try not to sell to people in high-risk groups. This last is direct discrimination, and would presumably be illegal. It is, however, very hard to control. The former (as we shall see, *infra* notes 154, 162), though it has a discriminatory effect, may not bespeak a discriminatory motive.

152. Residents of large metropolitan areas already pay considerably higher premiums than do residents of rural areas. They have ever since insurance companies first divided the United States into territories when charging insurance premiums in 1905. At that time, the United States consisted of only two territories: Greater New York, Boston and Chicago, and the rest of the United States. All-Industry Research Advisory Council, Geographical Differences in Automobile Insurance Costs 2 (October 1982). The number of territories used now varies by insurance company. The Insurance Service Office, an industry-wide data-gathering organization, divides the country into more than 700 territories, *id.* at 18. Premium per car and accident costs per car have both tended to be higher in territories with higher population densities (*i.e.,* urban areas), *id.,* Table 1 at 4, Table 5 at 14.

153. In California, § 11628 of the Insurance Code, *supra* note 148, prohibiting racial discrimination in motor vehicle insurance, was first passed in 1955. In 1967, the California legislature amended the statute to prohibit use of geographic areas of less than 20 square miles as actuarial categories. In 1982, the city of Los Angeles brought suit, unsuccessfully, to compel a number of insurance companies to alter their use of geographic areas as ac-

tuarial categories. Los Angeles County v. Farmers Ins. Exchange, 132 Cal. App. 3d 77, 182 Cal. Rptr. 879 (1982) (court found City of Los Angeles had not exhausted its administrative remedies).

154. The search for a surrogate category will occur whether or not the insurance company has any intent to discriminate on the basis of racial or any other improper classifications. The insurance company inevitably looks for actuarial categories that predict risk. It may willingly forego categories the law forbids, such as race or sex. But if these are strongly associated with risk, then there is a good chance that they will also be associated with any actuarial category that is closely associated with risk, that is any other category the company will come up with. *See also, infra,* note 162.

155. If discrimination is responsible for higher insurance rates for some categories, then the profit margin for insuring this category is likely to be higher than for other actuarial groups. In time one would expect at least one company to discover this and cut its rates, accepting a lower profit margin in return for a larger share of the category's business. Competing companies will either match these rates or be forced out of this sector of the market. One need not be a market fanatic to believe that discrimination will simply not survive the lure of cash over the long haul. *See* K. ABRAHAM, DISTRIBUTING RISK, INSURANCE, LEGAL THEORY AND PUBLIC POLICY 104–05 (review manuscript, 1983) (forthcoming, YALE U. PRESS).

156. The reader may, of course, question the extent to which we *are* a racist society. In response, I can only say that I don't know. I do remember a speech given by Dick Gregory some years ago; the part of the speech that impressed me was not Dick Gregory's saying "America is a Racist Society" (which he did). It was the audience's reaction to the statement and Mr. Gregory's response. When the audience visibly stirred in reaction to his statement, Mr. Gregory asked, "Did you think I said 'White America' or 'All America' was racist? Because if you heard the former, you have proven my point." I'm inclined to believe that the audience had interpreted Mr. Gregory to say the former; I know I did. The reason, I think, was simple: Dick Gregory is black, and furthermore, to a white audience, "America" means "White America." I don't know how much probative force this example has. We can, however, safely say it would be unwise to dismiss the hypothesis of continuing racism out of hand.

In any event, I am not really concerned here with what causes "riskiness". Indeed, I rather doubt that anybody at this point really knows. What I am concerned with here is factors that *can* be manipulated for safety and whether we *wish* to manipulate some of them or not. *See supra* note 143.

157. It is difficult to predict whether acknowledging or denying our continuing racism is preferable. Candor is often a double-edged sword. On the one hand, awareness of our own shortcomings often forces us to reme-

dial action. On the other, explicit recognition of the existence of discriminatory standards — even in criticism — may have the effect of legitimating those standards. It may lead people to say: "Everyone else discriminates, why shouldn't I?" *Cf.* The powerful argument against insurance categories directly based on sex made in Brilmayer, Hekeler, Laycock and Sullivan, *Sex Discrimination in Employer-Sponsored Insurance Plans: A Legal and Demographic Analysis,* 47 U. Chi. L. Rev. 505 (1980). *See also* Calabresi & Bobbitt, *supra* note 1 at 24–26, 74–77; Calabresi, A Common Law *supra* note 4 at chs. XIII–XV.

158. *Cf.* Note, *The Case for Black Juries,* 79 Yale L.J. 531 (1970) (arguing for a narrow definition of the constitutional term "vicinage" (neighborhood) for jury selection, which would ensure black juries for black defendants so long as blacks live in ghettos, but would cease doing so as soon as ghettos ceased to exist).

159. What I mean by "irrelevant" in this context is that there do exist some other bases on which they might be categorized that are neither more expensive to use nor less closely associated with riskiness but that are not used because they are forbidden.

160. *Reckless Insurance for Wreckless Drivers* N.Y. Times, Oct. 18, 1977, at 36, col. 1. (Editorial).

161. *See, e.g.,* a reprise of *supra* note 160; *Statistical Truth, Human Realities: Driving Records vs. Demographics* N.Y. Times, May 9, 1981, at 22, col. 1. (Editorial).

162. *Cf.* Abraham, *supra* note 155 at 143–44. The problem of predicting future accidents from past experience is a problem in probabilities. It is a characteristic of stochastic events that no single event is, strictly speaking, predictable. However, this probability of the event occurring over some number of trials can be predicted to fall within some interval with a specific probability. The greater the number of trials, the narrower this "confidence interval" becomes. Thus, if I flip a coin, I cannot be sure whether the coin will come up heads or tails. I can never be sure what the next toss of the coin will bring. I could flip 10 "heads" in a row. However, I can be confident that over a large number of coin tosses, about 50 percent of the time, I will toss a "head." Furthermore, the percentage will be more likely to approach 50 percent as the number of tosses increases. H. Blalock, Social Statistics 120–24 (2d ed. 1972).

We face a more difficult problem when we try to predict an individual's probability of having an accident on the basis of his or her past driving record. What pundits sometimes seem to be demanding is that we predict each individual's future likelihood of having an accident on his or her own past performance. This creates two problems apart from the fact that if we could do it, we would eliminate much of the desired "cost spreading" effects of insurance. First, for any one individual we will have few "trials" (*i.e.,* periods of time over which we can observe whether the individual has had an accident). Second, since an accident is a rare event (the average driver has one every 8–12 years), we wish to predict the accident rate with considerable accuracy. The difference between a predicted rate of 10 and 15 is of considerable significance to us. The difficulty is that we simply cannot develop sufficient observations for an individual driver to predict the accident rate within a narrow confidence interval.

There is a way to get more data. It is the device insurance companies already use. They pool the observations on a large number of drivers on the basis of a common characteristic in order to predict an accident rate for a group as a whole. When they do this, however, insurance companies are not predicting individual accident rates. They are predicting rates for a group; and that, despite their criticism of pooling on the basis of most characteristics, may ultimately be what the critics had in mind. They may want us to pool individuals — but solely — on the basis of their past accident rates (*i.e.,* treat all individuals with X number of accidents as one group). Unfortunately, it must be the case that past accident rates are not very good predictors of future accidents. If they were, we would imagine that insurance companies would be happy to use that characteristic more than to the limited extent they do now. *See supra* note 155. In fact, *all* variables in use predict only 22 percent of the variance in accident rates. Abraham, *supra* note 155 at 143 (citing NATIONAL ASSOCIATION OF INSURANCE COMMISSIONERS, D-3 ADVISORY COMMITTEE, PRIVATE PASSENGER AUTOMOBILE INSURANCE RISK CLASSIFICATION, n. 9 at 142 (1979)). Consequently, insurance companies are loathe to sacrifice predictors such as age and sex that they believe predict accident rates more powerfully than past driving record. *Id.*

This does not mean one cannot use past individual driver records to predict future accident rates and set insurance premiums accordingly. One can. It is just that one won't have a very good predictor. The result would be that individuals who have had an accident in the past would be forced to pay significantly higher insurance premiums, *despite* the fact that their past driving record gives us little information on their future driving record. Since, by definition people who have had such an accident will tend to be concentrated in accident-prone minority groups, using past records to set future rates becomes an arbitrary device that places the burden of subsidizing equal access to most in the minority on those in the minority, who have been chosen largely, though not entirely, at random: that is, those who happened to have been ill-starred.

163. "Irrelevant" merely in the sense that it is an extremely weak prediction of future accident rates. *See supra* note 162.

164. *See supra* notes 160, 161.

165. Two positions have tended to emerge in the current debate over

setting insurance and annuity premiums. One position is that there is no good reason in fact to charge different rates on the basis of demographic characteristics like gender. The other is that there are good actuarial reasons to use demographic characteristics to calculate rates and, consequently, we must do so. I adhere to neither position. The first suffers from wishful thinking. It is likely that there are sound reasons to use demographic characteristics to set rates. *See supra* notes 155, 162. The second refuses to acknowledge that we are not prisoners of statistical criteria. It may be true that there are good reasons to use demographic characteristics to set rates but we are not compelled to use them. If our values dictate that we set rates on some basis other than race, sex or age, then we certainly can do so. I do urge, however, that rather than blithely assuming such a decision is costless and can be effectuated simply by passing a law, we be aware that abandonment of these criteria is likely to be expensive and requires that we decide who should bear the cost and how we can enforce that cost allocation. *See* ABRAHAM, *supra* note 155, at 148–55.

166. There are a variety of ways in which a subsidy program could be administered. One possibility would be to have the government estimate actuarial rates and set desired rates for groups we wish to subsidize. The government could then pay the difference between the actual and desired rates to insurance companies for each member of the subsidized group insured.

167. When I was growing up, there was a great catcher for the Brooklyn Dodgers named Roy Campanella. He was usually described as black (actually, in the parlance of the time, "Negro"). However, he had an Italian name and he looked like a stereotypical Neapolitan. This puzzled me. I later learned that Mr. Campanella's father was Italian, and his mother was black. R. CAMPANELLA, IT'S GOOD TO BE ALIVE 28–29 (1959). What had happened, of course, is that American society classified Mr. Campanella and people like him as black rather than Italian or "both."

168. Assigned risk pools are a feature of state automobile insurance regulations in 43 states. Note, *Nipper v. California Assigned Risk Plan: The Duties of Care Owed to the Motoring Public by CAARP and Insurance Brokers,* 10 SW. U. L. REV. 1007, n. 1 (1978). They are meant to provide insurance coverage to drivers who are unable to obtain ordinary private insurance coverage at "reasonable rates" because they are considered bad risks. Such plans attempt to distribute the risk of insuring these drivers evenly by assigning them to insurance companies in numbers proportionate to each company's share of the state automobile insurance market. The problems of such a system are two-fold. First, it subsidizes all bad-risk drivers. It doesn't distinguish between those drivers we might wish to subsidize and those we do not. Second, the subsidy is only a partial subsidy as drivers in the assigned risk pool still

pay higher rates than those outside the pool. Those we wish to subsidize still end up paying high insurance rates. For these reasons, an assigned risk pool can be seen as an unhappy compromise between no subsidy and an explicit subsidy to selected groups.

169. If instead we limit the assigned risk pool to just those we wish to subsidize, then we are back to the subsidy of particular groups that, I have already suggested, is unlikely to be politically feasible.

170. Most states now require owners of motor vehicles to furnish proof that a vehicle is insured before it can be registered. However, the amount of insurance required is usually insufficient. For example, in Alabama, minimum insurance coverage required for bodily injury or death to one person is $5,000; for bodily injury or death of more than one person, $10,000; for property damage, $1,000. ALA. CODE § 32-7-22 (1977). Obviously, these figures are grossly inadequate given the damage an automobile accident can cause. More "generous" states do not do much better, however (e.g., California, whose comparable requirements are $15,000/$30,000/$5,000, or Arizona, $15,000/$30,000/$10,000. CAL. VEH. CODE § 16430 (West Supp. 1983), ARIZ. REV. STAT. ANN. § 28–1170 (1977, supp. 1983).

171. The loss and, therefore, the subsidy will be borne by those who buy uninsured motorist insurance if the victim is a driver, passenger, or car owner covered by such insurance. This might not be so bad if it weren't for two things. First, the limits on uninsured motorist insurance are often quite low. Note, *Twenty-Five Years of Uninsured Motorist: A Silver Anniversary Cloud with Tarnished Lining*, 14 IND. L. REV. 671, 675–76 (1981). Second, like assigned risk pools (*see supra* note 168) uninsured motorist insurance does not distinguish those injurers we wish to subsidize from those we don't. A system that allows all judgment-proof motorists to get away with not having insurance, because insurance is not required and losses are covered by uninsured motorist insurance, allows all high-risk drivers who are poor to avoid paying accident costs. This will be true whether we wish to subsidize them or not.

172. The student never doubts that even under anti-discrimination laws, one way or another, he or she would be able to discriminate on the basis of wealth. For some approaches to accident law which would lead insurers to increase the amount the wealthy would need to pay for insurance relative to the non-wealthy, *see* Calabresi, *First Party, Third Party, and Product Liability Systems supra* note 64.

173. *See supra* note 148.

174. U.S. CONST., amend. I.

175. *See supra* note 174. For indications of the difficulty of determining what these terms mean, operationally, *see, e.g.,* Everson v. Board of Education, 330 U.S. 1 (1947); McCollum v. Board of Education, 333 U.S. 203 (1948).

176. Of course, the Constitution does protect religious beliefs at the

national and—in time, after the passage of the 14th Amendment—at the local level as well. Cantwell v. Connecticut, 310 U.S. 296, 303 (1940). *See also, infra* note 219. However, the Constitution does not narrowly circumscribe every aspect of every area of law's treatment of religious beliefs. Nevertheless within the broad limits of what is constitutionally plausible, certain rules come to be preferred because they seem more to conform with what is perceived to be the spirit of the First Amendment.

177. CALABRESI, A COMMON LAW *supra* note 4 at 85; R. DWORKIN, TAKING RIGHTS SERIOUSLY 111 (1977) (Professor Dworkin speaks of a "gravitational force"). The analogy between a "gravitational field" and the way in which laws in formally unrelated areas may shape judicial decisions probably originated in Cohen, *Field Theory and Judicial Logic,* 59 YALE L.J. 238, 250 (1950).

178. As an example (albeit an unfortunate one), consider the response of the New Hampshire Supreme Court to the finding of the U.S. Supreme Court that a mother's decision to seek an abortion was constitutionally protected. Roe v. Wade, 410 U.S. 113 (1973). The New Hampshire Supreme Court had ruled in 1958 that a child could sue in tort for prenatal injuries without regard to its viability at the time of injury. However, in a post-*Roe* case, the same court declined to allow a nonviable fetus to sue in tort for its wrongful death in an automobile accident; remarking, "it would be incongruous for a mother to have a federal constitutional right to deliberately destroy a nonviable fetus [citation to *Roe* deleted] and at the same time for a third person to be subject to liability to the fetus for unintended but negligent acts." Wallace v. Wallace, 120 N.H. 675, 421 A.2d 134, 137 (1980).

179. Lange v. Hoyt, 114 Conn. 590, 159 A. 575 (1932).

180. I have simplified the actual *Lange* case, *id.,* in this discussion in one major regard. Minelda was actually a minor. It was her mother who failed to take her to a doctor. It was her mother who was a Christian Scientist. And it was her mother who stood not to recover for the extra expenses she had incurred due to the aggravation of Minelda's condition if the court found she had not acted reasonably to mitigate damages. (The court found that any failure of the mother to mitigate damages could not be imputed to Minelda or affect Minelda's recovery in her own right.) I have deleted these details from the discussion because they add little to the central issue: What values or beliefs can the hypothetical "reasonable" person of tort law have?

181. *Lange,* 114 Conn. at 596–597.

182. The defendant in *Lange, id.,* had appealed from the trial court on the grounds that the trial court had not issued proper instructions to the jury. Consequently, the appeals court was required to draw every reasonable factual inference in favor of the plaintiff.

183. *See supra* notes 100, 104.

184. *See supra* note 103.

185. *See Lange, supra* 114 Conn. at 596–597. The Supreme Court sacrificed its suffix "of Errors" in 1965, thus eliminating one of the more entertaining court titles from the lexicon.

186. *Id.*

187. *John* 18:38.

188. CALABRESI & BOBBITT, *supra* note 1 at 57–62.

189. *See Lange,* 114 Conn. at 596–597.

190. Encyclical Letter, *Humanae Vitae,* of Pope Paul VI, July 29, 1969.

191. *See* J. NOONAN, CONTRACEPTION: A HISTORY OF ITS TREATMENT BY THE CATHOLIC THEOLOGIANS AND CANONISTS (1965). The hypothetical Minelda's uncritical acceptance of the Church's teaching on contraception apparently would put her in a distinct minority among American Catholics. *See* A. M. GREELEY, THE AMERICAN CATHOLIC 141–43 (1977).

192. *See generally* Annot. 74 ALR 3d (1976). At common law, although a husband could generally bring suit for loss of a wife's "consortium," a wife could not sue for loss of a husband's consortium. Green, *Relational Interests,* 29 ILL. L. REV. 460, 465–67 (1934). It was only in 1950 that an American court first found that the wife had a right of action. Hitaffer v. Argonne Co., Inc., 183 F.2d 811 (D.C. Cir. 1950), *cert. den.* 340 U.S. 852 (1950). This rule is now accepted in most states. In certain cases, wives have collected large sums. Thill v. Modern Erecting Co., 292 Minn. 80, 193 N.W.2d 298 (1971) ($100,000); General Electric Co. v. Bush, 88 Nev. 360, 498 P.2d 366 (1972) ($500,000); Rodriguez v. McDonnell Douglas Corp., 87 Cal. App. 3d 626, 151 Cal. Rptr. 399 (2d Dist., 1978) ($500,000). The right of the woman to sue for loss of consortium is now so generally accepted in American legal culture that even Connecticut has come around. Hopson v. St. Mary's Hospital, 408 A.2d 260, 176 Conn. 485 (1979).

193. *Cf.* Little, *Suing Satan: A Jurisdictional Enigma,* 1 JOURNAL OF ATTENUATED SUBTLETIES 27 (1982).

194. My hypothetical example does not question the reasonableness of the first and second alternatives. Courts often do confront situations in which a party has to choose between various possibilities more than one of which may be perfectly reasonable. *See, e.g.,* Vincent v. Lake Erie Transp. Co., 109 Minn. 456, 458, 124 N.W. 221, 221 (1910).

195. Most Catholics would view abortion as far worse than contraception. C. J. McFADDEN, THE DIGNITY OF LIFE 93 (1976).

196. Assuming the statute of limitations has not run (and the issue of mitigation of damages, aside), Minelda, or her heirs, would have a good case. The issue raised is one of "proximate cause"—that is, are the damages in question sufficiently closely connected with the defendant's putatively neg-

ligent behavior for the defendant to be held responsible for it. And "proximity" runs fairly far in cases like this. An injurer will typically be liable, for example, for any disease or infection the victim contracts after the accident due to the victim's weakened state. Dickson v. Hollister, 123 Pa. 421, 16 A. 484 (1889); Wallace v. Ludwig, 292 Mass. 251, 198 N.E. 159 (1935). *See* RESTATEMENT (SECOND) OF TORTS § 458 (1965).

197. A widely accepted way of assessing the "reasonableness" of an actor's behavior is, in fact, a cost-benefit analysis. Posner, *A Theory of Negligence*, 1 J. LEG. STUD. 29, 32–33 (1972). The so-called Learned Hand test, named after the judge who first used it explicitly, *see* Conway v. O'Brien, 111 F.2d 611 (2d Cir. 1940), for example, involves weighing the burden on an actor of taking some set of precautions against the likely seriousness of damage, discounted by the probability of damage if the precautions are not taken. If the precautions cost less than the discounted damage, the actor is found to have acted unreasonably. *See* United States v. Carrol Towing Co., 159 F.2d 169, 173 (2d Cir. 1947); *Cf.* Walker-Flynn v. Princeton Motors 60 N.S.W. St. R. 488 (1960). This Australian case approximates the facts and findings of the "Catholic" case discussed here.

198. *See, e.g.,* Hastie v. Handeland, 274 Cal. App. 2d 599, 79 Cal. Rptr. 268 (1969); Jones v. Laird Foundation, Inc., 156 W. Va. 479, 195 S.E.2d 821 (1973).

199. An approach very similar to the Learned Hand test (*see supra* note 197) was proposed in Terry, *Negligence*, 29 HARV. L. REV. 40, 42–43 (1915). I know of no direct evidence to suggest that Learned Hand derived the test from Professor Terry. He did not cite Terry's article in U.S. v. Carroll Towing or Conway v. O'Brien, *see supra* note 197. It is true Terry's article predated the first of these cases by 25 years. Nevertheless, Hand being Hand, it is hard to imagine he had not read Terry's article.

200. *See* Posner, *supra* note 197 at 32–33.

201. Or, at least, so it seemed to his contemporaries. *See, e.g.,* Learned Hand's balancing test for the first amendment in Masses Pub. Co. v. Patten, 244 F. 535 (S.D.N.Y. 1917), *rev'd.* 246 F. 24 (2d Cir. 1917). Judge Hand's "balancing" test did gain some acceptance from a later generation of jurists. *See, e.g.,* Dennis v. United States, 341 U.S. 494, 510 (1951); Communication Ass'n. v. Douds, 339 U.S. 382, 394–400 (1950). *But see,* Barenblatt v. United States, 360 U.S. 109, 141–44 (Black, J., dissenting) for a discussion of the dangers of applying a balancing test to the first amendment.

202. *Cf.,* R. DWORKIN, TAKING RIGHTS SERIOUSLY 232–233 (1977) (moral preferences for treatment of others should not count in a utilitarian calculus); B. ACKERMAN, SOCIAL JUSTICE IN THE LIBERAL STATE, ch. 2 (1980) (individual moral preferences cannot justify particular distributions of resources).

203. Out of a total population of 3.1 million in Connecticut in 1983, 1.3 million were Roman Catholics. THE OFFICIAL CATHOLIC DIRECTORY App. p. 2 (1983) (General Summary).

204. In other words, the outlandishness of a belief can be recognized in the same way Justice Potter Stewart has chosen to recognize pornography. Jacobellis v. Ohio, 378 U.S. 184, 197 (1964).

205. Friedman v. New York, 282 N.Y.S.2d 858, 54 Misc.2d 448 (1967).

206. In Jewish religious tradition, religious injunctions need not be observed if they are life-threatening (*e.g.,* if observing them requires jumping off a ski lift at the risk of one's neck). Violation of certain very basic prohibitions such as murder, adultery, incest, and public desecration of God's name cannot be justified even on this basis. However, Ms. Friedman could probably safely assume that being on a ski lift with a boy after dark fit into none of these categories. *See Pikku'ah Nefesh,* 13 ENCYCLOPEDIA JU-DAICA 510 (1971).

207. The issue is not whether she was correct. If she could have reasonably held the belief she did, then it is quite reasonable for her to act on it. Blood v. Tyngsborough, 103 Mass. 509 (1870); Parrott v. Wells Fargo, & Co. 82 U.S. (15 Wall.) 524 (1872) (the nitroglycerine case).

208. Just as you cannot get blood out of a stone, you cannot get cash out of a pauper. Consequently, much of tort law involves the search for financially responsible parties to bear the cost of accidents. Since the decision to become a teacher is about as financially irresponsible a decision as one can make, there is good reason to believe teachers will usually be immune, in practice, to product liability suits. *But cf.* Stigler, *A Sketch of the History of Truth in Teaching,* 81 J. POL. ECON. 491 (1973).

209. Friedman, 282 N.Y.S. 2d at 862.

210. N.Y. Ct. of Cl. Act, §§ 9, 12(3) (McKinney 1963, Supp 1983).

211. Of course these students have a point. The fact that the courts have consistently treated victim beliefs found by the majority of Americans to be outlandish as reasonable cannot be lightly ignored. This may be because the common law reflects widely held values. Or it may be because in our legal-political systems common law courts are empowered to establish values, to create "oughts". *See* Calabresi, *The New Economic Analysis of Law: Scholarship, Sophistry, or Self-indulgence?,* 68 PROC. BRIT ACAD. 85 (1982).

212. 31 Mich. App. 240, 187 N.W.2d 511 (1971).

213. *Id.* at 514–16.

214. *Id.* at 519–20. The court's discussion explicitly extends to abortion although it was not legal in Michigan at the time of the suit. MICH. COMP. LAWS ANN. § 750.14 (West 1968). The defendants probably would have had little difficulty getting their child adopted at the time of the suit (1971). The ease with which adoptive parents could be found for white chil-

dren in the United States in the postwar years has been highly variable. In the 1950s, there were simply not enough adoptable white children to meet the demand. However, this situation was reversed in the early 1960s due to an increase in the illegitimate birth rate. However, in the late 1960s, supply again began to fall behind demand. C. DYUIASUK, ADOPTION — IS IT FOR YOU? 3–11 (1973). Reasons for this final reversal are unclear. Partly it was due to a uniform tendency of agencies to make it easier for people to become foster parents in response to the glut of the mid-'60s. *Id.* Adopting children had also become more socially acceptable during the 1960s and early 1970s. Bonham, *Who Adopts: The Relationship of Adoption and Social-Demographic Characteristics of Women,* 39 J. MARRIAGE AND THE FAMILY 295 (1977). There is also some fragmentary evidence to suggest that the increased availability of abortion in the late 1960s and, of course, early 1970s, simply reduced the availability of adoptable children. *Adolescent Pregnancy, 1978: Hearing on H.R. 12146 before the Subcomm. on Select Education of the House Comm. on Education and Labor* 95th Cong., 2d Sess. 202–04 (1978) (reprint of Population Bulletin by Dr. Wendy H. Baldwin).

215. Troppi v. Scarf 187 N.W.2d at 520.

216. The general rule is that the plaintiff is required to act "reasonably" to mitigate damages. *See generally,* DOOLEY, *supra* note 85, at § 10.05. In the context of the Learned Hand test, reasonable action to mitigate damages would mean action whose cost is less than the probable dimunition in damages it affects. *See supra* note 197 and text accompanying notes 199–200. The court in *Troppi,* 187 N.W.2d 511, by ruling that the plaintiffs were not required to get an abortion or place the child up for adoption, held that the subjective costs to the plaintiffs of abortion or adoption outweighed the reduction in monetary damages resulting directly from the birth of the unwanted child. Furthermore, by making this ruling as a matter of law, the court held, in effect, that the balance in this case was so clear-cut that there was no need to let the jury weigh the two sets of costs.

217. "The 'establishment of religion' clause of the first amendment means at least this: Neither a state nor the federal government can set up a church. Neither can pass laws which aid one religion, aid all religions, or prefer one religion over another." Everson v. Board of Education, 330 U.S. 1, 15 (1947).

218. The decision a judge or jury is asked to make when evaluating the reasonableness of a given action is seldom value-free. The test of a behavior's reasonableness involves balancing the interest achieved by the actor against the probable costs to potential victims. *See supra* note 197 and text accompanying notes 199–200. Balancing the two sets of interests involves only objective quantitative analysis if both are adequately measured on a single metric (*i.e.,* money). If, however, either of the interests involved can-

not adequately be converted into money, the decision-maker confronts the problem of comparing what cannot be compared except subjectively: just how important was the actor's interest in not having an abortion (or not running over the dog or maintaining a reputation for probity, etc.) compared to the costs that ensued? Such questions can be answered only by assigning relative weights to the competing sets of interests. But deciding, for example, that not having an abortion is a more valuable interest than some quantity of money is not a factual judgment. It is a judgment about the relative importance one should attach to certain activities. Consequently, it is an assertion about values.

The fact that judges and juries must make such value judgments in tort law raises first amendment issues when someone seeks to justify his or her behavior on the basis of religious beliefs. The decision-maker must then decide how much weight the religious beliefs should be given. If in the long run the beliefs of more popular religions are weighed heavily, while those of non-mainstream religions are weighed lightly or not at all, the legal system will have improperly, and perhaps unconstitutionally, favored certain religious beliefs over others. The problem is only partly ameliorated when these decisions are made by a jury. Since juries do not have to justify their decisions, the extent to which their decisions disfavor certain religious beliefs, will not be made explicit. *See* CALABRESI & BOBBITT, *supra* note 1 at 57–62. Of course, the constitutional issue doesn't go away. It is merely buried. In other words, the legal system will have treated the disfavored religious as non-conforming in both the literal and the historic sense. These religions are non-conforming because they are identified by their adherence to beliefs that are not widely held. They are also non-conforming religions in the historic sense: as in 17th and 18th century England when members of sects experienced civil disabilities because they failed to subscribe to the theological beliefs of the majority church. J. EUSDEN, PURITANS, LAWYERS AND POLITICIANS IN EARLY SEVENTEENTH CENTURY ENGLAND 67–84 (1958); A. LINCOLN, SOME POLITICAL AND SOCIAL IDEAS OF ENGLISH DISSENT, 1763–1800, ch. 2 (1938).

219. Ironically many of these same religions, non-conformist in England, *id.,* became state-supported, "established" religions in particular American states. This situation lingered on in some states until the early 19th century. For example, Congregationalism remained the established religion of Connecticut until the Constitution of 1818 — some 43 years after the beginning of the American Revolution. R. PURCELL, CONNECTICUT IN TRANSITION: 1775–1818, ch. IX (new ed. 1963). The survival of established religions in particular states was possibly because the first amendment's prohibitions applied only to the federal government (James Madison having been unsuccessful in his attempt to apply the no-establishment clause to state

governments as well. B. Schwartz, The Great Rights of Mankind: A History of the American Bill of Rights 165–77 (1977).) The limitations of the first amendment became applicable to state governments only after the passage of the 14th Amendment, and even then only as a result of slow doctrinal development. Cantwell v. Connecticut, 310 U.S. 296 (1940).

220. *See, e.g.,* Yania v. Bigan, 397 Pa. 316, 155 A.2d 343 (1959) (decedent, tauntd by defendant to jump into water-filled ditch apparently in order to demonstrate courage, was contributorily negligent). *Cf.* Steinman v. Di Roberts, 23 A. D. 2d 693, 257 N.Y.S.2d 695 (1965) (calling plaintiff a "liberal" does not constitute libel).

221. "[The first] Amendment requires the state to be a neutral in its relations with groups of religious believers and nonbelievers; it does not require the state to be their adversary. State power is no more to be used so as to handicap religions than it is to favor them." Everson v. Board of Education, 330 U.S. 1, 18 (1947). *See also* Sherbert v. Verner, 374 U.S. 398 (1963) (state must modify its unemployment compensation requirement of willingness to work Mondays through Saturdays in order to accommodate the needs of those religiously opposed to working on Saturdays but willing to work on Sundays instead).

222. McGowan v. Maryland, 366 U.S. 420 (1961); Two Guys v. McGinley, 366 U.S. 582 (1961); Braunfeld v. Brown, 366 U.S. 599 (1961).

223. Gillette v. United States, 401 U.S. 437 (1971).

224. The Supreme Court has justified failure to grant partial conscientious objectors exemption from conscription on two grounds: (1) The armed service's need for an adequate supply of manpower; (2) the difficulty of distinguishing between sincere religious objection and insincere or secular objections to particular wars; *id.* at 455–56.

Both problems would be solved if all conscientious objectors were simply required to register for a special lottery. Conscientious objectors would be inducted into the armed forces using this lottery only when the manpower requirements of the armed services were not being met from other sources. This system would satisfy manpower requirements and would also save the government from needing to assess the sincerity of the beliefs of partial conscientious objectors. Admittedly, it would also greatly burden the conscience of those conscientious objectors unfortunate enough to be drafted. But it would, at least, not arbitrarily discriminate between conscientious objectors whose pacifism is total and those who subscribe to the "just wars" doctrine.

225. In fact, four members of the court held that language in the Universal Military Training and Service Act which grounded conscientious objection in "religious training and belief" applied to any beliefs "held with the strength of traditional religious convictions." Welsh v. United States, 398

U.S. 333, 340 (1970). This interpretation had the attraction of relieving the Supreme Court of any need to declare the statute unconstitutional or to include non-religious conscientious objectors within its purview by widening the scope of the statute (a type of solution courts frequently find uncongenial, *see infra* note 234). This solution, of course, also totally lacked candor. The history and wording of the legislation made quite clear that Congress felt that valid conscientious objection could be grounded only in religious belief; *id.* at 351–54 (Harlan, J., concurring).

226. It is hard to characterize in any other way the attitudes that allowed the Court to justify the failure of Congress to grant conscientious objector status to partial conscientious objectors on the grounds that "[i]t does not bespeak an establishing of religion for Congress to forego the enterprise of distinguishing those whose dissent has some conscientious basis from those who simply dissent." Gillette v. United States, 401 U.S. 437, 457 (1971). It does not bespeak great respect for the theological position of any religion to characterize it as one particularly prone to fraud. (It is also not that convincing an argument. Real frauds will be quite indifferent to claiming total or partial conscientious objection.) Furthermore, it is hard to see how legislation that releases adherents of certain religions but not others from a particular civil duty, that is similarly onerous to both, does not unduly favor one religion over the other. Both positions, of course, affirm the superior social respectability of the "acceptable" religions over those of the others.

227. One must wonder what would have happened if a religion (e.g., Roman Catholicism) that took the doctrines of "just" wars more seriously than do most Christian churches, had been prominent in early American history. Would there now be a right to partial conscientious objection?

228. Undoubtedly, the most important pacifist sect in Colonial America was the Society of Friends. However, the Mennonites, the Amish, and certain other German sects who settled in America during the Colonial period were also pacifists. The history of religious conscientious objection in America prior to and during the Revolution is quite complex. Respect for pacifist religious principles was probably greatest in Pennsylvania and Rhode Island. The ease with which religious pacifists avoided military duty in other colonies varied with time, the political atmosphere, and the immediacy of the military threat. *See generally,* P. BROCK, PACIFISM IN THE UNITED STATES: FROM THE COLONIAL ERA TO THE FIRST WORLD WAR, Pt. I (1968). By the Revolution, most colonies recognized the right of pacifist sects to avoid conscription provided they either paid a fine or furnished a substitute, to both of which requirements, however, the Quakers objected on religious grounds; *id.* at 219–21.

229. I use "establish" here in a weak sense. Differential treatment of the moral theology of different churches does not fully confer on the favored

churches the institutional perquisites of what is normally called an "established" church.

230. There may be a moral in the fact that, as A. P. Herbert noted, it is frequently illegal for a man to dress as a woman but not for a woman to dress as a man. A. P. HERBERT, Aley v. Fish: *Justice for Men,* in STILL MORE MISLEADING CASES 125, 128 at n. 1 (4th ed. 1946). In any event, this was not always the case as the history of Joan of Arc demonstrates, M. WARNER, JOAN OF ARC, ch. 7 (1981). This in turn may suggest that bad laws applied equally or symmetrically may be little better than biased ones.

231. Certainly it has been used for this purpose. In Pierce v. Society of Sisters, 268 U.S. 510 (1925), the Court struck down an Oregon statute that required all children to be sent to public schools. The statute was quite explicitly aimed against Catholic schools and was only passed after a public campaign against immigrants by the Ku Klux Klan. W. MARNELL, THE FIRST AMENDMENT: THE HISTORY OF RELIGIOUS FREEDOM IN AMERICA 170–73 (1964).

232. *See, e.g.,* McCollum v. Board of Education, 333 U.S. 203 (1948) (a released-time program in which regular public school classes end early so that religious instruction may be given in public classrooms found unconstitutional), Committee for Public Education v. Nyquist, 413 U.S. 756 (1973) (tax-relief program for parent of New York nonpublic school children, most of whom were in parochial schools, found unconstitutional); Epperson v. Arkansas, 393 U.S. 97 (1968) (statute banning teaching of evolution in public schools, where sole reason for prohibition is religious beliefs of some churches, is unconstitutional).

233. Welsh v. United States, 398 U.S. 333, 342–44 (1970).

234. *See id.* at 340 (where Court attempted to define qualifying nonreligious philosophical beliefs).

Technically, of course, the Court's position was not inescapable. The Court could have avoided the alleged favoring of religion by striking down the statute allowing conscientious objection. Generally, courts prefer this approach and narrow rather than widen the application of a "discriminatory" statute. It has the advantage of not extending the statute to individuals the legislature did not intend to cover. Usher v. Schweiker, 666 F.2d 652, 661 n. 17 (1st Cir. 1981). It also does not require expenditure of funds not appropriated by the legislature. Thus, narrowing of a statute is traditionally viewed as less of an infringement on the legislature's prerogatives than would widening it. Nevertheless, the Court chose to expand the coverage of the conscientious objection statute even though recognition of conscientious objection may well not be a Constitutional *requirement.* Welsh, 398 U.S. at 356 (Harlan, J., concurring); Jacobson v. Massachusetts, 197 U.S. 11, 29 (1905) dictum). Apparently, the Court was loathe to abolish a legal status so closely linked with the historical development of the American conception of religious freedom (*see* Brock, *supra* note 229) as to seem almost a Constitutional right. The Court has shown similar willingness to expand the coverage of statutes in cases where failure to do so would leave a statute totally at war with the rest of the legal landscape. For example, the Social Security Act originally provided that widows of men who had contributed to the system were automatically eligible to receive survivor's benefits, while widowers of women who had contributed were not eligible unless they had been dependent on their spouse when she died. When the constitutionality of this statute was challenged in the mid-'70s, the court expanded coverage of the statute so that widowers thereafter needed to meet only the same minimal requirements as widows to receive survivor's benefits. Califano v. Goldfarb, 430 U.S. 199 (1977). The interesting thing about this holding was that despite the fact that it required the federal government to spend more money than had been appropriated by Congress and thereby intruded, in a very real way, upon the power of the purse, the opinion created little stir. Evidently the Court's assessment of what was consistent with the legal landscape, even if not legislated by Congress, was correct.

235. The classic case is Vaughan v. Menlove, 3 Bing. (N.C.) 468, 132 Eng. Rept. 490 (C.P. 1837) (defendant's good faith belief that hay rick would not ignite would not excuse defendant for negligently constructing the hay rick). The objective nature of the standard of reasonableness was settled in American law by a series of articles published in the Harvard Law Review during the second and third decade of this century. *See* Seavey, *Negligence—Subjective or Objective?*, 41 Harv. L. Rev. 1 (1927); Terry, *Negligence*, 29 Harv. L. Rev. 40, 47–49 (1915); Edgerton, *Negligence, Inadvertence, and Indifference*, 39 Harv. L. Rev. 849 (1926).

236. This problem, although not in this precise format, is not unknown. A relatively small number of individuals find the wearing of a helmet when driving a motorcycle personally offensive. It has been argued that such a failure to wear a helmet should constitute contributory negligence and/or failure to mitigate damages. *See* Graham, *Helmetless Motorcyclists—Easy Riders Facing Hard Facts: The Rise of the "Motorcycle Helmet Defense"*, 41 Ohio St. L.J. 233 (1980).

237. *See, e.g.,* Warrington v. New York Power and Light, 252 A. D. 364, 367, 300 N.Y.S. 154, 158 (1937) ("The standard is not what the jurors individually or collectively would have done, but the standard is that of the typically prudent man").

238. I used a white racist as an example, but the same conclusion would apply to a member of a black nationalist group who refused to be treated by a white doctor. The proportion of the population holding the belief would also not be relevant.

239. *Cf. e.g.,* Kennedy v. Bureau of Narcotics and Dangerous Drugs,

459 F.2d 415 (9th Cir. 1972), *cert. denied,* 409 U.S. 1115, *reh'g denied* 410 U.S. 959; (Church of Awakening not entitled to exemption from law prohibiting use of peyote although court concedes it is valid religion); People v. Weber, 19 Ca. App. 598, 97 Cal. Rptr. 150 (1971) (use of marijuana as part of sincere religious practice is not protected). The implication is, of course, that first a group must show that it is a valid religion, and even then some of its *practices* may be regulated. *See infra* note 241.

240. For a general discussion of why the distinction between speech and conduct is unconvincing, *see* L. TRIBE, AMERICAN CONSTITUTIONAL LAW § 12-7 (1978). The distinction between speech and conduct may nevertheless serve a useful purpose. It may be inevitable that freedom of speech must be balanced against other interests, *e.g.,* prevention of someone "falsely shouting fire in a theatre" to use Holmes' famous example in Schenck v. United States, 249 U.S. 47, 52 (1919). However, by refusing to acknowledge that we engage in such balancing, we may strengthen the presumption against regulation of speech. This point was illustrated in a trenchant example given by Charles Black. There is, of course, an absolute prohibition against torture in the American legal system. Suppose, nevertheless, that a judge is faced with the claim that a prisoner is being tortured. The police admit the fact but conclusively demonstrate that the prisoner has hidden a hydrogen bomb in a major city which will explode in an hour and that the only thing the prisoner fears is hideous pain. Black suggested that, under these circumstances, the judge will allow the torture to continue through use of some subterfuge. Then, Black asks, does this mean there is not an *absolute* prohibition against torture in the American legal system? Whether one should answer this question affirmatively may perhaps depend on what one means by the term "absolute." Black, nevertheless, gives good reason to prefer answering the question: "Yes, there is an absolute prohibition against torture." Whom, Black asks, would you prefer to have decide torture cases, generally: A judge who in easy as well as hard cases declares that we must balance the costs and benefits of torture or a judge who announces an absolute prohibition on torture? Black suggests quite convincingly that it is the latter judge who is to be preferred. Black, *Mr. Justice Black, The Supreme Court, and the Bill of Rights,* HARPER'S MAGAZINE Feb. 1961 at 63.

241. When pushed to allow the regulation of religious beliefs, courts typically speak as though they are regulating actions but not beliefs. The classic statement of this position is Chief Justice Waite's, that "laws are made for the government of actions, and while they cannot interfere with mere religious belief and opinions, they may with practices." Reynolds v. United States, 98 U.S. 145, 166 (1878) (adherence to Church of Latter Day Saints is not a defense against charge of polygamy). The action-belief distinction still flourishes in interpreting the First Amendment. It has been invoked,

for instance, in cases that hold that, while adults may adhere to any religious beliefs they wish, this does not justify withholding medical treatment from their children. Craig v. State, 220 Md. 590, 155 A.2d 684 (1959); Kennedy Memorial Hospital v. Heston, 58 N.J. 576, 279 A.2d 670 (1981). Similarly, courts have found that while prisoners have an unconditional right to their religious beliefs, this does not justify activity that interferes with prison discipline, Ron v. Lennane, 455 F. Supp. 98 (D. Conn. 1977). This distinction between action and belief is not terribly convincing when dealing with religion. Although some religious beliefs are purely cosmological, most have a moral component. They urge certain types of activities and condemn others. Consider the Roman Catholic obligation to attend mass. It involves any number of acts. Could the government validly pass a law forbidding some of them, for example, consecration of the host? It seems unlikely. Yet if the First Amendment means anything, it means that government cannot favor certain religions at the expense of others, *see supra* note 217. But, if an integral component of religious belief is to guide behavior, how can one say that a legal practice that allows the beliefs of some religions to be translated into behavior while prohibiting the same for others does not favor the first? This does not mean we should not make a distinction between religious practices and beliefs. It may be true that we are forced sometimes to balance our interest in freedom of religion against the costs imposed. We may be unable to accommodate the predilections of a sect worshipping Hermes, god of thieves, that truly believes bank robbery to be a blessed sacrament. Nevertheless, there may be good reasons when we prohibit such robberies not to acknowledge that we are infringing on freedom of religious belief. *See supra* note 240.

242. The discussion in text focused on beliefs discordant with the spirit of the Constitution. Similarly, however, a belief that was sufficiently disfavored by a set of statutes or with the whole "legal topography" would also be considered unreasonable in a victim. For a discussion of the concept of legal topography, *see* CALABRESI, A COMMON LAW *supra* note 4 at 129–31 (1982).

243. *See infra* Ch. 4.

244. *Compare,* for example, Carter v. Gallagher, 452 F.2d 315, 4 FEP 84 (8th Cir. 1971) (affirmative action required to offset effect of past racially discriminatory action) with Regents Of The University of California v. Bakke, 438 U.S. 265, 300–02 (1978) (Powell, J., opinion of court, 1-4-4 decision) (use of affirmative action in institutions not openly approved in absence of proved constitutional or statutory violation).

245. *See, for example,* Green, *Illinois Negligence Law II: Contributory Negligence,* 39 ILL. L. REV. 116 (1944); Loundes, *Contributory Negligence,* 22 GEO. L.J. 674 (1934); James, *Last Clear Chance: A Transitional Doctrine,* 47 YALE L.J. 704 (1938). Most states during the 1970s apparently decided that it did not.

In the latter 1960s, only seven states (plus the federal government) had abandoned contributory for comparative negligence. By 1980, this number had reached 35. Wade, *Comparative Negligence — Its Development in the United States and Its Present Status in Louisiana*, 40 LA. L. REV. 299, 302–04 (1980).

246. Sovereign immunity means simply that neither the federal nor state governments in the United States may be sued without their consent. The doctrine arose out of the medieval English conception of the law courts as extensions of the king's power to which he himself was bound only at his discretion. This doctrine, although it makes little sense under modern conditions, was transferred to the United States early in its history and remains reasonably vigorous in the tort law. *See, generally,* Jaffe, *Suits Against Governments and Officers*, 77 HARV. L. REV. 1 (1963); James, *Tort Liability of Government Units and Their Officers*, 22 U. CHI. L. REV. 610 (1955). In the actual *Friedman* case, 54 Misc. 2d 448, 282 N.Y.S. 2d 858 (1967), the state allowed itself to be sued. The suit was brought in the Court of Claims because this was the only forum in which the state allowed suits to be brought against it. *See supra* note 210.

247. *See, e.g.,* Craig v. State, 220 Md. 590, 155 A.2d, 684 (1959); Kennedy Memorial, Hospital v. Heston 58 N.J. 576, 279 A. 2d 670 (1971).

248. For one suggestion of why intentional and negligent wrongs should be treated differently, *see* Calabresi and Melamed, *Property Rules, Liability Rules, and Inalienability: One View of the Cathedral,* 85 HARV. L. REV. 1089, 1124-1127 (1972). There are numerous differences in the way that tort law actually treats negligent and intentional torts. For example, lack of foreseeability is less likely to be considered a bar to recovery if the injurer's act is intended to inflict harm. Punitive damages may only be awarded to victims of intentional torts. Emotional damages may be awarded to victims of intentional torts in far more circumstances than to victims of negligent torts. *See generally* W. PROSSER, THE LAW OF TORTS 9–12, 55–60, 263 (1971).

249. The concept of causation in tort law is itself functional. The range of events that can be considered a cause of something else expands and contracts in order to serve underlying substantive purposes. *See, e.g.,* F. HARPER & F. JAMES, 2 THE LAW OF TORTS 1132-134 (1956).

250. Of course, the parents owe a variety of duties to prevent harm to their child. *See, e.g., Kennedy Memorial Hospital,* 58 N.J. 576 (1971). The implication of this would be to strengthen the child's case. The fact that we would not give the child recovery for harms caused it by not being given in adoption suggests that we strongly approve of the desire of parents to keep even "unwanted" children.

251. Although there are quite a few cases in which religious belief has played a role in the victim's defense, *e.g., Lange* 114 Conn. 590 (1932), cases in which the injurer's belief is even raised as a bar to victim's recovery are

rare. There are, however, a few recent cases in which injurer's rather idiosyncratic beliefs have been argued unsuccessfully. *See, e.g.,* Interbank Card Assoc. v. Simms, 431 F. Supp. 131 (D.N.C. 1977) (injunction granted to prevent distribution of cards and stickers which closely resembled "Master Charge" credit cards to proselytize for fundamentalist Christian group); Bear v. Reformed Mennonite Church, 462 Pa. 330, 341 A.2d 105 (1975) (Plaintiff might bring suit in tort for damages incurred by business and family when plaintiff was excommunicated and literally ostracized by Mennonite Church). The ruling in the latter case is somewhat surprising. There has been a long line of cases involving expulsion from churches (many of them admittedly more "established" or at least more "popular" than the Mennonite Church.). In most of these cases recovery has been denied. Annot. 20 ALR2d 421, 499–500 (1951).

252. O. W. Holmes, The Common Law 94–95 (1881). The use of the term "act of God" to refer to accidents resulting from natural causes (*see, e.g.,* Parrish v. Parrish, 21 Ga. App. 275, 277, 94 S.E. 315, 316, [1917]), is peculiarly inapposite. It seems rather questionable theology to assign to divine intervention a natural occurrence whose most notable effect is to leave bodies strewn about.

253. Holmes v. Mather, 10 L.R.-Ex. 261, 267 (1875).

254. *See supra* text accompanying notes 47–48.

255. *Cf.* Prosser and Keeton *supra* note 103 at § 135, *See also supra* note 147 and accompanying text, and *supra* note 251.

256. *See* Calabresi, *Too Much, Too Little, or Both,* Oxford J. Legal Studies (forthcoming) Blackstone Lecture at Oxford); on the unwillingness of legislatures to face such issues, *see generally,* Calabresi, A Common Law *supra* note 4.

257. This would be a variety of assigned-risk pool, *see supra* note 168.

258. This fund should tax both injurer activities and victim activities. In other words, it should tax activities likely to cause injury to others (*e.g.,* driving) and those likely to cause injury to the participants (*e.g.,* skiing or riding ski lifts). *Cf.* R. Keeton & J. O'Connell, Basic Protection for the Traffic Victim; A Blueprint for Reforming Automobile Insurance 263–65 (1965).

259. *See supra* note 61.

260. We would, in fact, elect to subsidize unusual religious beliefs by means of a small tax placed on other members of society.

261. In other words, we would use the same strategy as the New Zealand plan. *See supra* note 61.

262. *See* Calabresi, Costs, *supra* note 48 at Ch. 9; *see also* Calabresi & Bobbitt, *supra* note 1 at 32.

263. *See* F. Harper & F. James, 2 The Law of Torts § 18.4 (1956).

264. *See, e.g.,* Jeppsen v. Jensen, 47 Utah 536, 155 P.429 (1916) (defen-

dant threatens plaintiff's husband in her presence); Enright v. Groves, 39 Colo. App. 39, 560 P.2d 851 (1977) (false arrest of plaintiff).

265. In recent years there has been a significant widening of the circumstances that allow recovery of emotional damages from a negligent injurer. The majority view during the early decades of this century was that material damages could be awarded only if there had been actual physical injury or "impact." The impact rule originated in the United Kingdom in the case of Victorian Railway Commissioners v. Coultas, 13 App. Cas. 222 (P.C. 1888) (no recovery from mere fright occasioned by near-collision with train). The impact rule was quite short lived in the U.K. although it lingered on in many American jurisdictions for years. Only 13 years later, a pregnant woman was awarded damages for fright and consequent injuries to her unborn child when the defendant's vehicle hit the tavern where she was employed. Dulieu v. White [1901] 2 K.B. 669. However, even for jurisdictions following *Dulieu,* recovery was limited to situations in which plaintiff was threatened with actual physical injury. *See, e.g.,* Waube v. Warrington, 216 Wis. 603, 258 N.W. 497 (1935). Only recently have courts begun to award damages for emotional injury resulting from witnessing threatened or actual harm to another. Most of these cases have involved threats to close relatives, *e.g.,* Dillon v. Legg, 68 Cal.2d 728, 69 Cal. Rptr. 72, 441 P.2d 912 (1968) (mother and daughter witness death of second daughter, run over by automobile); Barnhill v. Davis, 300 N.W.2d 104 (Iowa S. Ct. 1981) (son witnesses mother involved in automobile accident); Corso v. Merrill, 119 N.H. 647, 406 A.2d 300 (1979) (parents in vicinity of, though did not actually witness, car hitting and injuring daughter). Generally speaking, recovery has not been extended to situations in which the threatened or injured party is not a close relative of the plaintiff. A number of recent California cases have also refused to extend *Dillon* to allow recovery when the parents did not actually observe the injury done to their child. Justus v. Atchison, 19 Cal.2d 564, 139 Cal. Rptr. 97, 565 P.2d 122 (1977); Hathaway v. Superior Court of Fresno County, 112 Cal. App. 3d 728, 169 Cal. Rptr. 435 (1980). *See generally* Bell, *Immoral Subsidy: Hiding The Cost of Psychic Injury,* 3 U. FLA. L. REV. (1984) at nn. 32–40 and accompanying text. Bell provides a cogent argument that recovery for emotional injury should be expanded further rather than limited.

266. Campbell v. Animal Quarantine Station, 63 H. 557, 632 P.2d 1066 (1981). A learned professor who, I'm sure, would rather remain anonymous, gave me the following "poem" about the case:

> In the tropic isles beyond Mex
> Slain was the pet of one Rex
> Hot tears of his young
> The judiciary wrung
> To the visible change of the Lex.

In fact, such "animal" cases are not that new or unusual. Since damage to the animal constitutes economic loss to the owner, emotional damages attendant on such tangible damages are recoverable without much stretching of traditional doctrine. *See* Bell, *supra* note 265 at n. 59.

267. *See* DWORKIN, *supra* note 204 at 232–33.

268. Bork, *Neutral Principles and Some First Amendment Problems,* 47 IND. L. J. 1, 9–10 (1971).

269. *Cf., id.* Such "public acts of indecency" are, of course, for better or worse, still violations of criminal statutes. *See, e.g.,* CAL. PENAL CODE §§ 314, *et seq.* (West 1970, Supp. 1983); N.Y. PENAL LAW §§ 245.00–245.11 (Consol 1977).

270. It is hard to find statutes that actually make sale of live organs illegal. In practice, however, such sales are blocked. *See, e.g., Doctor Blocks Sale of Kidney,* New Haven Register, January 18, 1978, at 9, col. 3. *See also* Susan Rose-Ackerman, *Inalienability and the Theory of Property Rights,* 85 COLUM. L. REV. (1985).

271. *See, e.g.,* Richards, *Commercial Sex and the Rights of the Person: A Moral Argument for the Decriminalization of Prostitution,* 127 U. PA. L. REV. 1195 (1979); Comment, *Human Rights in an International Context: Recognizing the Right of Intimate Association,* 43 OHIO ST. L. J. 143 (1982); Comment, *Decriminalization of Prostitution: The Limits of Criminal Law,* 55 OR. L. REV. 553 (1976); Kaplan, *The Edward G. Donlevy Memorial Lecture: Non-victim Crime and the Regulation of Prostitution,* 79 W. VA. L. REV. 593 (1977). *But see,* Abramson, *A Note on Prostitution: Victims Without Crime — Or, There's No Crime But the Victim is Ideology,* 17 DUQ. L. REV. 355 (1979).

272. *See, e.g., Man in Debt Offers His Eyes for $5,000,* New Haven Register, March 15, 1975, at 14, col. 1. Of course, it may be possible that these individuals do not intend to sell their organs at all. An offer to sell an organ may be merely a bid for publicity to obtain charitable contributions.

273. The issue of whether suicide should be permitted or not is a much-debated topic. *See, e.g.,* Englehardt and Malloy, *Suicide and Assisting Suicide: A Critique of Legal Sanctions,* 36 SW. L. J. 1003 (1982). Suicide and attempted suicide were criminal offenses at common law in England from at least the 14th until the 19th century. (It was an offense against canon law well before that.) Hoffman and Webb, *Suicide as Murder at Common Law,* 19 CRIMINOLOGY 372, 373–74 (1981). Only three state courts — Alabama, Oregon, and South Carolina — have followed the common law tradition and held suicide to be a crime, though other states forbade attempted suicide. Englehardt and Malloy, *supra,* at 1018, nn. 66, 67. Most states, however, treat aiding and abetting suicide as a crime; *id.* at 1019.

Except for the fact that both prohibitions attempt to prevent affront to community values, there is no clear conceptual linkage between the prohibitions on suicide and sale of body parts. One can certainly argue that both prohibitions, for the sake of the community, prevent individuals from doing something that they believe is in their self-interest. Of course, the law often does that. For an argument based partly on moralisms for preventing behavior more clearly in the individual's self-interest than either suicide or self-mutilation, *see* Burt, *Why We Should Keep Prisoners From the Doctors,* HASTINGS CENTER REP. February 1975, at 25 (arguing that prisoners should not be given psychosurgery even with their consent and even if it increases likelihood of release from jail).

274. When the legal system deals with moralisms, it tends to do so in an all-or-nothing manner. When we decide to protect moralisms, the offensive activity is often flatly prohibited. If we decide not to offer protection, we often allow the offending activity to occur freely (*i.e.,* without cost). Given that individuals may have a strong interest in limiting offenses to their moral sensitivities and that other individuals may also have a strong interest in doing things others find offensive, it is interesting that we do not attempt to balance these two interests. It is only in those relatively rare instances in which moralisms are allowed to count in tort law that a cost-benefit analysis of these two competing interests occurs, via the medium of the Learned Hand test. *See supra,* notes 102, 197, and text accompanying notes 199–200.

275. *Cf.* Kelman, *Choice and Utility,* 1979 U. WIS. L. REV. 769; *cf. also* R. TITMUS, THE GIFT RELATIONSHIP: FROM HUMAN BLOOD TO SOCIAL POLICY (1971).

276. One can readily see that most people will claim special affection for property once it has been damaged.

277. Fraud is frequently given as the reason for banning certain types of lawsuits. Nevertheless when social conditions change sufficiently to make such suits seem desirable, fraud no longer seems to stand in the way. Consider, for example, the fate of intra-family torts immunity—the doctrine that spouses could not sue each other nor could children sue parents for torts. This doctrine arose out of notions that such suits undermined family unity or discipline. After the development and spread of liability insurance, however, it came to be (and still is) frequently justified on the grounds that intra-family suits are peculiarly prone to collusion and fraud. *Cf., e.g.,* Raisen v. Raisen, 379 So.2d 352, 355 (Fla. Sup. Ct., 1979), U.S. Cert. den. 449 U.S. 886; Briere v. Briere, 107 N.H. 432, 224 A.2d 588, 590 (1966); Kobe v. Kobe, 61 Ohio App.2d 67, 399 N.E.2d 124, 125 (1978). The practical effect of intra-family immunity then had become to deny the family's recovery from the insurance company of money needed to care for one of its members. Badigian v. Badigian, 9 N.Y.2d 472, 474, 215 N.Y.S. 2d 35, 37 (N.Y. 1961) (Fuld, J., dissenting). It is not surprising that, in time, the doctrine of intra-family immunity was abrogated in many jurisdictions, primarily in the last two

decades. *See* J. DOOLEY, 1 MODERN TORT LAW §§ 11.01.50, 13.09 (rev. ed. 1982). Nevertheless, the rapidity of the doctrine's passing makes one wonder how serious the courts were in using the danger of fraud as a justification in the first place.

In any event, items of damages like pain and suffering are as open to fraud as any that we have been discussing. Nevertheless, we allow such damages. *Cf., e.g.,* Schwartz v. United States, 230 F. Supp. 536 (D.C. Pa. 1964). In practice, we rely on juries to be highly skeptical of claims of damage in such cases. If the danger of fraud were the only barrier to awarding emotional damages, surely it could be surmounted by such skepticism combined with a presumption against such injuries having occurred that could be overcome only by presentation of evidence of actual pain and suffering. For a highly effective criticism of the use of fraud as a ground for denying emotional damages, *see* Bell, *supra* note 265, at text accompanying n.n. 203–213.

278. *See, generally,* CALABRESI, COSTS, *supra* note 48 at 148–49, 244–46.

279. This is the essence of the argument for the doctrine of assumption of risk. It explains why "assumption of risk" or "lack of duty" is a defense even if the defendant was negligent. *See supra* notes 95–97 and accompanying text. This kind of situation is the exact obverse of situations in which the party with the greater knowledge is the defendant. In such situations (*e.g.,* situations covered by various doctrines imposing strict injurer liability), the contributory negligence of the plaintiff is frequently not a defense. Calabresi and Hirschoff, *Toward A Test for Strict Liability in Torts,* 81 YALE L. J. 1055, 1060–67 (1972).

280. Of course, to what situations we will decline to extend the doctrine of assumption of risk or its obverse (*see supra* note 279) depends on what activities we believe individuals should be able to participate in "freely." Among the classic examples of assumption of risk are the cases in which plaintiffs attend some sporting event, *e.g.,* Brown v. San Francisco Ball Club, 99 Cal. App.2d 484, 222 P.2d 19 (1950) (plaintiff, woman unfamiliar with game of baseball, is struck by misthrown baseball). In *Brown,* the plaintiff was found to have assumed the risk of being hit since she declined to purchase a seat in the screened-in portion of the stands. It is interesting, however, that the court suggested that the defendant ball club might have been liable had they provided no screened-in seats; *id.* at 21 (*dicta*). This suggestion implies either that, in the absence of a screened-in portion, people would be unaware of the risks of sitting in the stands or, a more plausible interpretation, that the ability to attend baseball games is so important a part of American civil culture that we will not alow baseball clubs to force people to assume the risk of being bopped on the head when they go to a baseball game. The right to bring Amnesia's watch on a freeway is apparently not treated as being equally

fundamental. The right of devout Christian Scientists, and of Catholics who abjure contraception, to drive is. One might question whether the right to go on ski lifts with members of the opposite sex should be accorded analogous protection. Fortunately for Mrs. Eider, however, the court in *Friedman v. New York,* 282 N.Y.S.2d 858, focused on whether she acted reasonably in jumping and not on whether, given her belief, she had assumed the risk of her injury by going on the ski lift in the first place.

281. For a discussion of the side effects of various contraceptives (with emphasis on the pill) *see, e.g.,* B. SEAMAN & G. SEAMAN, WOMEN AND THE CRISIS IN SEX HORMONES (1977). These side effects, per se, are not considered design defects (*but see infra* note 282), despite the fact that many other products that produce injuries or illness or failure to do the job they are designed to do have been considered defectively designed, *see, e.g.,* Gilmore v. St. Anthony Hosp., 598 P.2d 1200 Okla. 1979 (hepatitis contracted from blood transfusion); Chrysler Corp. v. Miller, 310 So.2d 356 (Dist. Ct. App. Fla. 1975) (engines on houseboats recommended by defendant were insufficiently powerful and subject to breakdown). In such cases, contributory negligence is typically not a defense. *See generally* W. KIMBLE & R. LESHER, PRODUCTS LIABILITY § 242 (1979).

282. There are, of course, cases in which people have sued for illnesses caused by side effects of contraceptives. The mere fact that a contraceptive was a proximate cause of the side effect has not been sufficient to sustain recovery. Plaintiff must, in addition, demonstrate that the manufacturer failed to give adequate warning of the potential hazards of the drug. *See, e.g.,* McEwen v. Ortho Pharmaceutical Corporation, 270 Or. 375, 528 P.2d 522 (1974) (warning inadequate); Leibowitz v. Ortho Pharmaceutical Corp., 224 Pa. Super 418, 307 A.2d 449 (1973) (same oral contraceptive, similar side effect as above case; warning found adequate); *see generally* W. KIMBLE & R. LESHER, PRODUCTS LIABILITY §§ 372, 374–76 (1979).

283. The danger of fraud is small if the side effect at issue is illness. Loss of pleasure, in contrast, is quite prone to fraud because it is entirely subjective and hard to monitor. The side effect of unwanted pregnancy is also prone to fraud simply because it is difficult to determine if a pregnancy is, in fact, unwanted. It would be quite easy for people who want children to fail to use contraceptives, claim the pregnancy was unwanted, and cite *Troppi* to establish that they are not required to mitigate damages by either having the child adopted or getting an abortion. *See supra* notes 212 *et seq.* and accompanying text.

284. *See supra* note 103.

285. The system envisioned parallels Workmen's Compensation laws in that the legislature would fix by statute the size of awards according to a schedule of the severity of "injury." *See supra* note 103. A system of sched-

uled damages eliminates incentives for victims to exaggerate their feelings. Their recovery is determined not by their subjective experience, but by the objective standard given in the schedule. Of course, I suppose there may be a problem of the cold-hearted going out of their way to witness particularly gruesome accidents so as to recover damages. This problem can be ameliorated by limiting recovery to those who pass by the scene of the accident immediately after its occurrence. Admittedly, this will exclude from recovery some people who pass by after the time limit has elapsed and are genuinely upset. Nevertheless, it would arguably be better than the current system which excludes not only these people but everybody no matter when they encounter the accident.

286. The problem is illustrated by the seemingly paradoxical nature of the question: "How much must I offer to get you to love me for myself quite apart from my offer?" McKean, *Economics of Trust, Altruism and Corporate Responsibility*, ALTRUISM, MORALITY AND ECONOMIC THEORY 30 (Edmund Phelps ed. 1975); *see also* Calabresi, *Comment, id.* at 59. It is at least plausible to believe that people will attribute to themselves more emotional pain as they devote more attention to that pain. *See generally* Ofshe and Christman, *supra* note 19. *Cf.* Bell, *supra* note 265 at text accompanying nn. 311–315. There is, however, evidence that allowing such damages in certain circumstances will ameliorate emotional suffering; *id.* at text accompanying nn. 316–324. In any event, it is clear courts do worry about the possibility that awarding emotional damages will increase sensitivity to psychic injury. *See, e.g.,* McLoughlin v. O'Brian and Others [1981] 1 All E.R. 809, 828 (C.A.) (Griffiths, L.J.); *cf. also* Magruder, *Mental and Emotional Disturbance in the Law of Torts,* 49 HARV. L. REV. 1033, 1035 (1936).

287. Of course, the persistence of anguish would cause actual injury to increase but this would be unlikely to cause cheating in the individual case. Assuming that the amount of damages in the schedule is periodically revised to accord with actual victims' self-reports, the effect of self-reports that exaggerate the extent of suffering, would be to increase future awards. Victims, however, have little incentive to magnify the extent of their emotional injury when doing so has no effect on their compensation at the present and provides only the shadowy possibility of greater recovery in some completely hypothetical future lawsuit.

288. For some idea of how the topic of adultery figured in the novels of the period, *see, e.g.,* G. MEREDITH, THE ORDEAL OF RICHARD FEVEREL (1859); F. MADDOX FORD, THE GOOD SOLDIER (1915); S. ANDERSON, WINESBURG, OHIO (1919) (particularly the short story, "Respectability").

289. In the course of judicially abolishing the action for alienation of affection, a recent Iowa opinion noted that 17 states and the District of Columbia had already done so by judicial decision. Louisiana had never recog-

nized this tort. Six states deny recovery of money damages, three states view such actions with disfavor. Two more have abolished the action with exception. Fundermann v. Mickelson, 304 N.W.2d 790 (Iowa Sup. Ct. 1981). Most of these jurisdictions acted during the 1970s. However, the probability of successfully pursuing a suit for alienation of affection in these jurisdictions seems to have been quite low prior to the action's formal abolition, as seems also to be the case in jurisdictions that have yet to abolish the action. For a description of the similar fate of the similar action for criminal conversion and seduction, *see* Kline v. Ansell, 287 Md. 585, 414 A.2d 929, 931 (1980).

290. I am not here arguing that there is anything wrong with more liberal divorce laws. I merely note that they may well have had the effect of weakening the sense of proprietal loss attendant on the breaking up of a marriage.

291. To say that one is surprised to see certain language or sexual acts become commonplace in the media is totally different from saying one would censor such acts. There are any number of reasons why a person might disapprove of extremely explicit treatment of such behavior in popular culture and yet not believe in censorship (*e.g.,* difficulty of enforcement of censorship laws; inevitable spreading of censorship to areas where it is extremely undesirable). What is interesting, though, is the extent to which permitting various forms of cultural expression in the United States leads to these forms being considered desirable rather than merely to be tolerated even if tawdry.

As to how dramatic the changes have been, I would only note that recently, while flying, I found the movie available to everyone was "An Officer and a Gentleman". The movie was well acted and not a bad movie. It was, however, full of "vulgar" language, sexually explicit discussions and situations, and nudity. No one but me seemed surprised. I couldn't help remembering how shocked people were to learn that Clark Gable did not wear an undershirt (in "It Happened One Night") or that he could actually say, "Frankly my dear, I don't give a damn" ("Gone With The Wind").

292. It is quite plausible to believe that the demand for sexually explicit entertainment is not an intercultural constant. It may well expand (and under some circumstances also contract) as the availability and acceptability of such material increases. Nevertheless, the existing of thriving, albeit underground, prostitution and pornography industries in the United States and England during the Victorian era suggests there is an irreducible and not inconsiderable minimum demand for such entertainment even under the most repressive of cultural regimes. *See, e.g.,* D. CROW, VICTORIAN WOMEN, ch. 13 (1971); G. TAYLOR, THE ANGEL-MAKERS, ch. 4 (1958).

293. *E.g.,* Dillon v. Legg, 68 Cal.2d 728, 69 Cal. Rptr. 72, 441 P.2d 912 (1968); Archibald v. Braverman, 275 Cal. App. 2d 253, 79 Cal. Rptr.

723 (1969); Barnhill v. Davis, 300 N.W.2d 104 (Iowa Sup. Ct. 1981); *see also supra* note 265.

294. If we do not wish to allow recovery for purely emotional damages to unrelated passers-by on the grounds this will tend unnecessarily to increase emotional distress, we may, nonetheless, decide to charge the injurer a set amount payable to the state in lieu of such damages. This might have the effect of increasing the incentives for safety without increasing the damages to the emotional victims. *See* Bell, *supra* note 265. It may be, however, that by recognizing that there has been emotional harm, we may still increase the salience and, consequently, the extent of emotional injury even though we have not awarded compensation for it. Thus, when our law limits (by license or zoning) the location of sex shops, it in a sense tells people they have a right to be shocked by sex shops, which they are.

295. *Cf., e.g.,* Koehler v. United States, 187 F.2d 933 (7th Cir. 1951); Roedder v. Rowley, 28 Cal. 2d 820, 172 P.2d 353 (1946); Fordon v. Bender, 363 Mich. 124, 108 N.W.2d 896 (1961); Faught v. Washam, 329 S.W.2d 588 (Mo. 1959).

296. This is called the "contingent-fee" system. *See* F. B. MacKinnon, Contingent Fees for Legal Services, 28–29 (1964); Schwartz and Mitchell, *An Economic Analysis of the Contingent Fee in Personal Injury Litigation,* 22 Stan. L. Rev. 1125, 1147–54 (1970).

297. Three major criticisms of the contingent-fee system are worth mentioning. The first is that the contingent fee clogs the court system by encouraging frivolous suits. *See* L. Patterson & E. Cheatham, The Profession of Law 275 (1971); R. Hunting & G. Neuwarth, Who Sues in New York City? 50–51 (1962); MacKinnon, *supra* note 296 at 201. The second is that lawyers typically charge overly high fees using the contingent-fee system. Note, *The Contingent Fee: Disciplinary Rule, Ethical Consideration, or Free Competition?,* 1979 Utah L. Rev. 547, 551–53. The third is that there is an inherent conflict of interest between lawyer and client once the lawyer has gone to the trouble of preparing a case for trial. At this point, it may well be in the client's interest to settle, but it may not be in the interest of the lawyer, who, for what may be a relatively minor extra investment of time and energy, has a chance at a much larger fee; *id.* at 561–62; Schwartz and Mitchell, *supra* note 296, at 1139. The first two criticisms are the most common and are easily answered. *See infra,* notes 298, 299. The last may have some merit but hardly seems sufficient to invalidate the whole contingent-fee system, particularly as there may well be ways to ameliorate this problem. *See* Note, *The Contingent Fee,* 1979 Utah L. Rev. 547, 562–74.

298. The contingent-fee system acts as a mutual insurance system among plaintiffs for downside risks. Those who collect nothing pay no lawyer's fees. Those who collect pay a substantially higher fee than they would

under a set-fee system to compensate their lawyer for the risk of losing the case and collecting nothing. There would be no need for the contingent-fee system if we had legal aid for everyone — not just the poor, but also those who hesitate to risk a significant proportion of their income or wealth in order to bring a suit they might lose. The cost of bringing a lawsuit in the absence of some form of legal aid or of a contingent-fee system acts in many ways like a regressive tax on the use of the legal system.

In the United Kingdom there is no contingent-fee system; instead losers typically pay the lawyer's fees for the winner. H. C. COLLINS, ROBINSON'S COUNTY COURT COSTS 2–3 (5th ed. 1976). This is not an adequate substitute for the contingent-fee system. It does not protect the relatively less prosperous against the economic consequence of bringing a suit that fails and so encourages such people to bring only those suits they are quite sure to win. This might not sound like so serious a consequence. Some might even welcome it as a check on frivolous lawsuits. But there is an enormous difference between a frivolous suit and an uncertain one. This is certainly true in torts, where just what happened is frequently unclear until the facts are brought out during trial. Since the money penalty for a mistake in bringing a suit is the same for rich and poor, the burden of a lost suit will weigh regressively on the poor. The net effect is that the poorer one is, the less likely one will be to seek redress in court. It is this aspect of the English system that seems most unacceptable in the United States. The English system (like the American one, *see supra* note 297) is also subject to conflicts of interest. *See infra* note 299.

The principal problem of the contingent fee system is that it is expensive. Fees frequently take a significant chunk (usually around one-third) of any award. This is partly because the fee, as noted above, includes a premium to compensate the attorney for all the cases he or she didn't win. This premium, in practice, requires the award of pain and suffering damages that are quite expensive to prove. As a result, already expensive litigation under a fault system is made even more costly. For a discussion of the advantages of systems (like the contingent-fee system) which put the costs of allocating burdens on those who "win" rather than those who "lose," *see* CALABRESI & BOBBITT, *supra* note 1 at 131–34 (1978).

299. Rather than using the subterfuge of awarding damages for pain and suffering in order to cover lawyer's fees, it might be possible to award a fixed percentage of damages over and above economic losses to pay attorney's fees. The percentage awarded would have to be sufficient not only to compensate the lawyer for the time spent on that case but also for time spent on the normal proportion of losing cases as well. Apart from some problems of its own, this reform would not address the frequent criticism that the contingent-fee system encourages frivolous suits, *see supra* note 297. Frankly,

that criticism is not convincing. In fact, the contingent-fee system provides some incentive not to bring weak cases as a lawyer has nothing to gain from a suit he or she loses. This would not be true if the lawyer were paid a time-based fee. In such a system, the lawyer would have an incentive to bring frivolous suits, since he or she would be paid no matter how weak the case is. The same can be said also of the variation of the argument against the contingent-fee system that suggests that there exists a mass of underemployed lawyers in the legal system who have an incentive to bring even relatively weak cases since their time is under-occupied. These lawyers, it is said, can at least hope to get lucky and win an occasional case; and even weak cases may have some "settlement value" since it may be cheaper for a defendant to settle on a small award than to litigate. The trouble with this argument is that the problem it foresees would not be ameliorated by moving from a contingent to a fixed-fee system. Underemployed lawyers could be expected to charge very low hourly rates, and clients might still flock to them for the settlement value the client could collect. Certainly such lawyers on a fixed (though paltry) fee would have no incentive to discourage clients from frivolous suits. Thus, the argument against the contingent-fee system cannot be based on the proposition that it encourages weak suits; it must be based on the proposition that it encourages a greater volume of cases, strong as well as weak. In other words, it makes the law more accessible to those with limited funds. But this either becomes an argument that recovery is not justified in most torts suits, or that the "masses" should be excluded from the legal system. Either position may be argued (though not, I think, very convincingly), but neither is an argument primarily against the contingent-fee system. Those who hold such positions are, in fact, going after bigger game!

300. *See, e.g.,* O'Connell, *A Proposal to Abolish Payment for Pain and Suffering in Return for Payment of Attorney's Fees,* 1981 U. ILL. L. REV. 333.

301. One may wonder why such systems sometimes allow (typically low) recovery for emotional damages or dignitary losses (i.e. non-economic damages due to loss of limbs or members), *e.g.,* CAL. LAB. CODE § 4658 *et seq.* (West, 1971; Supp. 1983); ILL. ANN. STAT., Ch. 48, § 138.8 (Smith-Hurd 1969; Supp. 1983) (dignitary losses in Workmen's Compensation laws). One reason may be to compromise with the system they replaced which allowed damages for pain and suffering. Retaining scheduled damages for such losses in a worker's compensation system has few of the drawbacks it would have if emotional damages were made central in litigation. Because these damages are fixed, they are also unlikely to be made more salient and consequently exacerbated by the recovery process.

302. The reason why pain and suffering damages are allowed in England, which does not have a contingent-fee system, is harder to understand. Roughead v. Railway Executive, 65 T.L.R. 435 (K.B. 1949); Jones

v. Livox Quarries, Ltd. [1952] 1 T.L.R. 1377 at 1382 (C.A.) (opinion of Singleton, L.J.).

303. In general, administrative costs should be allocated to the party whom we decide should bear the substantive cost. CALABRESI, COSTS, *supra* note 48 at 226 (1970).

304. Of course, the interests at stake in the case of pornography may be somewhat different. Those offended by pornography may in some sense desire that there be some material by which they can be shocked. If so, the gradual loosening of controls on pornography has probably served all parties well. Those who desire explicit sexual depictions can find them far more easily and (one imagines, given a larger market and consequently increased returns to scale) more cheaply. Those who wish to be offended by aspects of sex can continue to be, although the explicitness or tawdriness of the display required to elicit offense has probably been increased. This is no great hardship since more graphic and tawdry material inevitably is produced. Thus, even if one becomes inured to *Playboy*, *Hustler* becomes available to give offense.

305. *See* Barenblatt v. United States, 360 U.S. 109, 134–62 (1959) (Black, J., dissenting). This case symbolized for Justice Black how quickly the courts and the country adjusted to constitutionally doubtful infringements of the civil liberties of so-called Communists during the McCarthy era. The Supreme Court, itself, had approved far more limited restrictions in earlier cases on the grounds that more stringent restrictions would never be imposed "while this Court sits." Yet, as Justice Black noted, "This Court still sits!" and acquiesced to the use of the congressional subpoena to hound citizens whose political opinions failed to find favor with the members of the House Un-American Activities Committee; *id.* at 153. The moral seemed obvious to Justice Black: any infringement of constitutional liberties places us on the proverbial slippery slope. The case also suggested to him the importance of clear language and a written Constitution. He hoped that the clear language of the constitution might shock us into reconsidering what case after case had not so slowly led us to think was permissible. By comparing what others called the law with the original language of the Constitution, he hoped to keep us from too readily sliding down the slippery slope, and perhaps even to induce us to ratchet our way back up; *id.* at 140–41.

306. As recently as August of 1962, 74 percent of a national sample, when asked if abortion should be legal for parents who could not afford another child, said no. Blake, *The Abortion Decisions: Judicial Review and Public Opinion* in ABORTION: NEW DIRECTION FOR POLICY STUDIES 51, Table 1 at p. 58 (E. Manier, W. Liu, D. Solomon eds. 1977).

307. This is according to a 1981 Yankelovich Survey. *Abortion in America: ABCs of a Raging Battle,* 94 U.S. NEWS AND WORLD REPORT Jan. 24, 1983

at 47, 48. Percentages supporting abortion vary considerably with how the question is phrased. *Id. See also,* Blake, *supra* note 306 at 54, 55–66.

It remains clear, nevertheless, that these percentages represent a complete reversal from the 74% disapproval rating recorded in 1962. *See supra* note 306. The turn-around in opinion over 20 years was quite gradual but also steady. As measured by answers to the same questions repeated in the Gallup poll, disapproval of legalization of abortion decreased from 74% in 1962 to 68% in 1969, to 55% by 1972. In 1974, two years after the Supreme Court announced its decision limiting restrictions on abortion in Roe v. Wade, disapproval showed a further statistically significant drop to 47%. *See* Blake, *supra* note 306 at 57, Table 1 at 58. There is some evidence to suggest that the decline in opposition to abortion was accompanied by the debate becoming increasingly ideological and polarized. During the middle 1970s, men's attitude toward abortion became increasingly strongly associated with religious and sexual attitudes. This was apparently not the case for women for whom abortion was already a highly ideological issue by the middle 1970s. *See* Barnett and Harris, *Recent Changes in Predictions of Abortion Attitude,* 66 SOCIOLOGY AND SOCIAL RESEARCH 320 (1982).

308. As mentioned earlier, I am not dealing here with the question of censorship (*see supra* notes 122, 291). Thus, we may feel certain behavior is undesirable yet be unwilling to try to suppress it or to censor it. There are various devices that allow us to discourage behavior without making criminals of those who wish to engage in it. In some societies certain actions are permitted but are generally acknowledged to be tawdry, immoral, and undesirable, consigned to shady places, and shady people. In others certain forms of expression are prohibited, but the laws are systematically not enforced. In still others, behavior is prohibited in "good" parts of town, but allowed elsewhere. The advantages and disadvantages of each of these strategies are obvious. I can only add that when I was a student, the last strategy was employed in a noteworthy fashion in Boston. At that time, even the most harmless literature could be "Banned in Boston" (which meant merely that you bought it elsewhere), but a less seemly part of Boston was also the site of the "best" (*i.e.,* most explicit) burlesque shows on the East Coast.

309. *See* Calabresi, *The New Economic Analysis of Law — Scholarship, Sophistry or Self-Indulgence, supra* note 211. One of the contributions of the Critical Legal Studies school is to have focused attention on the role of the legal system in shaping tastes. One of its weaknesses is to have asumed that traditional, liberal, and "Law and Economics" scholarship (which they tend to lump together) has nothing to contribute to this subject. *See* Kelman, *Choice and Utility,* 1979 WISC. L. REV. 769.

310. Calabresi, *Comment,* in ALTRUISM, MORALITY, AND ECONOMIC THEORY 57 (E. S. Phelps ed. 1975).

311. *See supra* note 265. Courts, however, have frequently cautioned that there are rather narrow limits on the situations in which they will award psychic damages. *Cf., e.g.,* Keck v. Jackson, 122 Ariz. 114, 593, P.2d 668 (1979); Stadler v. Cross, 295 N.W.2d 552 (Minn. Sup. Ct. 1980); Yandrich v. Radic, 495 Pa. 243, 433 A.2d 459 (1981).

312. These all too frequently look to short-run efficiency only. For a discussion and bibliography of economic analysis of law and of its use of the efficiency concept, *see* C. G. VELJANOVSKI, THE NEW LAW-AND-ECONOMICS: A RESEARCH REVIEW (1982).

313. When one is not talking about beliefs or attitudes, short-run cost avoidance may be sufficiently powerful so that achieving it becomes a significant long-run value. In this manner, short-run cost avoidance may be incorporated into our concept of justice. *Cf.,* CALABRESI, COSTS, *supra* note 48 at ch. 15; Calabresi and Melamed, *Property Rules, Liability Rules, and Inalienability: One View of the Cathedral,* 85 HARV. L. REV. 1089, 1102–05 (1972). For some, it can even become almost coextensive with justice. *See, e.g.,* Posner, *Utilitarianism, Economics, and Legal Theory,* 8 J. LEG. STUD. 103 (1979); Posner, *The Value of Wealth: A Comment on Dworkin and Kronman,* 9 J. LEG. STUD. 243 (1980).

314. *See generally,* CALABRESI & BOBBITT, *supra* note 1. (1978).

315. *Cf.* Tribe, *Ways Not to Think About Plastic Trees: New Foundations for Environmental Law,* 83 YALE L.J. 1315 (1974). In this celebrated article Laurence Tribe examines all the errors that could be made in a cost-benefit analysis designed to determine whether or not a society should replace real with plastic trees. Tribe's conclusion is that, even if the analysis favored plastic trees and even if all the errors have been corrected, the substitution should not be made. Tribe's critique is splendid; his conclusion, problematic—at least for a liberal (as he would, I think, describe himself). If what Tribe is saying is that when society decides to do something that is morally wrong, even though it is justified by the best possible cost-benefit analysis, he would have the right and duty to dissent, rebel, emigrate, or otherwise invite martyrdom, then Tribe is saying what I am asserting in text. If, however, he is saying that he would have a right to impose his moral preferences on society, rather than attempt to sway others by his example, then he may be correct in some transcendental sense but is not a liberal.

316. *See,* CALABRESI & BOBBITT, *supra* note 1; *see also* CALABRESI, A COMMON LAW, *supra* note 4 at 172–75.

317. *See* Repouille v. United States, 165 F.2d 152 (1947); People v. Roberts, 211 Mich. 187, 178 N.W. 690 (1920).

318. *See* Sherlock, *For Everything There is a Season: The Right to Die in the United States,* 1982 B.Y.U. L. REV. 545, 569–70; Survey, *Euthanasia: Criminal, Tort, Constitutional, and Legislative Considerations,* 48 NOTRE DAME LAW. 1202, 1213–15 (1973).

319. *See* CALABRESI & BOBBITT, *supra* note 1 at 57–64.

320. *Cf.,* Black, *Mr. Justice Black, The Supreme Court, and the Bill of Rights,* HARPER'S MAGAZINE Feb. 1961 at 63; CALABRESI, A COMMON LAW, *supra* note 4 at 173–74.

321. *See, e.g., Nassau Man Freed In "Mercy Killing,"* N.Y. Times, Oct. 19, 1938, at 46, col. 1; *Carol Paight Acquitted As Insane At Time She Killed Ailing Father,* N.Y. Times, Feb. 8, 1950, at 1, col. 2; *Jury Frees Son In Mercy Death of Sick Mother,* Chicago Tribune, Jan. 25, 1969, at 1, col. 1; People v. Wiener, Crim. No. 58-3636 (Cook Co. Ct. Ill. 1958) (A portion of the transcript of this case is presented in Williams, *Euthanasia and Abortion,* 38 U. COLO. L. REV. 178, 184–87 (1966)).

322. *Cf.,* Grimshaw v. Ford Motor Co., 119 Cal. App. 3d 757, 174 Cal. Rptr. 348 (1981). In this case, the jury awarded $125 million in punitive damages (later reduced to $3½ million) for a design defect in the plaintiff's Ford Pinto that caused it to burst into flames when struck from the rear. The Ford Motor Co. claimed all it had done was analyze the cost of reducing the likelihood of fire in a rear-end collision and the value of the likely reduction in injury and deaths. Ford claimed the cost-benefit analysis demonstrated a design change was not justified. This cost-benefit analysis may well be what offended the jury sufficiently to produce its award. *Cf.* Wheeler, *The Public's Costly Mistrust of Cost-Benefit Safety Analysis,* NAT'L L.J., Oct. 13, 1980, at 26. It is also possible, however, the Ford had done the wrong cost-benefit analysis. It may have compared the cost of modifying the Pinto to prevent fires in rear-end collisions with the damages they expected to pay if the Pinto was left unmodified. In other words, they may have deleted from the analysis the damage to victims who didn't know enough to sue or who lost their suit. If so, the award of punitive damages might have had the effect of saying to Ford: "If you do Cost-Benefit Analysis, make sure you do it right because, the few times you do get caught, we will make you pay for all the accidents in which you don't get caught." While appealing, this legal theory probably did not motivate the jury. They were probably just offended by the "costly" fact that the pricing of human life had been made too obvious.

323. Regents v. Bakke, 438 U.S. 265 (1978); *see* Calabresi, *Bakke as Pseudo-Tragedy,* 28 CATH. U. L. REV. 427 (1979).

324. *Bakke,* 438 U.S. at 310.

325. *Id.* at 311–12.

326. *Id.* at 318–19.

327. And perhaps by none more assiduously than the "Big Three" of the Ivy League. *See generally* M. SYNNOTT, THE HALF-OPENED DOOR: DISCRIMINATION AND ADMISSIONS AT HARVARD, YALE, AND PRINCETON, 1900–1970 (1979). Consequently, it is ironic that the Supreme Court chose to praise publicly the process at Harvard, and the weight it gives to diversity, as a model of non-discriminatory admission in *Bakke,* 438 U.S. at 316–19.

328. Calabresi & Bobbitt, *supra* note 1 at 57–58 (1978).

329. *See supra* note 327.

330. *See supra* note 323; *see also* Calabresi, *Bakke: Lost Candor,* N.Y. Times, July 6, 1978, at A19, col. 1.

331. I believe such a solution was available in *Bakke; see* Calabresi, *supra* note 323, at 432–44.

332. "Pro-choice" groups support and "pro-life" groups oppose legalized abortion. Selection of these labels gives some idea of how bitter the controversy between the two sides is. Opponents of abortion call themselves "pro-life" in order to emphasize what they want us to consider to be the salient characteristic of their opponents: that they oppose life or, to put it less charitably, condone murder. That their opponents gleefully murder innocent babes whose sole crime is to be, as yet, unborn is often quite frankly avowed in "pro-life literature":

> Photos show this human life aborted, dropped onto surgical gauze or into plastic-bagged garbage pails. Take that human life by suction abortion and the body is torn apart, becoming a jumble of tiny arms and legs. In a D and C abortion, an instrument slices the body to pieces. Salt poisoning at nineteen weeks? The saline solution burns away the outer layer of the baby's skin. The ultimate is the hysterectomy. . . . Often, this baby fights for its life, breathes, moves, and even cries. To see this, or the pictures of a plastic-bagged garbage can full of dead babies, well, it makes believers in right-to-life. It is unfair to write this way, cry the super-abortionists, or to show the horrible photos. But Buchenwald and Dachau looked terrible, too. Abortions are always "grisly murders."

Thimmesch, *The Abortion Culture,* in Life or Death —Who Controls? 141, 142 (N. Ostheimer and J. Ostheimer eds. 1976).

Supporters of abortion have chosen the label "pro-choice" in retaliation. The implication is that their opponents would deny to women the freedom to control their own destinies and lives. That this is (in their view) due either to narrow-minded religious fanaticism or dogmatic authoritarianism is also made quite clear:

> By continuing to cut a woman off from real and authoritative communication at this time, anti-abortionists help prevent *her* from making a decision based on her alternatives. Where problems are not individualized, the only benefits go to self-righteous people who have inflated their own self-esteem. . . .
>
> Marie [a diabetic woman for whom pregnancy was dangerous] called the local pro-birth office and got a dose and a half of what she probably hoped to hear: How wonderful a good Christian woman she was for resist-

ing the temptation of the easy, sinful way out. She was told not to worry about her family and health. Everyone knows the Lord will provide. If He didn't want her to carry the pregnancy, He would not have allowed it. "See your doctor and pray real hard. Don't fall into sin and everything will be just fine," she was told. [Note: in this tale, Marie and her baby both die in the eighth month of pregnancy.]

S. Barr, A Woman's Choice 224–26 (1977).

The bitterness of the controversy undoubtedly reflects the fact that both sides are trying to impose their values on the other. "Pro-life" proponents are undoubtedly sincerely troubled by others having abortions. "Pro-choice" proponents are undoubtedly sincerely opposed to limitations on a woman's right to be sexually active without losing control over her own reproductive capacity. The trouble is that the two sides are currently so polarized that there is little room left for compromise. One side claims to represent "life," the other "liberty," and both deny that the other represents either. Under the circumstances, it is hard to see what is left to discuss (except, perhaps, who has cornered the pursuit of happiness).

333. *See supra* notes 179, 205, 212, and accompanying text.

334. This argument has been made, although with little success, in Women's Services v. Thone, 483 F. Supp. 1022 (D. Neb. 1979), *aff'd* 636 F.2d 206 (8th Cir. 1980), *vacated and remanded,* 452 U.S. 911 (1981), *aff'd* 690 F.2d 667 (8th Cir. 1982), *vacated and remanded* 103 S. Ct. 3102 (1983); Akron Center for Reproductive Health, Inc. v. City of Akron, 479 F. Supp. 1172 (N.D. Ohio 1979), *modified,* 651 F.2d 1198 (6th Cir. 1981), *aff'd in part, rev'd in part,* 103 S. Ct. 2481 (1983).

335. Roe v. Wade, 410 U.S. 113 (1973).

336. *See* my discussion of the "Uses and Abuses of Subterfuge," in Calabresi, A Common Law, *supra* note 4 at ch. 14.

337. *See* Calabresi & Bobbitt, *supra* note 1 at 73–74.

338. *See, Federal Judge Blocks Utah Abortion Law,* N.Y. Times, Oct. 17 (1981), at A20, col. 6 (District Court Judge David K. Winder issues injunction to prevent enforcement of Utah state law requiring women to look at color photographs of various fetuses prior to obtaining abortion).

339. *Id.*

340. *See Birth Control Parley Shaken as Protesters Display Two Fetuses,* N.Y. Times, Feb. 16, 1979, at B7, col. 6.

341. It is far more likely to lead to highly emotional and politically divisive show-trials. *See* Note, *Obstructionist Activities at Abortion Clinics: A Framework for Remedial Litigation,* 8 N.Y.U. Rev. L. & Soc. Change 325, 336–42 (1979).

342. Roe v. Wade, 410 U.S. 113, 158 (1973).

343. U.S. Const. Amend XIV, § 1. *Cf.* Levy v. Louisiana, 391 U.S. 68 (1968); Glona v. American Guaranty and Liability Ins. Co., 391 U.S. 73 (1968); Weber v. Aetna Casualty and Surety Co., 406 U.S. 164 (1972) (forbidding discrimination against illegitimate children on equal protection grounds).

344. *See* J. CASNER & B. LEACH, CASES AND TEXT ON PROPERTY 358–59 (1951) (discussing doctrine of "abeyance of the seisin").

345. C. FEARNE, AN ESSAY ON THE LEARNING OF CONTINGENT REMAINDERS AND EXECUTORY DEVISES 308–09 (8th ed., London, 1824) (1st ed. London, 1772).

346. Reeve v. Long, 3 Lev. 408 (1695).

347. I've taken this version of the toast from CASNER & LEACH, *supra* note 344, at 359, n. 11.

348. Tort law's increasingly less solicitous attitude toward injurers has been much commented on. A classic discussion is Gregory, *Trespass to Negligence to Absolute Liability*, 37 VA. L. REV. 359 (1951). As part of this development courts have become increasingly willing to award damages to children for injuries they sustained prior to birth, at least where the child was viable and born alive. Parents are also increasingly likely to recover for injuries to unborn children although some jurisdictions still deny recovery if the fetus was not viable at the time of injury or was stillborn. *See generally* JAMES DOOLEY, 1 MODERN TORT LAW §§ 14.02.50-14.04 (Rev. Ed. 1982).

349. *See supra* note 178. *See also* Justus v. Atchison, 19 Cal.3d 564, 139 Cal. Rptr. 97, 565 P.2d 122 (1977) (fetus not person for purpose of wrongful death statute). *But see Missouri Court Rules that a Fetus is a Person,* N.Y. Times, Aug. 18, 1983, at C11, Col. 1 (discussing case of O'Grady v. St. Joseph's Hospital, 654 S.W.2d 904 (Mo. 1983). Interestingly, Missouri is one of the jurisdictions most active in passing laws seeking to establish the importance of fetal life and to restrict the applicability of Roe v. Wade. *See, e.g.,* Planned Parenthood v. Danforth, 428 U.S. 52 (1976) (striking down portions of Mo. Ann. Stat. § 188 (Vernon, 1978), requiring spousal or parental consent to abortions, banning saline amniocentesis, and requiring physician to preserve life and health of fetus whatever the stage of pregnancy); Frieman v. Ashcroft, 584 F.2d 247 (8th Cir. 1978), *aff'd* 440 U.S. 941 (1979) (striking down Mo. Ann. Stat. § 188.045 (Vernon 1978), that requires physician to inform woman seeking abortion that infant born alive will be ward of state and requires woman to acknowledge in writing that she has been so informed); Planned Parenthood v. Ashcroft, 655 F.2d 848 (8th Cir. 1981), *supplemented* 664 F.2d 687 (8th Cir. 1981), *cert. granted* 102 S.Ct. 2267 (1982) (striking down sections of Missouri code governing abortion. Mo. Ann. Stat. §§ 188.010 *et seq.* (Vernon 1982), that requires second and third trimester abortion to

be performed in hospital, 48-hour waiting period prior to abortion, notice to parents of minors seeking abortion, etc.).

350. A number of recent cases have found that intentional or unintentional actions that kill a fetus (*e.g.,* beating the mother, reckless speeding while drunk) do not constitute homicide; People v. Greer, 37 Ill. Dec. 313, 402 N.E.2d 203, 79 Ill.2d 103 (1980); State v. Larsen, 578 P.2d 1280 (Utah Sup. Ct. 1978); State v. Brown, 378 So.2d 916 (Sup. Ct. La. 1979); State v. Gyles, 313 So.2d 799 (Sup. Ct. La. 1975); A five month fetus has also been found not to qualify as a "person" under a Texas statute that permits the use of "deadly force" in defense of a third person. Ogos v. State, 655 S.W.2d 322 (1983). This ruling is particularly troublesome because the court simultaneously ruled that the deceased's action had not constituted a sufficient threat either to the mother or to the fetus to justify use of deadly force in response. Consequently, the ruling that the fetus was not a person for the purposes of the statute was entirely gratuitous. *But cf.* People v. Apodaca, 142 Cal. Rptr. 830, 76 Cal. 3d 479 (Ct. App. 1978) (killing of *viable* fetus constitutes murder), which suggests some movement in the other direction. Note also that there were a number of cases prior to *Roe* that declared killing of a fetus was not murder. *See, e.g.,* Keeler v. Superior Court of Amador County, 2 Cal. 3d 619, 87 Cal. Rptr. 481, 420 P.2d 617, (1970); State v. Prude, 24 So. 871, 76 Miss. 543 (1899).

351. *E.g.,* Paul Ramsey, *The Morality of Abortion,* in LIFE OR DEATH: ETHICS AND OPTIONS, 60 (Daniel Lably ed. 1968) (fetus should be treated as alive); D. SHULDER & F. KENNEDY, ABORTION RAP 107–15 (1971) (quoting testimony of Rabbi David Feldman to effect that fetus is not alive under Jewish law); S. BARR, A WOMAN'S CHOICE 253–54 (1977) (Appendix A: medically speaking, fetus should not be considered alive until 24–33 weeks of gestation); Harrington, *Human Life and Abortion,* 17 CATH. LAW. 11 (1971) (fetus is human life and abortion is murder); J. T. NOONAN, A PRIVATE CHOICE: ABORTION IN AMERICA IN THE SEVENTIES (1979) (fetus is alive; *see* chs. 7, 15, particularly); Dorsen, *Crushing Freedom in the Name of Life,* 10 HUM. RIGHTS 19 (Spring 1982).

352. Approval of abortion is closely linked to religion and religiosity. Roman Catholics are more opposed to legalized abortion than Protestants or Jews. However, opposition to abortion increases with religiosity in all these groups. Members of fundamentalist Protestant sects are particularly strongly opposed to abortion. Consequently, fundamentalist Protestants and Roman Catholics are probably the backbone of the anti-abortion movement. *See* Granberg and Granberg, *Abortion Attitudes, 1965–80: Trends and Determinants,* 12 FAMILY PLANNING PERSPECTIVES 250 (September/October 1980). It is widely recognized that both these groups are increasingly alienated from American society. In both cases, this alienation has resulted in a political style that

is a symbolic rejection of majoritarian culture. For some of the relatively recent immigrants who are Roman Catholic, the result has been the very conservative urban ethnic politics exemplified by Frank Rizzo, former mayor of Philadelphia. *See generally,* M. NOVAK, THE RISE OF THE UNMELTABLE ETHNICS (1971). For fundamentalist Protestants who are more typically rural, less recent immigrants, the comparable political movement has been the "New Right" exemplified by Jerry Falwell and the Moral Majority. *See generally,* Lienesch, *Right-Wing Religion: Christian Conservatism as a Political Movement,* in 97 POL. SCI. Q. 403 (1982). I am not arguing, of course, that the abortion issue produced these two political movements. Clearly, many other factors were also responsible for the emergence of these two varieties of the politics of disenchantment. Furthermore, the development of conservative ethnic politics preceded *Roe* v. *Wade.* Nevertheless, the decision in *Roe* can hardly be said to have had a palliative effect on their sense of alienation, and has undoubtedly swelled their ranks with people who previously had not felt themselves to be excluded from the mainstream.

353. *See supra* notes 113, 114, 124, 125, and accompanying text. I do not mean to suggest that Justice Blackman, the author of the opinion in *Roe,* was insensitive to such issues. Indeed, one cannot read *Roe* without feeling his own anguish and sensing that he was trying to write in a way that would not exclude those who lost. That is probably part of the reason for his refusal to affirm when fetal "life" begins. The other part, I think, was due to the fact that "science" had not answered the question for him. I suspect it was the same scientistic way of thinking that led him to write the statement that excluded fetuses (not independently viable) from the protection of the due process clause of the Constitution. There is an odd ring of certainty about that part of his opinion, almost as if, at last, he had found something verifiable that he could say. Our Constitution, however, is rarely that unambiguous, and to read it as if it gives scientific answers can be extraordinarily offensive to those who do not accept those answers or that kind of legal science.

354. *See, e.g.,* Ely, *The Wages of Crying Wolf: A Comment on Roe v. Wade,* 82 YALE L.J. 920 (1973). The reference is, of course, to the wing of the abolitionist movement that viewed the Constitution as a pro-slavery document and, consequently, "a covenant with death and an agreement with Hell." *See* R. NYE, FETTERED FREEDOM: CIVIL LIBERTIES AND THE SLAVERY CONTROVERSY, 1830–1860, 238 (1972).

355. Fundamentalist Mormons are the classic American case of a small sect being driven beyond the pale and ultimately (more or less) suppressed. During the middle of the 19th century, the uniform hostility of outsiders led the majority of Mormons to migrate to Utah. It was about this time that the Church formally adopted the institution of polygamy. Although only about 10% of Mormon families were polygamous, polygamous marriage was con-

sidered the ideal and was nearly universal among leaders of the Church. In the latter part of the 19th century, the federal government began to imprison Mormons for bigamy. *See* Reynolds v. United States, 98 U.S. 145 (1879). Under severe pressure, the Mormon Church renounced polygamy in 1890, but sects of fundamentalist Mormons continued to practice polygamy. T. O'DEA, THE MORMONS 108–10, 245–49 (1957). These fundamentalist sects have been driven underground and are seldom heard from. They did, however, recently emerge from obscurity in a spectacular murder case in Utah in 1980 when the leader of "The Church of the Lamb of God" was found guilty of having a rival murdered. *See, 2 in Utah Say Polygamist Leader Ordered "False Prophets" Killed*, N.Y. Times, May 19, 1980, at A16, col. 5. *See also* N.Y. Times, May 23, 1980 at 12, col. 6; May 29, 1980 at A20, col. 3; June 3, 1980 at A14, col. 6.

Early abolitionists were also driven underground and even, in the case of John Brown, hanged. They were, however, one small group which, despite its emargination, eventually triumphed. One can legitimately wonder if the abolitionists would have seen their goals realized had not the polarization of North and South led to attempted secession, Civil War, and the consequent radicalization of opinion on the slavery issue in the North.

356. *See* O'DEA, *supra* note 355.

357. *See* Dred Scott v. Sanford, 60 U.S. (19 How.) 393 (1857). The court declared both that the provisions of the Constitution did not apply to Negroes and that no state had the power to confer the rights of a citizen on a Negro. The implication was not only that Negro slavery was enshrined by the Constitution but that no state could act to ban slavery in its own territory. This reading of the Constitution led not only abolitionists but also those who had only opposed the spread of slavery to demand the changing of the Constitution so as to bar all slavery. The analogy with the current controversy is obvious. Anti-abortion forces are also attempting to amend the Constitution to achieve their political goals. *See infra* note 360. And the laws against abortion would, in fact, be far stronger after such an amendment was passed than they were before *Roe*. Such an amendment would not only prohibit abortion in all the states but would also allow promulgation of laws enforcing such a prohibition to be at the federal rather than state level.

One moral of this story is that the legitimacy of a representative democracy is, if not necessarily negated, at least eroded if a significant segment of the population is thrust "outside" the Constitution. The difficulties of such a situation are obvious to any student of recent Italian history. In Italy, for a long period, many pro-clerical Catholics considered themselves excluded from the kingdom that had seized Rome from the Pope, and from its secular Constitution. This exclusion certainly weakened the state and contributed to the successful fascist revolution. More recently, the far left and the far right were effectively excluded from possible participation in government coalitions. This situation which (with regard to the left) may have begun to change in the last few years virtually assured the dominance of one party, the Christian Democrats. *Cf., The New Opening in Italy,* N.Y. Times, August 20, 1983, at 20, col. 1. (Editorial).

358. *See, e.g.,* N.Y. PENAL LAW § 125.05(3) (McKinney 1975) (passed 1970) which permits abortion at any time within 24 weeks of conception. For a discussion of the extent to which *Roe v. Wade* both galvanized and embittered anti-abortion forces, *see* Williams, *The Power of Fetal Politics* SATURDAY REVIEW June 9, 1979 at 12.

359. A dramatic example of this was in Rhode Island. Prior to *Roe v. Wade,* Rhode Island banned abortion counseling and abortion except to protect the life of the mother. In March 1973, immediately after *Roe* was decided, the Rhode Island legislature passed legislation that not only declared that the fetus was a person within the meaning of the 14th Amendment, but imposed draconian penalties on anyone guilty of performing an abortion except to protect the life of the mother: 1–7 years in prison if the mother survived; 5–20 if she died. R. I. GEN. LAWS §§ 11-3-1 to 11-3-5 (1975). This legislation was immediately struck down in Doe v. Israel, 358 F. Supp. 1193 (D.R.I. 1973), *cert. den.,* 416 U.S. 993 (1974). Although the repudiation of *Roe* was less dramatic in other states, it is notable that 31 other states had passed legislation attempting to restrict or regulate access to abortions within 3 years after *Roe v. Wade. See* Witherspoon, *The New Pro-Life Legislation: Patterns and Recommendations,* 7 ST. MARY'S LAW JOURNAL 637, n. 31 at 646 (1976).

360. The recent failure of a proposed constitutional amendment to ban abortions to get a majority, let alone two thirds, of the vote in the U.S. Senate suggests the political foes of abortion may lack sufficient political strength to reverse the court. *See Foes of Abortion Beaten in Senate on Amendment Bid,* N.Y. Times, June 29, 1983 at A1, col. 1.

361. *See* Novak, *supra* note 352, at ch. 4.

362. Like blacks, women required a constitutional amendment (the XIXth) to get the suffrage. This fact, and the implications it has for equal protection of law by itself suffices to make abortion an issue in which two sets of constitutional values are placed in conflict. *See* Calabresi, *Bakke as Pseudotragedy,* 28 CATH. U. L. REV. 427 (1979).

363. It might seem that federalism offers a solution which enables both sets of metaphysics to prevail, though only some of the time; that is, only in some states. The advantage of a federalist solution is that it may allow deeply conflicting values to be accommodated within the same nation. Both sets of values would be accommodated, however, only if a significant number of states permitted abortions and another significant number barred them. Since each set of values would be dominant in large parts of the country,

a federalist solution is unlikely to be acceptable to those who hold uncompromisingly to one set of values and see no merit in the opposing set. As our country has become more centralized, moreover, the federalist solution has seemed to be acceptable less often. "We are one nation, and it is offensive to have fundamental [decisions] depend on the chance of where in the land one lives. The judicial history of the Fourteenth Amendment may be characterized as the development of the sense that whatever its advantages, this kind of decentralization will not be permitted when certain fundamental values are involved." CALABRESI & BOBBITT, *supra* note 1.

The federalist solution, finally, has a special problem in the abortion context. It is all too easy for women of means to go to another state to have an abortion. At the same time, it is all too difficult for the very poor to do the same thing. The result is that many opponents of abortion tend to view the federalist approach as an obvious sell-out, unless bolstered by laws restricting travel to procure an abortion. (Such travel restrictions by states would be of doubtful constitutionality, to put it mildly. Analogous federal laws would, I expect, be greeted with the same opprobrium that attended the fugitive slave laws before the civil war.) It follows that the values that "pro-life" groups seek to affirm would be given little protection even in the states in which they were nominally upheld. A short train trip would often be sufficient to override them. Conversely, the equality values, that I contend *infra* are at the heart of the "pro-choice" position, would be severely undermined by a federalist solution that made abortions significantly less available to those too poor to travel.

364. *See* Wellington, *Common Law Rules and Constitutional Double Standards: Some Notes on Adjudication,* 83 YALE L. J. 222, 308–09 (1973).

The Roman Catholic position has been that any direct attack on the fetus is murder. Both mother and child are patients of the doctor and have an equal right to live. The mother, however, is not morally required to forego treatment she requires even though such treatment will cause the death of her child. Thus, while the mother could not procure an abortion at any time and under any circumstances, even to save her own life, she could have a cancerous uterus removed even though this would mean the death of the fetus. D. CALLAHAN, ABORTION: LAW, CHOICE AND MORALITY, Ch. 12 (1970). The Catholic position would deny that there are similarities between the distinction that is made in the cancer case and the distinction Professor Judith Thompson makes between the intent of a woman to be separated from the fetus (even if death of the fetus follows almost certainly) and the intent to destroy the fetus. See *infra* notes 399–409 and accompanying text. Some might want to make another distinction and treat differently those cases in which the death of the fetus, though not desired in itself, is necessary (and accomplished) in order to induce the separation-abortion, from those situations in which the desired separation-abortion inevitably (or almost inevitably) results in the (not desired) death of the nonviable fetus. Nevertheless, the more one thinks about it, the more all these cases seem to rest on analogous notions that intent is more important than results.

365. *See* Wellington, *supra* note 363 at 308–09.

366. *See supra* notes 195, 364; *see also* MODEL PENAL CODE § 207.11 (Tentative Draft No. 9, 1959) (justifying less severe penalties for non-therapeutic abortions performed prior to twenty-sixth week of pregnancy). CALLAHAN, *supra* note 364 at 496–501 (abortion is least desirable method of controlling births). B. SARVIS & H. RODMAN, THE ABORTION CONTROVERSY, Ch. 8 (2d ed. 1974) (contraception, not abortion, is preferred method of family planning).

367. *See, e.g.,* L. GORDON, WOMAN'S BODY, WOMAN'S RIGHT (1976); D. SCHULDER & F. KENNEDY, ABORTION RAP 20–36 (1971) (a "Commodity Producing Another Commodity," testimony of Lucy Wilcox); see also *supra* note 364.

368. *See supra* notes 270, 272, and accompanying text.

369. *See, e.g.,* Doe v. Commonwealth's Attorney, 403 F. Supp. 1199 (E.D. Va. 1975), *aff'd mem.* 425 U.S. 901, *reh'g denied,* 425 U.S. 985 (1976) (Va. statute making sodomy a crime is not unconstitutional); *see also* State of Ohio ex rel. Grant v. Brown, 39 Ohio 2d 112, 313 N.E.2d 847 (1974), *cert. dismissed,* 420 U.S. 916 (1975) (Secretary of State need not approve article of incorporation for gay rights organization since homosexuality is against public policy of state).

370. The litigation strategy of gay rights groups has centered almost entirely on attacks on discrimination against homosexuals. This strategy has met with some success. *See, e.g.,* Gay Law Students Association v. Pacific Telephone & Telegraph, 24 Cal. 3d 458, 595 P.2d 592, 156 Cal. Rptr. 14 (Cal. Sup. Ct. 1979) (homosexual employees may challenge privately-owned public utility policy of not hiring homosexuals); Doe v. Doe, 284 S.E.2d 799 (Va. Sup. Ct., 1981) (fact mother was lesbian insufficient reason to terminate parental rights).

371. *Cf.* Griswold v. Connecticut, 381 U.S. 479 (1965) (state ban on contraceptives is unconstitutional). This case was decided, in part, on privacy and it was the basis of the privacy argument in *Roe* v. *Wade.* But, just as one swallow does not a summer make, neither does one case a jurisprudence of sexual privacy establish. Furthermore, in *Griswold,* two out of the six-person majority (Justices White and Harlan) did not endorse the concept of a protected sphere of marital privacy and decided the case on substantive due process grounds. Consequently a minority of the court (Justices Douglas, Goldberg, Brennan, and Warren) endorsed a right to sexual privacy in that case. The embarrassing absence of any link between the con-

cept of a protected zone of sexual privacy and specific constitutional provision such as the IVth Amendment, led Justice Black to join in dissent against the striking down of what he conceded to be an uncommonly silly law. 381 U.S. at 507–09.

372. *See e.g.,* J. ELY, DEMOCRACY AND DISTRUST (1980); SUNSTEIN, infra note 373. To give some idea how developed, indeed almost Ptolemaic in its epicycles, this jurisprudence of equality is, I simply note that classifications based on gender have been subject to "heightened" but "intermediate" rather than "strict" scrutiny by the Supreme Court. Blattner, *The Supreme Court's "Intermediate" Equal Protection Decisions: Five Imperfect Models of Constitutional Equality,* 8 HASTINGS CONST. L.Q. 777, 791–94 (1981).

373. Sunstein, *Public Values, Private Interests, and the Equal Protection Clause,* 1982 SUP. CT. REV. 127 (1983).

374. It may seem that most of the cases in which we sacrifice lives involve omission rather than commission. That is, we let people die rather than kill them. Certainly it is easier to hide the fact that lives are being sacrificed when they are lost through failure to act than through direct actions, since often the choices and intents involved are less clear in such omission cases. Oliver Wendell Holmes long ago argued that what ought to matter is not action or inaction, but the clarity of the choice involved in either the omission or the commission. O. W. HOLMES, THE COMMON LAW 76–78, (1881) (Howe edition 1963). To kill people by starving them to death intentionally is no less to murder them than poisoning them is. Moreover, it is not true that the only sacrifices we require *are* in cases of omission. Sending troops into battle is surely commission, and so is sending troops to enforce desegregation—as in *Cooper v. Aaron, infra* notes 384–386 and accompanying text. In none of these cases, of course, do we *wish* to kill but only to do that which necessarily or very likely results in killings. The distinction is important, but it can also apply in abortion situations to the difference between the intent to separate oneself from a fetus and the intent to destroy the fetus. *See supra* note 364, and *infra* notes 399–409, and accompanying text.

375. "No ordinary bystander is under a duty to attempt the rescue of a child from drowning in what he knows to be shallow water." WINFIELD, CASES ON THE LAW OF TORTS 404 (4th ed. 1948); *see* HARPER & JAMES, *supra* note 83 at 1046–47; Regan, *Rewriting Roe v. Wade,* 77 MICH. L. REV. 1569, 1569–70 (1979).

376. *See e.g.* Art. 593, Italian Criminal Code of 1930. Minnesota has recently passed a law making it a petty misdemeanor to fail to come to someone's aid. Good Samaritan Law, ch. 319, H.F. No. 380, 1983 Minn. Law. 2329 (to be codified as MINN. STAT. § 604.05). This gives rise to speculation that since Minnesota is a "negligence *per se*" state (*i.e.,* a state in which statutes defining criminal behavior establish the standard of care to which in-

dividuals are held in torts suits), the civil law duty to be a Good Samaritan might now exist in Minnesota. Vermont also has a similar statute. Vt. Stat. Ann. tit. 12, § 519 (1973).

377. Landes and Posner, *Altruism in Law and Economics,* 68 Am. Econ. Rev. 417, 421 (Papers and Proceedings Issue, May 1978).

378. While it is true that the legal duty to rescue in Italy is currently found in Article 593 of the Italian Criminal Code of 1930, which was promulgated under Fascism, the duty to rescue in Italian law far antedates Fascism in Italy. It was formulated in Article 389 of the Italian Criminal Code of 1889 which in turn followed an old Tuscan police regulation. *See* Rudzinski, *The Duty to Rescue: A Comparative Analysis,* in The Good Samaritan and the Law 91, 98 (J. M. Ratcliffe ed. 1981).

379. Though originally arrived at independently, the following argument has been much influenced, and for the better, by Regan, *supra* note 375.

380. Although statutes that classify individuals on the basis either of race or gender are subject to heightened scrutiny, classification on basis of gender is said to be subject to a less strict standard of scrutiny than is race. *See supra* note 372.

381. *See supra* note 373. In McFall v. Shimp, 10 Pa. D &C 3d 90 (1978), a plaintiff dying from a rare bone marrow disease asked the court to compel the best available donor to provide marrow for a transplant. The court refused despite the fact that being a donor entailed little danger and only a modicum of pain. In fact, the judge expressed his horror at the idea of "a society which respects the rights of one individual, . . . sink[ing] its teeth into the jugular vein or neck of one of its members and suck[ing] from it sustenance for another member." *Id.* at 92. The judge did not say whether a statute allowing an injunction under these circumstances would be unconstitutional. He did not need to in order to decide the case. The judge, however, left no doubt that he would never issue such an injunction in the absence of a statute. The depth of judicial antipathy to any attempt to force individuals to provide medical aid to others may be gauged by Head v. Colloton, 331 N.W.2d 870 (Iowa Sup. Ct. 1983). In this case, the court refused to order a hospital to release the name of a suitable bone marrow donor to a leukemia victim so he could plead with her personally to save his life. It is worthwhile to note that the potential donor had originally volunteered her marrow for another donor, had been found unsuitable, and had simply indicated a preference not to be a donor in the future. She was almost certainly unaware of the plaintiff's particular plight.

382. Sickle cell anemia is a hereditary blood disease that usually, though not invariably, occurs in blacks. Individuals who are heterozygous (*i.e.,* have one normal hemoglobin gene and one sickle cell gene), are partly protected from a severe form of malaria, and typically suffer no ill effects of sickle cell

anemia. However individuals unfortunate enough to be homozygous for the sickle cell gene (*i.e.,* have two sickle cell genes) experience severe side effects and are unlikely to survive to maturity except with constant medical attention. Some have speculated that the concentration of the trait among blacks is due to the survival power of individuals who were heterozygous and came from parts of Africa where this form of malaria was common. *See Sickle Cell Trait and Sickle Cell Anemia,* IX ENCYCLOPEDIA BRITANNICA 182 (15th ed. 1974).

383. Consider, for example, the clear unconstitutionality of automobile insurance categorizations based directly on ethnic or racial identity. *Cf. also* Arizona Governing Committee v. Norris, 103 S.Ct. 3492 (1983) (per curiam; striking down state pension plan that provided higher monthly benefits to men than women since women tend to live longer). *Cf. also supra* note 153. This means that people in these groups will drive more than they otherwise would even though we might be able to predict with a fair degree of certainty that they will have high accident rates. As a result, more lives will be lost than would have happened had insurance rates been based on racial or ethnic identity. *See supra* text at notes 140–42. Nevertheless, we (quite properly, I think) elect to sacrifice these lives rather than burden a disfavored group, just as in *Norris,* we demonstrate an unwillingness to burden women with lower pension benefits despite the alleged actuarial appropriateness of doing so.

384. Cooper v. Aaron, 358 U.S. 1 (1958).

385. *Id.* at 12.

386. The opinion of the court in this case was unusual in that it was stated to be the opinion of every member of the court. *Id.* at 4. It was neither an opinion by one member whom everyone joined nor a "per curiam" opinion whose author was unknown. Unlike a "per curiam" opinion which stresses anonymity, this opinion stressed unanimity.

387. Sometimes we do make distinctions that favor actual over statistical lives. (*See supra* notes 28–30 and accompanying text.) But that differentiation cannot be invoked here. For a discussion of omission versus commission, *see supra* note 374.

388. The essence of rape is, of course, lack of consent. This is true also of statutory rape *de jure,* and frequently, given the youth of the victim, *de facto* as well. Very similar considerations apply in cases of incest, which often involve a younger female and older male who has considerable power over her. In such situations, consent on the part of the woman would seem to be a misnomer. *See* Cormier, Kennedy and Sangowicz, *Psychodynamics of Father-Daughter Incest* in DEVIANCY AND THE FAMILY 97 (C. Bryant and J. G. Wells eds. 1973). Some writers have recently argued that given socio-economic realities, all or virtually all heterosexual intercourse derives from a coerced caring on the part of the woman. *See* e.g., C. MACKINNON, SEXUAL HARASS-

MENT OF WORKING WOMEN: A CASE OF SEX DISCRIMINATION 54–55 (1979). If one accepts this position most unwanted pregnancies could be described as lacking consent even though there is no overt coercion.

389. Consequently, abortions performed under the American Law Institute's pre-*Roe* model penal code for victims of rape or incest were not criminal. MODEL PENAL CODE § 230.3(2) (proposed official draft, 1962). Similarly, when the "Hyde Amendment," cutting off Medicaid funding for abortions was passed, funding for therapeutic abortions and abortions for victims of rape and incest were specifically excluded from the cut-off. J. NOONAN, A PRIVATE CHOICE 115–16 (1979). Many states have also preserved Medicaid funding for such abortions even after cutting off state funding of other types of abortions. *See* Note, *Medicaid Funding for Abortions: The Medicaid Statute and The Equal Protection Clause,* 6 HOFSTRA L. REV. 421 (1978).

390. Certainly, this seems to be the position of the Catholic Church. *See supra* note 364. As late as 1980, 17% of American adults surveyed in a national poll would refuse abortion to victims of rape (incest not surveyed). *See* Granberg and Granberg, *supra* note 352 at Table 1, p. 252.

391. Tay Sachs disease is a rare hereditary disease characterized by a disorder of fat metabolism. Sufferers seldom survive beyond early childhood. It is most common among the Jewish population. *See Lipid Storage Diseases,* VI ENCYCLOPEDIA BRITANNICA 250 (15th ed. 1974).

This whole hypothetical situation is entirely fanciful. I have used Jewish people in it for several reasons. First, I wanted a group of real people who would suffer discrimination. Had I used Xs or Ys none of us would worry about the discriminatory impact as much for we would not know real people who would be injured by the discrimination. Second, I needed a group of people who have suffered mightily from past discrimination. Third, I wished here, as in my earlier speeding examples involving Italians, to use a group with which I have close links, lest anyone think I was being snide about the group.

392. One could imagine, I suppose, that the reason only the children of carriers, and only some of them, could get the disease was the genetic similarity between carriers and potential victims.

393. This may help explain why compulsory registration for military service, which applies only to males, has been held to be constitutional. *See* Rostker v. Goldberg, 453 U.S. 57 (1981). Interestingly, a significant argument against the constitutionality of such registration was that it discriminated against women by perpetuating stereotypes that caused women to be treated unequally. That women were willing to make such an argument, even though the equality they sought could readily lead to loss of life in case of war, suggests again that equality is at times considered more important than life itself. (I am assuming that military service is dangerous to life even for

those not directly involved in combat duties). The Court did not, however, accept the argument. *Id.* at 74 note 11; *But see,* the dissenting opinion of Justice Marshall, *id.* at 86. For a case in which eight members of the Supreme Court seemed to agree that the constitutionality of a statute depended on whether it discriminated against men or women (though they disagreed as to which), *see* Califano v. Goldfarb, 430 U.S. 199 (1977). For a discussion of this aspect of the case, *see* CALABRESI, A COMMON LAW, *supra* note 4 at 9–10.

394. *See supra* notes 364, 374 and *infra* notes 399–409 and accompanying text.

395. *E.g.,* Conlin, *Equal Protection Versus Equal Rights Amendment — Where Are We Now?,* 24 DRAKE L. REV. 259 (1975). *See also supra* note 372.

396. *Cf.* Korematsu v. United States, 323 U.S. 214 (1944), which, tragically, upheld fierce war-time discrimination against Japanese-Americans. The result in the much criticized case was properly termed "a disaster". *See* Rostow, *The Japanese American Cases — A Disaster* 54 YALE L. J. 489 (1945). Nevertheless, the language used in the opinion, because it emphasized the importance of the very values the case failed to uphold in the opinion, has been the source of many of today's equal protection holdings. (This point was made to me by my colleague Professor Paul Gewirtz.) As a result, in contexts other than wartime, even as disastrous a case as *Korematsu* has led to a strengthening of equal protection values. Likewise, one might have hoped that had *Roe v. Wade* been written differently it might have strengthened society's sense that fetal life is important and worthy of protection — even while reaching the same result. This in turn might have led to rules of law, in other contexts (such as cases involving tortious injuries to the unborn, felonious attacks on pregnant women which killed non-viable as well as viable fetuses, aborted fetuses who survived, state expenditures for care of the unborn) which would further emphasize the values being attached to the life of the unborn. The climate fostered by such cases might in time even lead to legislative action recognizing these values in non-abortion situations. The net result might be that a decision legalizing abortion could come to be seen, years later, to have induced respect rather than callousness for the values it found impossible to uphold in the specific context. It is impossible to say, quantitatively, whether *Korematsu's* language has come to prevent more discrimination than the case itself permitted. Neither, however, can one demonstrate the opposite. It is undoubtedly wishful thinking to suppose that such uncertainty might some day have attached to the fetal life values involved in *Roe v. Wade.* Yet, if one thinks of the many unborn who do not survive because of inadequate pre-natal care, and of the possibility that in time early fetuses could be separated simply and safely from women seeking abortions and then be brought to term, even the wishful seems possible. The opinion as written,

instead effectively demeaned the losing values and made such desirable wishful thinking impossible.

397. The Italian Constitution of 1948 recognized the Lateran Pacts signed between Mussolini and the Roman Catholic Church in 1928. Cost. Art. 7. These pacts gave the Roman Catholic Church a privileged position in the Italian State. They recognized Vatican City as an independent state, granted Catholic priests the right to perform marriage ceremonies that have civil validity, reserved to church courts control over marriage annulments, committed the Italian State to subsidizing the Church in Italy and granted a number of other concessions to the church. M. CAPPELLETTI, J. MERRYMAN & J. PERILLO, THE ITALIAN LEGAL SYSTEM 60 (1967). Consequently, one can reasonably call the Roman Catholic Church the "established" church in Italy. In Italy, in 1978, a law was passed allowing abortion for all women over 18 years of age in the first 90 days of pregnancy, if there was a threat to the physical or psychological health of the mother. Therapeutic abortions and abortion in cases of rape or incest were also available. This position was in many ways the moderate position. Certain groups wished abortion to be freely available. The Roman Catholic Church opposed abortion being made available at all. In 1981, a referendum was held to determine if the abortion law should be upheld. The Roman Catholic Church and Pope John Paul II (who was shot and seriously injured just before the referendum was held) actively campaigned for repeal. The Christian Democratic Party, initially for repeal, more or less withdrew from active campaigning. Most other political parties supported the abortion statute. In the end, the Italian voters voted against repeal by a 2-1 margin. The availability of abortion was neither expanded nor eliminated. The moderate position, backed by most political parties, had won. *See, On Abortion, Italian Voters are Less Catholic Than the Vatican,* N.Y. Times, May 24, 1981, at E3, col. 1.

398. In 1974, Senator James Buckley was able to have a bill which sought to create a Federal Death Penalty amended, so that a sentence of death could not be carried out on a pregnant woman. 120 CONG. REC. 6711–12 (1974).

399. *See, e.g.,* Rosen, *Psychiatric Implications of Abortion: A Case Study in Social Hypocrisy,* in ABORTION AND THE LAW 82, 93–5 (David Smith ed. 1967) (arguing that women should never be forced to bear children merely to give them up for adoption because of deleterious impact on mother's mental state).

400. *Cf.,* Thomson, *A Defense of Abortion,* 1 PHIL. & PUB. AFFAIRS 47, 66 (1971).

401. Planned Parenthood v. Danforth, 428 U.S. 52, 69 (1976) (Missouri statute requiring spousal consent for abortion is unconstitutional); Harris v. State, 356 So.2d 623 (Ala. Sup. Ct. 1978) (father of illegitimate child cannot compel mother to get an abortion).

402. Commonwealth v. Edelin, 371 Mass. 497, 359 N.E.2d 4 (1976).

403. Dr. Edelin was convicted of manslaughter in the trial court. This conviction was reversed by the Supreme Judicial Court of Massachusetts. *Id.* That court found that there was insufficient evidence of wanton or reckless conduct for the case to have gone to the jury.

404. *See supra* note 350.

405. Harris v. McRae, 448 U.S. 297 (1980) federal government may restrict use of federal Medicaid funds to pay for abortions); Williams v. Zbaraz, 448 U.S. 358 (1980) (state may restrict use of state funds and pay only for those abortions necessary to preserve life of mother); Maher v. Roe, 432 U.S. 464 (1977) (state may restrict use of Medicaid funds to paying only for first trimester abortions that are "medically necessary"); Poelker v. Doe, 432 U.S. 519 (1977) (per curiam; city need not provide publicly financed hospital services for abortion although it does so for childbirth).

406. Senator Daniel Patrick Moynihan, for instance, who is a Roman Catholic and is opposed to abortion, has nevertheless criticized denial of federal aid for abortion. He has been quoted on the front page of the New York Times as saying: "There are minimum social services that everyone must be provided with, and access to abortion as a last resort is one of them." N.Y. Times, July 13, 1977 at A1, col. 4.

407. The ethical issues raised by the use of abortion as a "quality control" device are discussed in Nolan-Haley, *Amniocentesis and the Apotheosis of Human Quality Control,* 2 J. LEGAL MEDICINE 347 (1981).

408. Thompson, *supra* note 400.

409. *See supra* pp. 251–52.

Index

IDEALS, BELIEFS, ATTITUDES, AND THE LAW

was composed in 11-point Digital Compugraphic Baskerville and leaded 2 points,
with display type in Baskerville, by Metricomp;
printed by sheet-fed offset on 55-pound, acid-free Glatfelter Antique Cream,
Smythe-sewn and bound over binder's boards in Joanna Arrestox B,
also adhesive bound with paper covers by Maple-Vail Book Manufacturing Group, Inc.;
with jackets and paper covers printed in 2 colors by Philips Offset Company, Inc.;
and published by

SYRACUSE UNIVERSITY PRESS

SYRACUSE, NEW YORK 13210